DEADPOOL & THE MERC$ FOR MONEY

"MO' MERCS, MO' MONKEYS"

CULLEN BUNN
writer

IBAN COELLO
artist

GURU-eFX
colorist

IBAN COELLO & NOLAN WOODARD
cover art

VC's JOE SABINO
letterer

HEATHER ANTOS
assistant editor

JORDAN D. WHITE
editor

Deadpool created by Rob Liefeld & Fabian Nicieza

collection editor JENNIFER GRÜNWALD
assistant editor CAITLIN O'CONNELL
associate managing editor KATERI WOODY
editor, special projects MARK D. BEAZLEY
vp production & special projects JEFF YOUNGQUIST
svp print, sales & marketing DAVID GABRIEL
book designer ADAM DEL RE

editor in chief AXEL ALONSO
chief creative officer JOE QUESADA
publisher DAN BUCKLEY
executive producer ALAN FINE

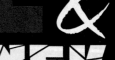

DEADPOOL & THE MERCS FOR MONEY VOL. 1: MO' MERCS, MO' MONKEYS. Contains material originally published in magazine form as DEADPOOL & THE MERCS FOR MONEY #1-5. First printing 2017. ISSN# 978-1-302-90263-6. Published by MARVEL WORLDWIDE, INC., a subsidiary of MARVEL ENTERTAINMENT, LLC. OFFICE OF PUBLICATION: 135 West 50th Street, New York, NY 10020. **Printed in Canada.** ALAN FINE, President, Marvel Entertainment; DAN BUCKLEY, President, TV, Publishing & Brand Management; JOE QUESADA, Chief Creative Officer; TOM BREVOORT, SVP of Publishing; DAVID BOGART, SVP of Business Affairs & Operations, Publishing & Partnership; C.B. CEBULSKI, VP of Brand Management & Development, Asia; DAVID GABRIEL, SVP of Sales & Marketing, Publishing; JEFF YOUNGQUIST, VP of Production & Special Projects; DAN CARR, Executive Director of Publishing Technology; ALEX MORALES, Director of Publishing Operations; SUSAN CRESPI, Production Manager; STAN LEE, Chairman Emeritus. For information regarding advertising in Marvel Comics or on Marvel.com, please contact Vit DeBellis, Integrated Sales Manager, at vdebellis@marvel.com. For Marvel subscription inquiries, please call 888-511-5480. **Manufactured between 12/23/2016 and 1/30/2017 by SOLISCO PRINTERS, SCOTT, QC, CANADA.**

10 9 8 7 6 5 4 3 2 1

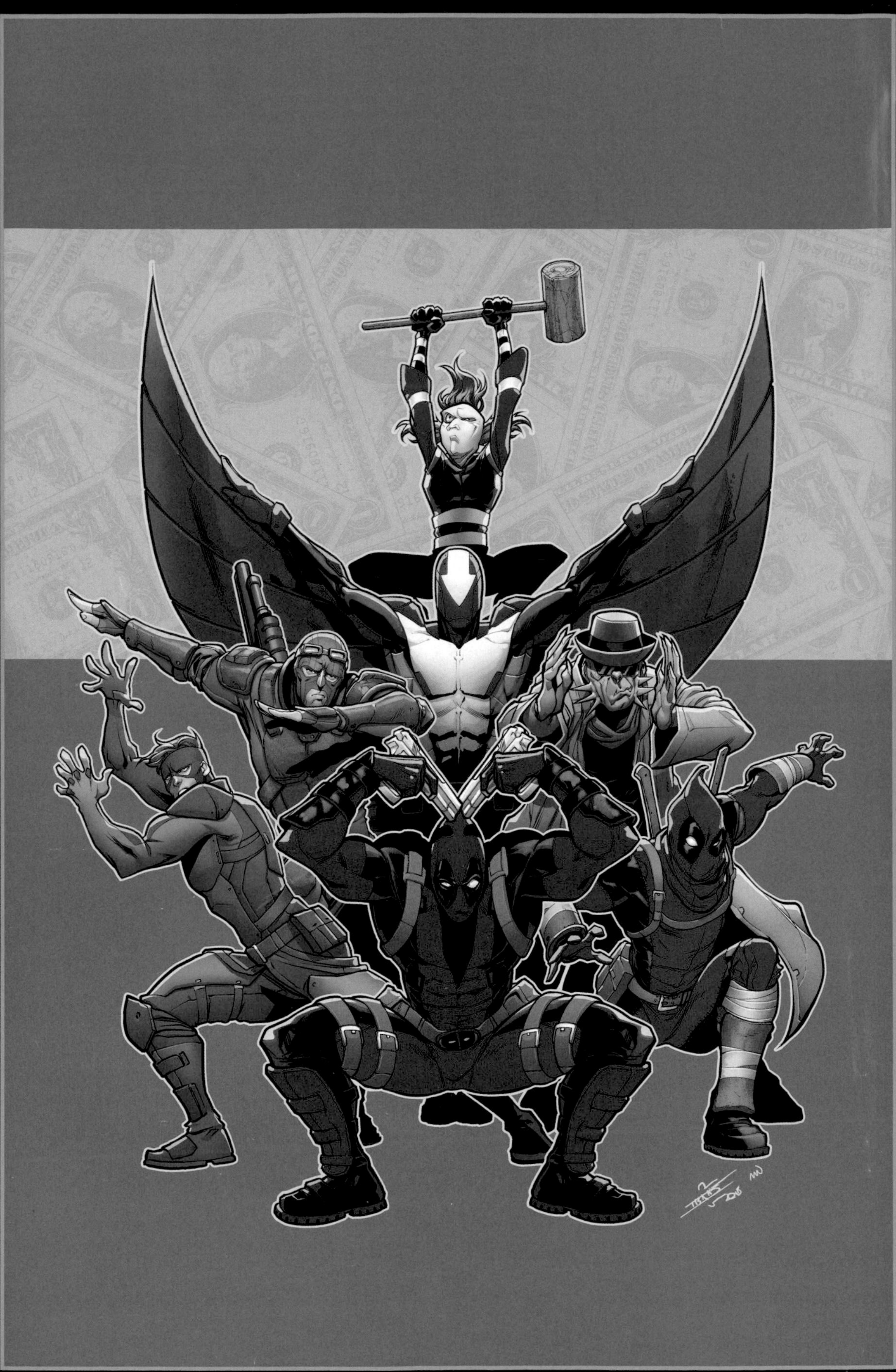

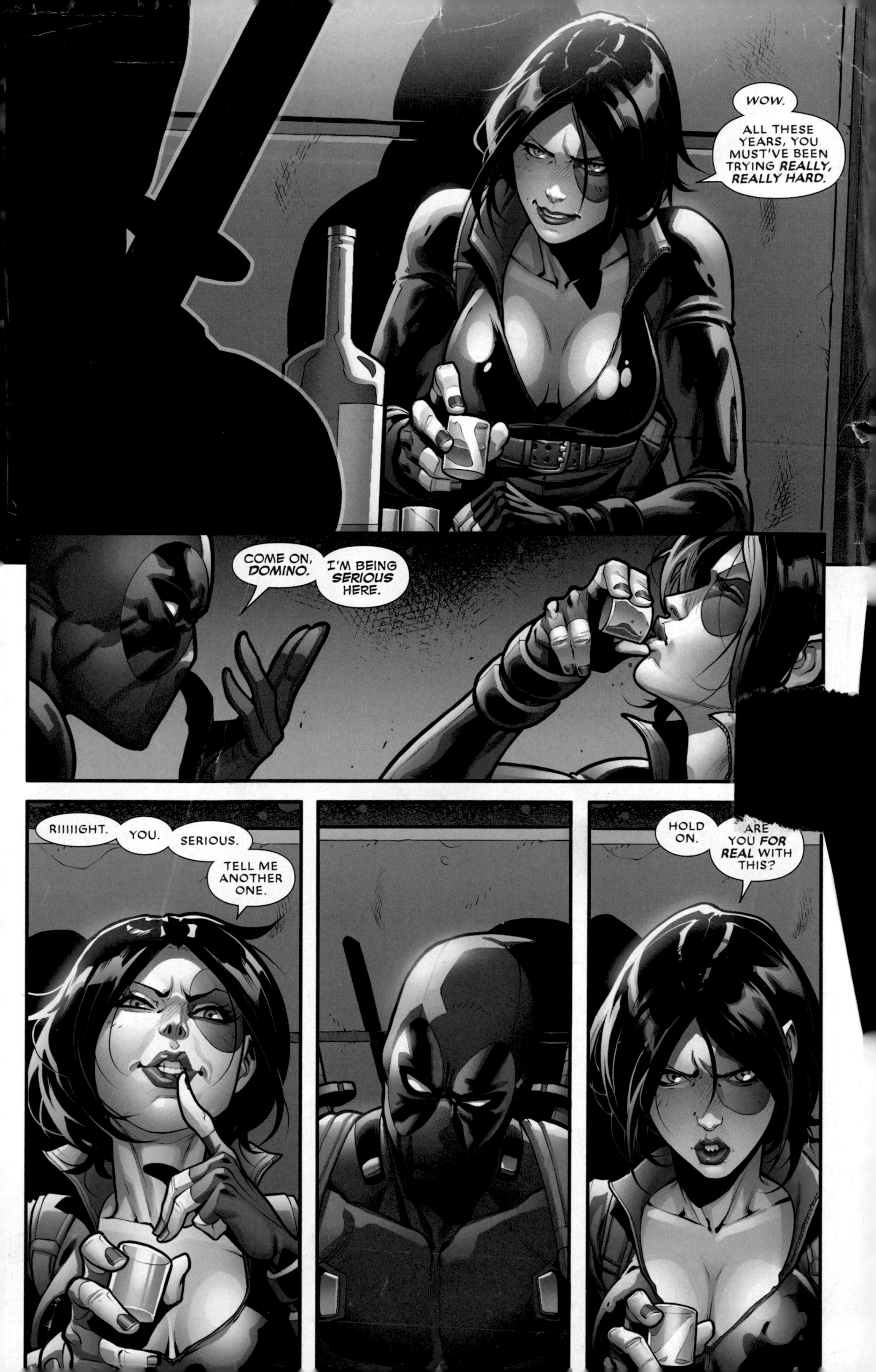
WOW.
ALL THESE YEARS, YOU MUST'VE BEEN TRYING REALLY, REALLY HARD.
COME ON, DOMINO.
I'M BEING SERIOUS HERE.
RIIIIIGHT.
YOU.
SERIOUS.
TELL ME ANOTHER ONE.
HOLD ON.
ARE YOU FOR REAL WITH THIS?

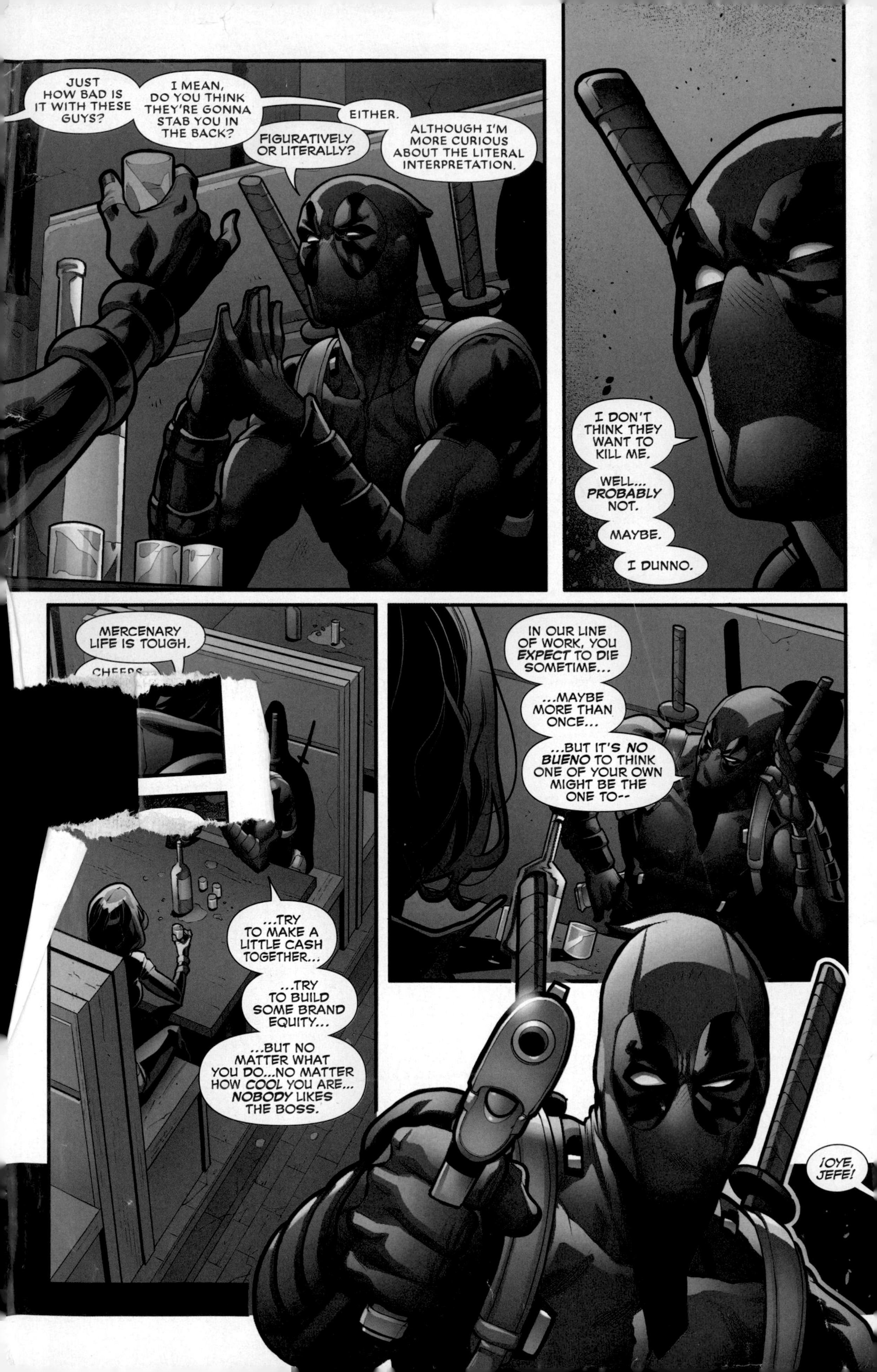
JUST HOW BAD IS IT WITH THESE GUYS?
I MEAN, DO YOU THINK THEY'RE GONNA STAB YOU IN THE BACK?
FIGURATIVELY OR LITERALLY?
EITHER.
ALTHOUGH I'M MORE CURIOUS ABOUT THE LITERAL INTERPRETATION.
I DON'T THINK THEY WANT TO KILL ME.
WELL... PROBABLY NOT.
MAYBE.
I DUNNO.
MERCENARY LIFE IS TOUGH.
...TRY TO MAKE A LITTLE CASH TOGETHER...
...TRY TO BUILD SOME BRAND EQUITY...
...BUT NO MATTER WHAT YOU DO...NO MATTER HOW COOL YOU ARE... NOBODY LIKES THE BOSS.
IN OUR LINE OF WORK, YOU EXPECT TO DIE SOMETIME...
...MAYBE MORE THAN ONCE...
...BUT IT'S NO BUENO TO THINK ONE OF YOUR OWN MIGHT BE THE ONE TO--
¡OYE, JEFE!

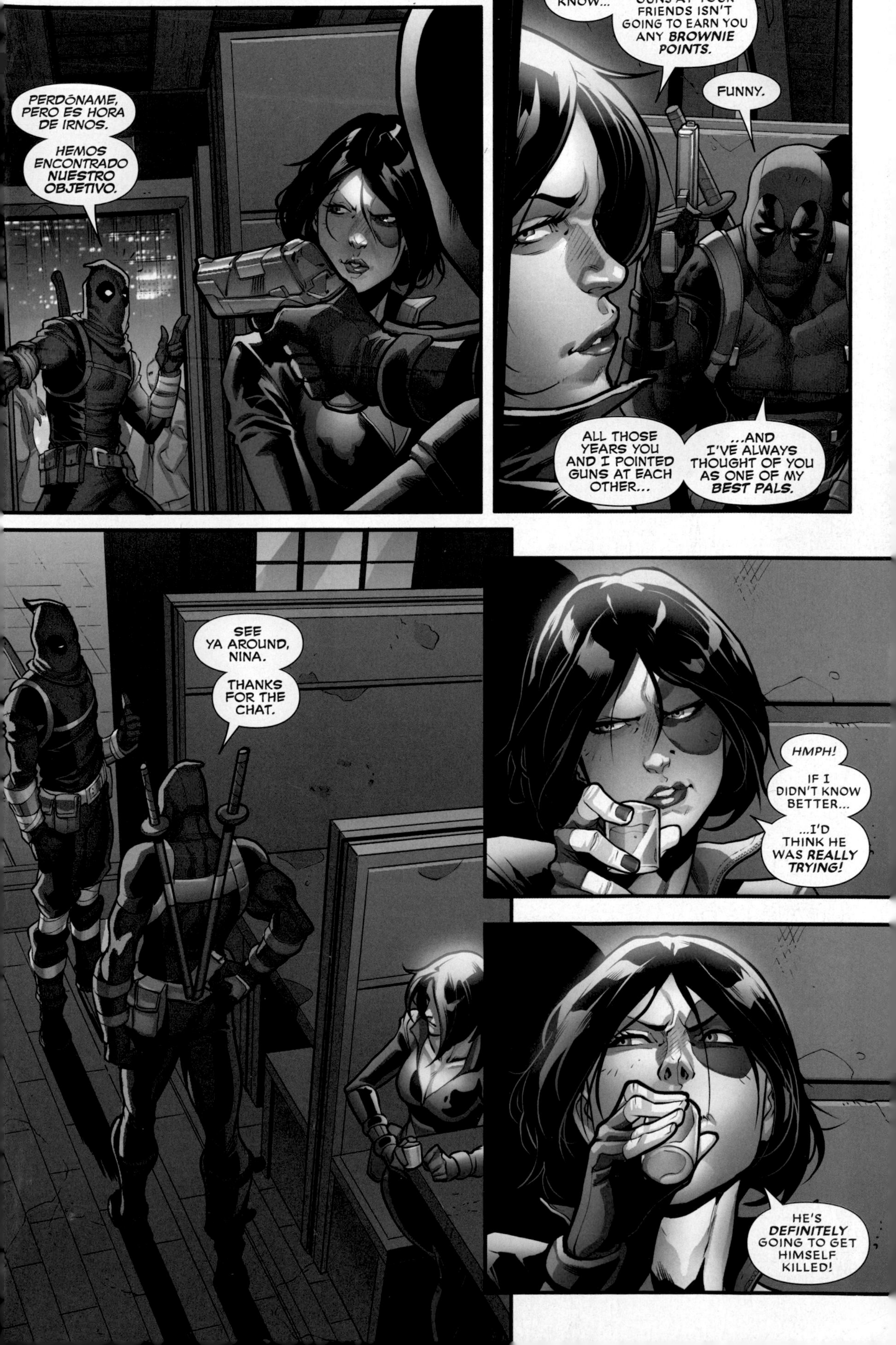
PERDÓNAME, PERO ES HORA DE IRNOS.
HEMOS ENCONTRADO NUESTRO OBJETIVO.
YOU KNOW...
...POINTING GUNS AT YOUR FRIENDS ISN'T GOING TO EARN YOU ANY BROWNIE POINTS.
FUNNY.
ALL THOSE YEARS YOU AND I POINTED GUNS AT EACH OTHER...
...AND I'VE ALWAYS THOUGHT OF YOU AS ONE OF MY BEST PALS.
SEE YA AROUND, NINA.
THANKS FOR THE CHAT.
HMPH!
IF I DIDN'T KNOW BETTER...
...I'D THINK HE WAS REALLY TRYING!
HE'S DEFINITELY GOING TO GET HIMSELF KILLED!

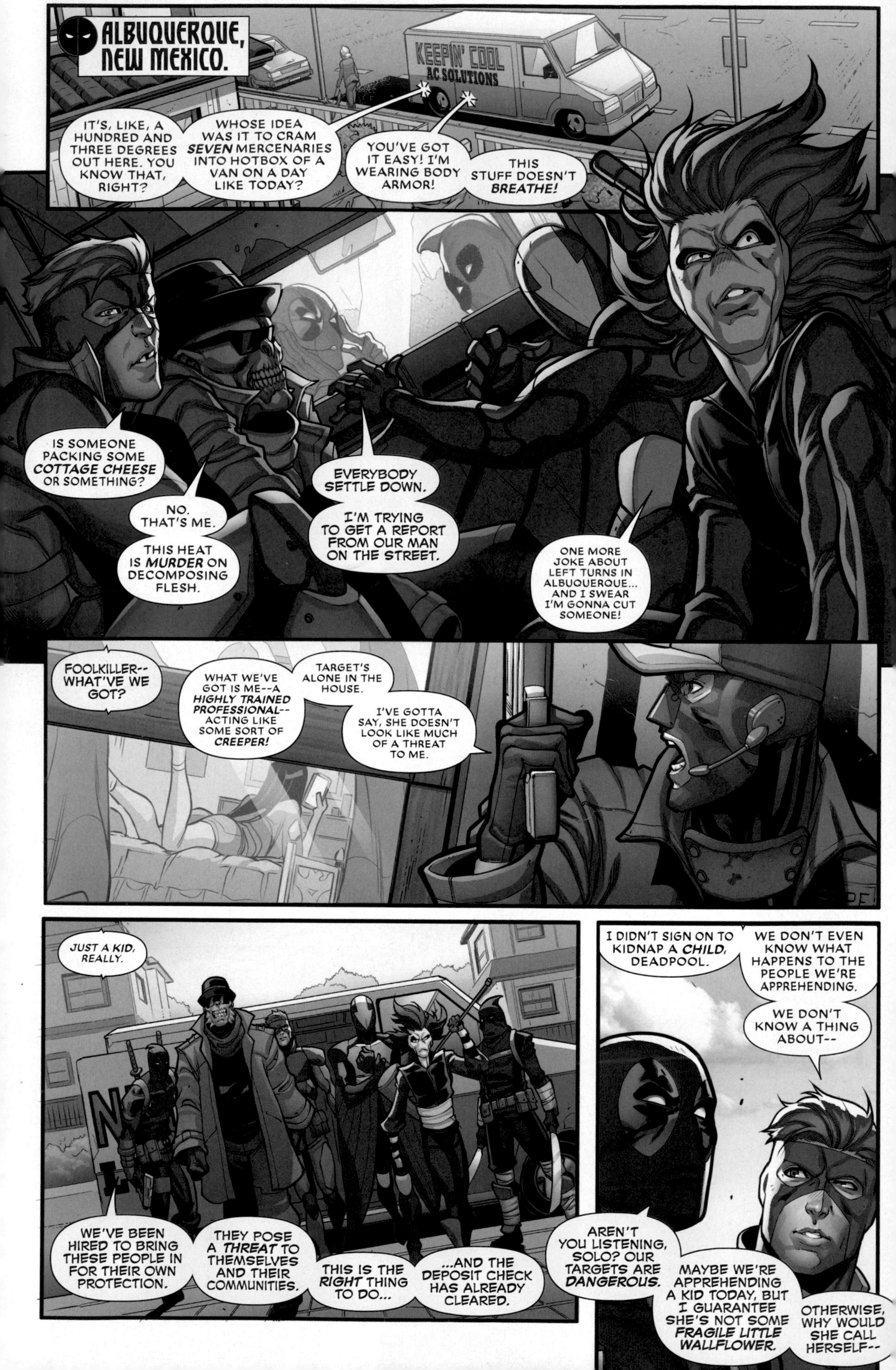
ALBUQUERQUE, NEW MEXICO.
KEEPIN' COOL AC SOLUTIONS
IT'S, LIKE, A HUNDRED AND THREE DEGREES OUT HERE. YOU KNOW THAT, RIGHT?
WHOSE IDEA WAS IT TO CRAM SEVEN MERCENARIES INTO HOTBOX OF A VAN ON A DAY LIKE TODAY?
YOU'VE GOT IT EASY! I'M WEARING BODY ARMOR!
THIS STUFF DOESN'T BREATHE!
IS SOMEONE PACKING SOME COTTAGE CHEESE OR SOMETHING?
NO. THAT'S ME.
THIS HEAT IS MURDER ON DECOMPOSING FLESH.
EVERYBODY SETTLE DOWN.
I'M TRYING TO GET A REPORT FROM OUR MAN ON THE STREET.
ONE MORE JOKE ABOUT LEFT TURNS IN ALBUQUERQUE... AND I SWEAR I'M GONNA CUT SOMEONE!
FOOLKILLER-- WHAT'VE WE GOT?
WHAT WE'VE GOT IS ME--A HIGHLY TRAINED PROFESSIONAL-- ACTING LIKE SOME SORT OF CREEPER!
TARGET'S ALONE IN THE HOUSE.
I'VE GOTTA SAY, SHE DOESN'T LOOK LIKE MUCH OF A THREAT TO ME.
JUST A KID, REALLY.
WE'VE BEEN HIRED TO BRING THESE PEOPLE IN FOR THEIR OWN PROTECTION.
THEY POSE A THREAT TO THEMSELVES AND THEIR COMMUNITIES.
THIS IS THE RIGHT THING TO DO...
...AND THE DEPOSIT CHECK HAS ALREADY CLEARED.
I DIDN'T SIGN ON TO KIDNAP A CHILD, DEADPOOL.
WE DON'T EVEN KNOW WHAT HAPPENS TO THE PEOPLE WE'RE APPREHENDING.
WE DON'T KNOW A THING ABOUT--
AREN'T YOU LISTENING, SOLO? OUR TARGETS ARE DANGEROUS.
MAYBE WE'RE APPREHENDING A KID TODAY, BUT I GUARANTEE SHE'S NOT SOME FRAGILE LITTLE WALLFLOWER.
OTHERWISE, WHY WOULD SHE CALL HERSELF--

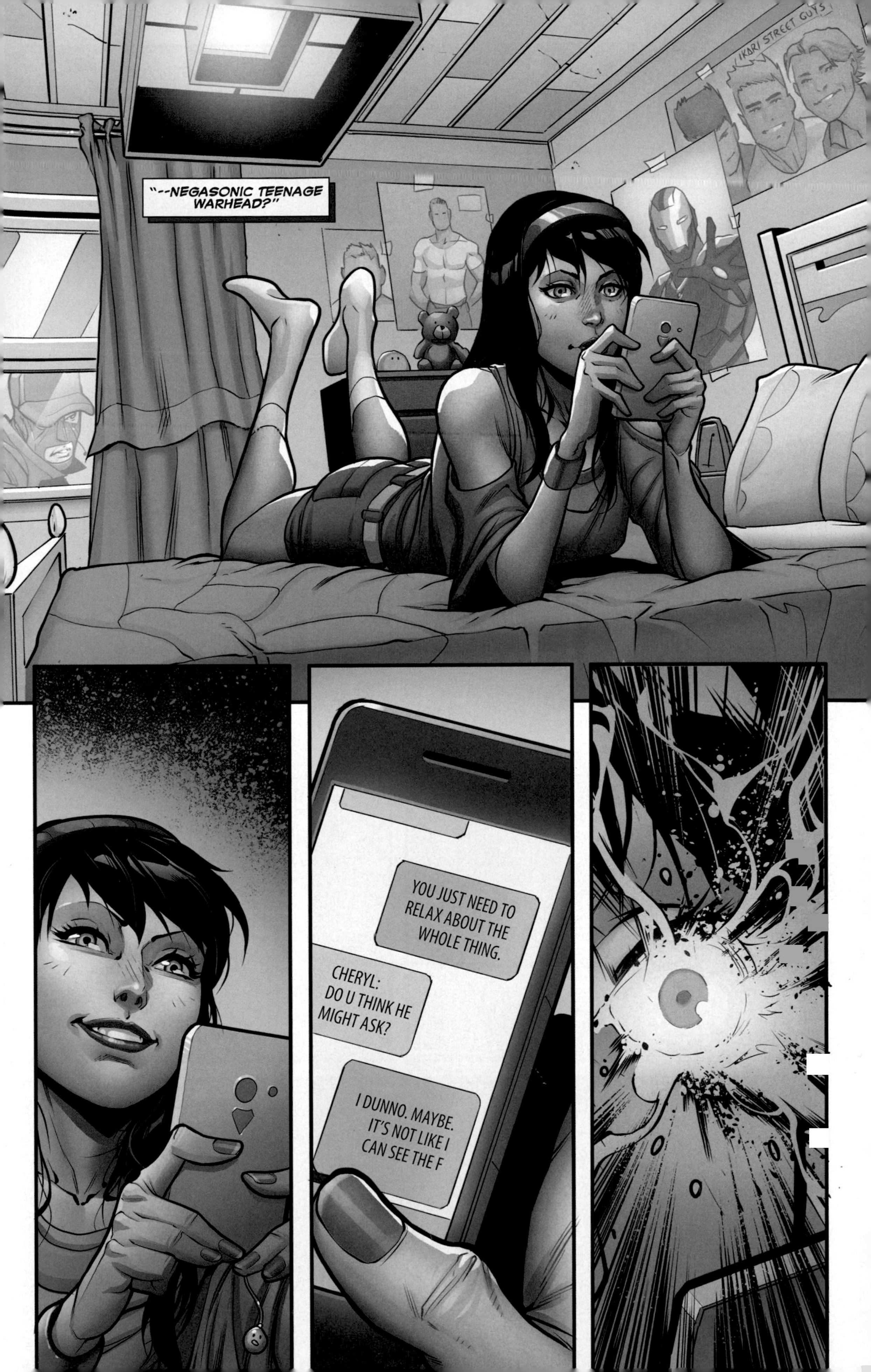

"--NEGASONIC TEENAGE WARHEAD?"
IKARI STREET GUYS
YOU JUST NEED TO RELAX ABOUT THE WHOLE THING.
CHERYL: DO U THINK HE MIGHT ASK?
I DUNNO. MAYBE. IT'S NOT LIKE I CAN SEE THE F

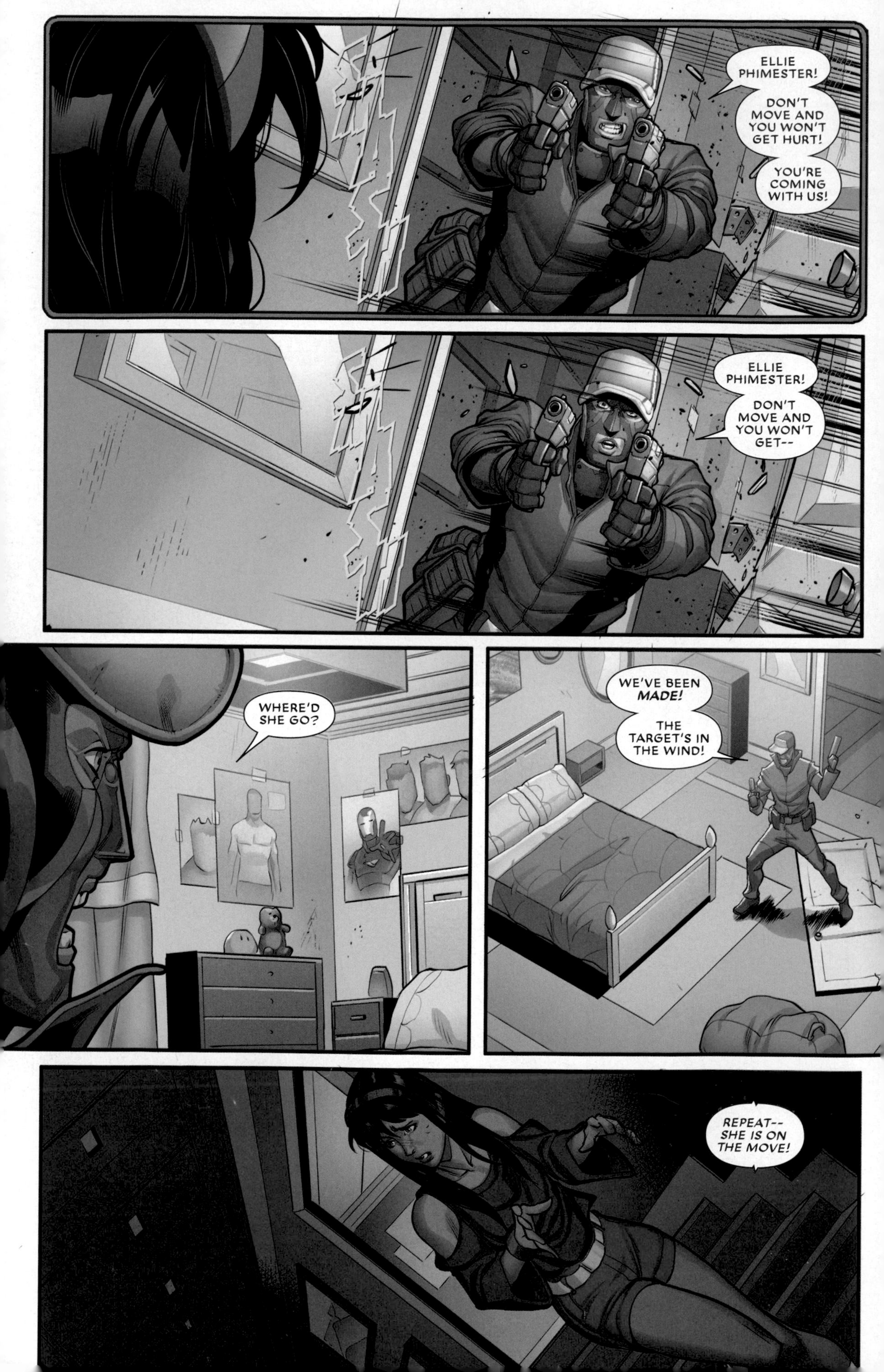
ELLIE PHIMESTER!
DON'T MOVE AND YOU WON'T GET HURT!
YOU'RE COMING WITH US!
ELLIE PHIMESTER!
DON'T MOVE AND YOU WON'T GET--
WHERE'D SHE GO?
WE'VE BEEN *MADE!*
THE TARGET'S IN THE WIND!
REPEAT-- SHE IS ON THE MOVE!

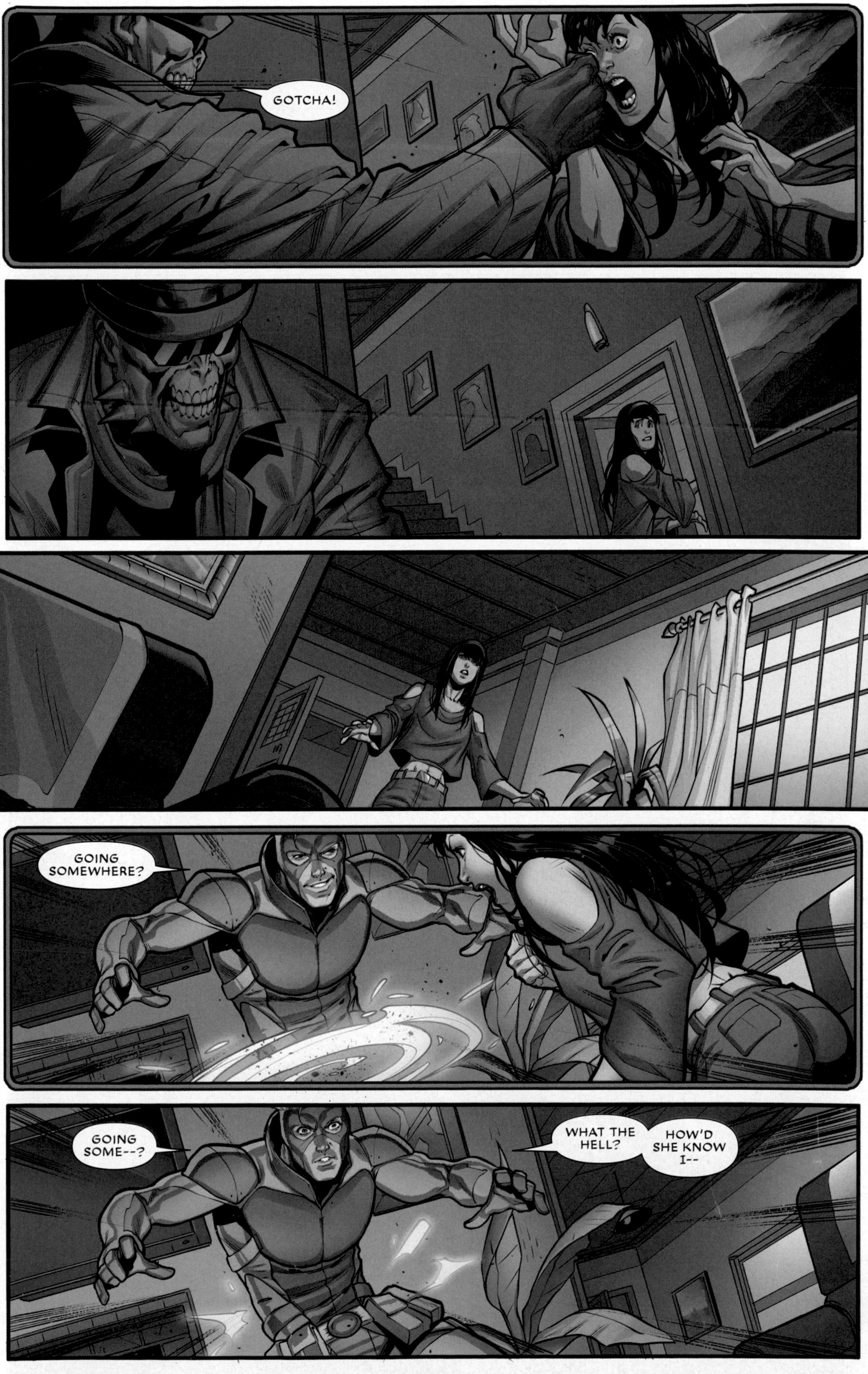
GOTCHA!
GOING SOMEWHERE?
GOING SOME--?
WHAT THE HELL?
HOW'D SHE KNOW I--

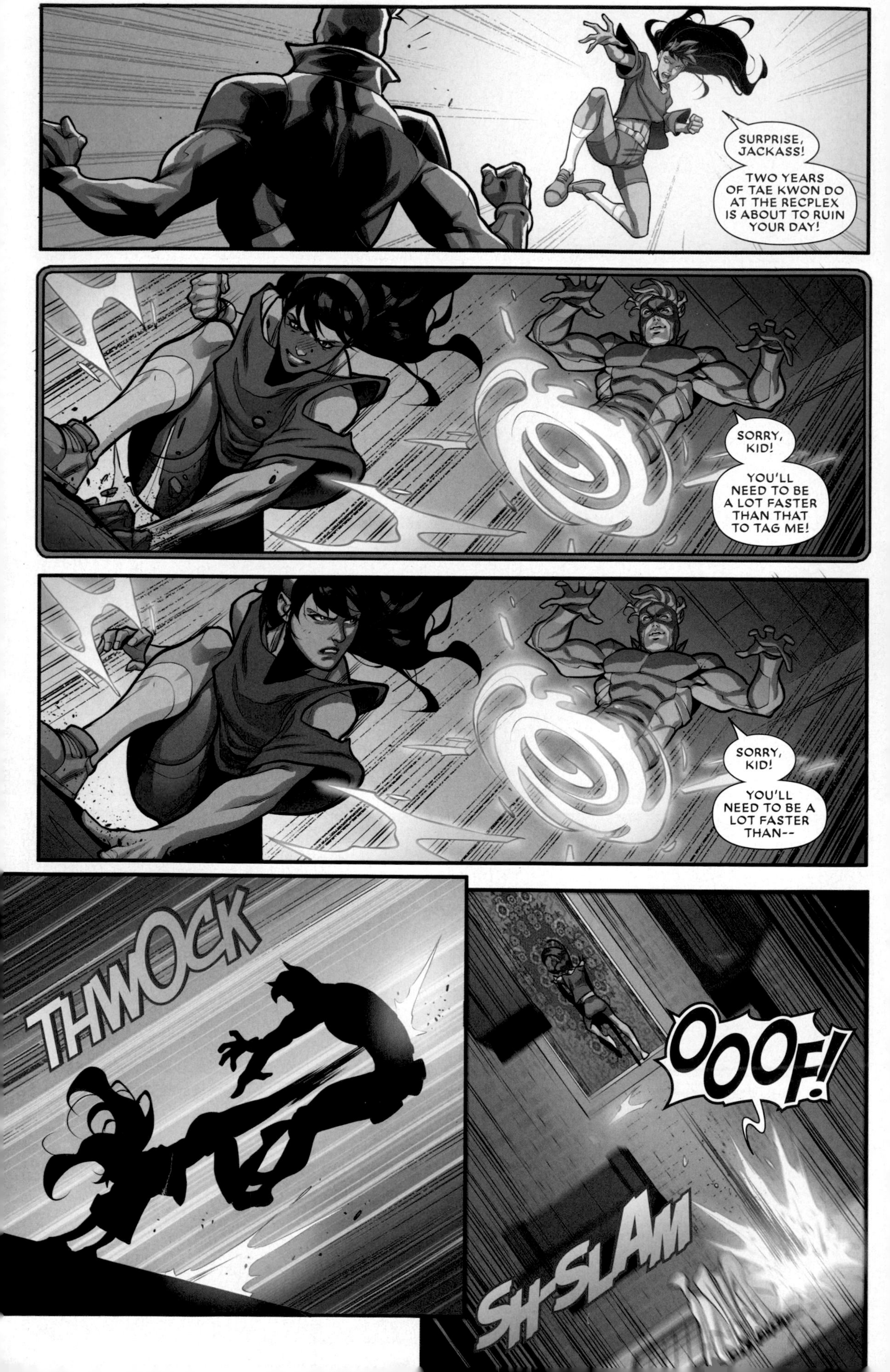
SURPRISE, JACKASS!
TWO YEARS OF TAE KWON DO AT THE RECPLEX IS ABOUT TO RUIN YOUR DAY!
SORRY, KID!
YOU'LL NEED TO BE A LOT FASTER THAN THAT TO TAG ME!
SORRY, KID!
YOU'LL NEED TO BE A LOT FASTER THAN--
THWOCK
OOOF!
SH-SLAM

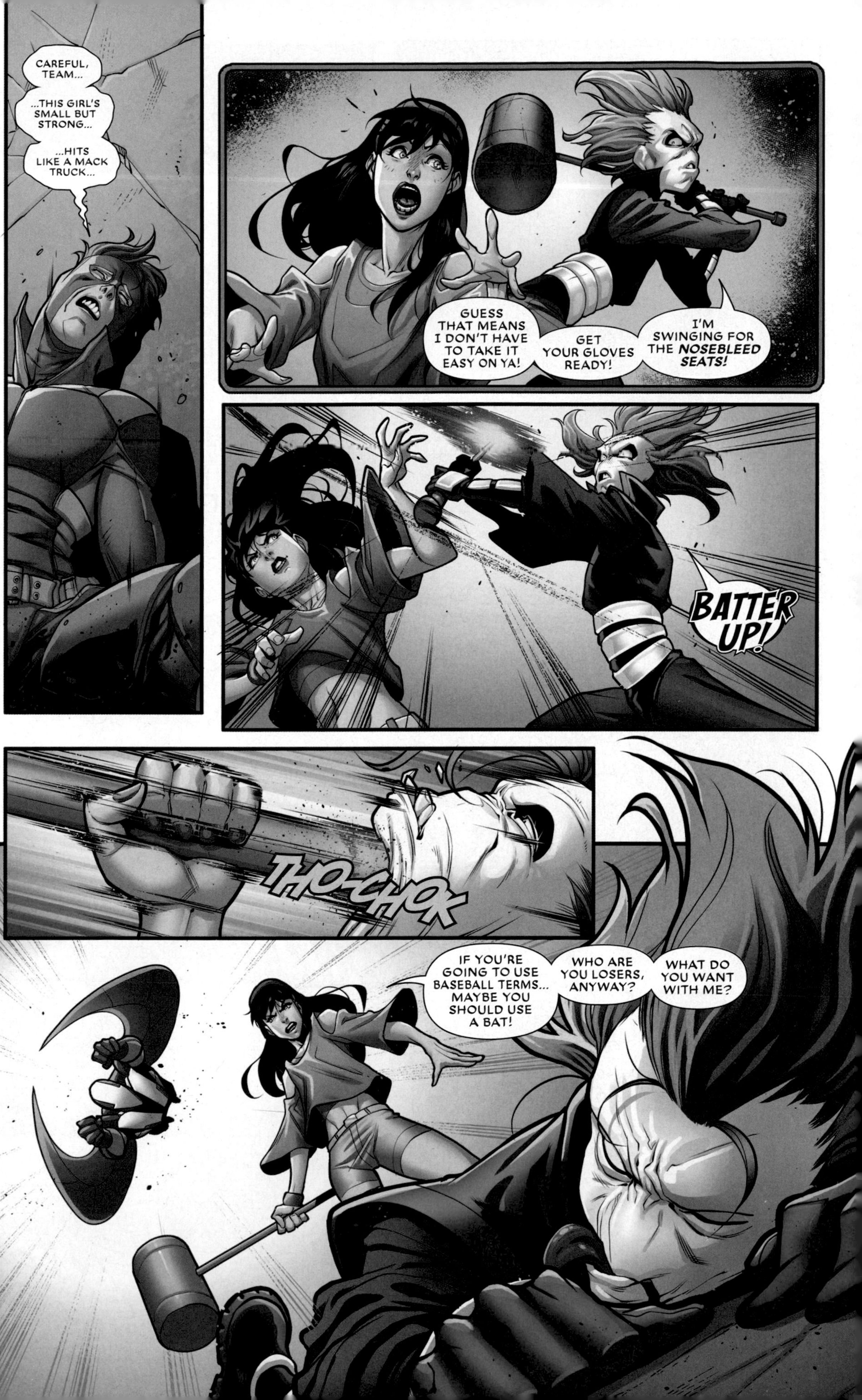
CAREFUL, TEAM...
...THIS GIRL'S SMALL BUT STRONG...
...HITS LIKE A MACK TRUCK...
GUESS THAT MEANS I DON'T HAVE TO TAKE IT EASY ON YA!
GET YOUR GLOVES READY!
I'M SWINGING FOR THE NOSEBLEED SEATS!
BATTER UP!
THO-CHOK
IF YOU'RE GOING TO USE BASEBALL TERMS... MAYBE YOU SHOULD USE A BAT!
WHO ARE YOU LOSERS, ANYWAY?
WHAT DO YOU WANT WITH ME?

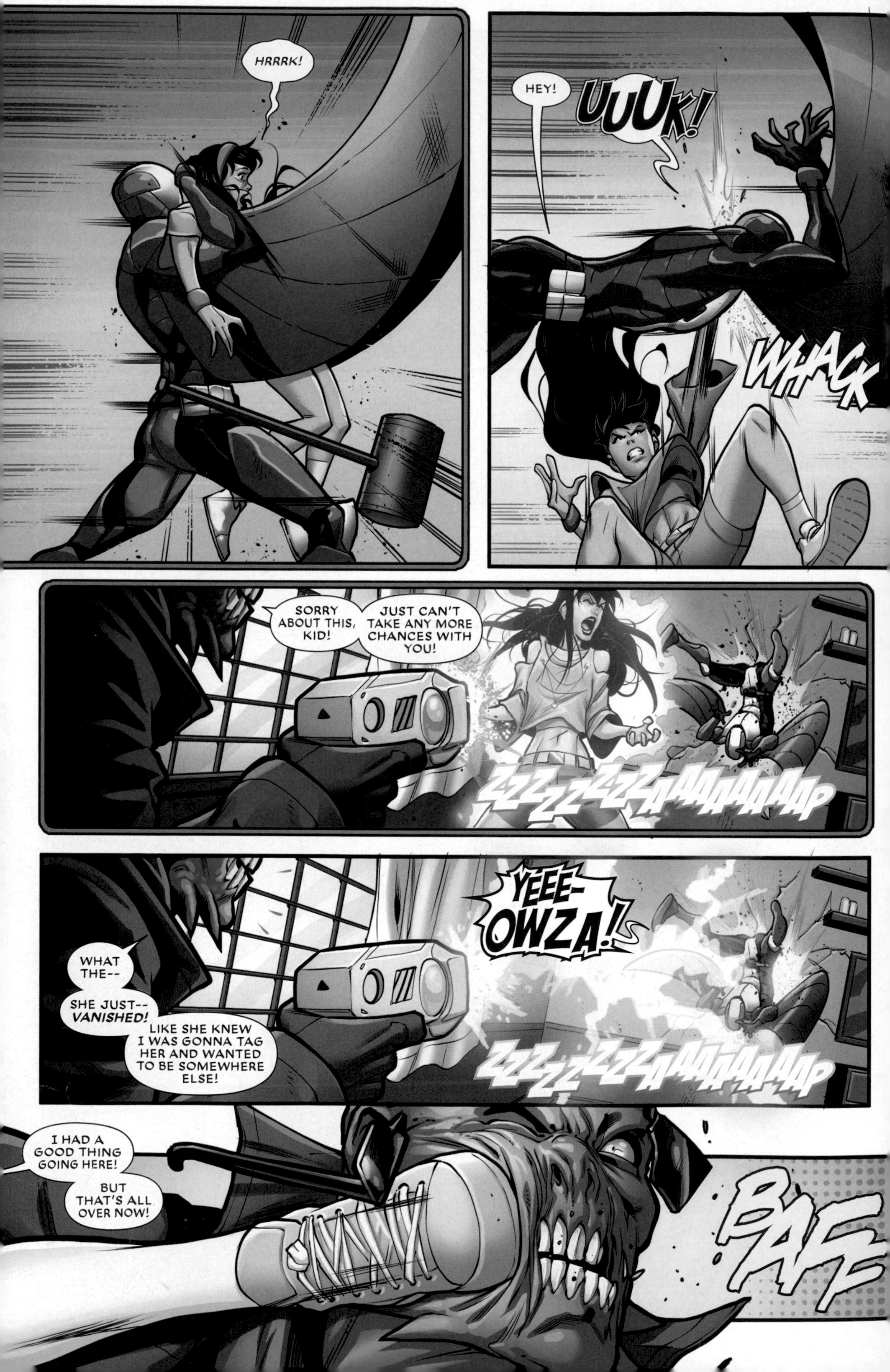
HRRRK!
HEY!
UUUK!
WHACK
SORRY ABOUT THIS, KID!
JUST CAN'T TAKE ANY MORE CHANCES WITH YOU!
ZZZZZZZZZAAAAAAAAP
YEEE-OWZA!
WHAT THE--
SHE JUST-- *VANISHED!*
LIKE SHE KNEW I WAS GONNA TAG HER AND WANTED TO BE SOMEWHERE ELSE!
ZZZZZZZZZAAAAAAAAP
I HAD A GOOD THING GOING HERE!
BUT THAT'S ALL OVER NOW!
BAFF

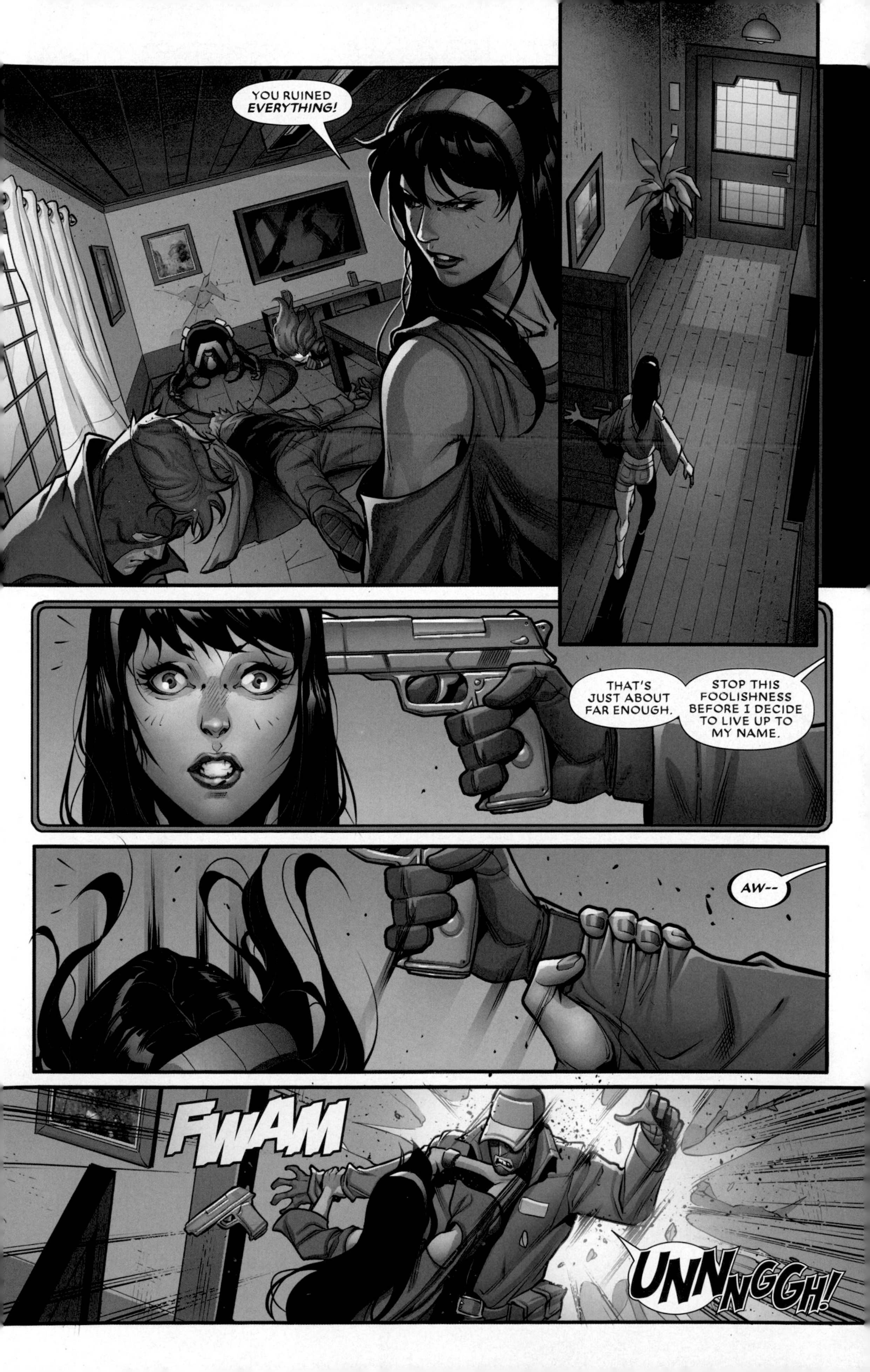
YOU RUINED EVERYTHING!
THAT'S JUST ABOUT FAR ENOUGH.
STOP THIS FOOLISHNESS BEFORE I DECIDE TO LIVE UP TO MY NAME.
AW--
FWAM
UNNNGGH!

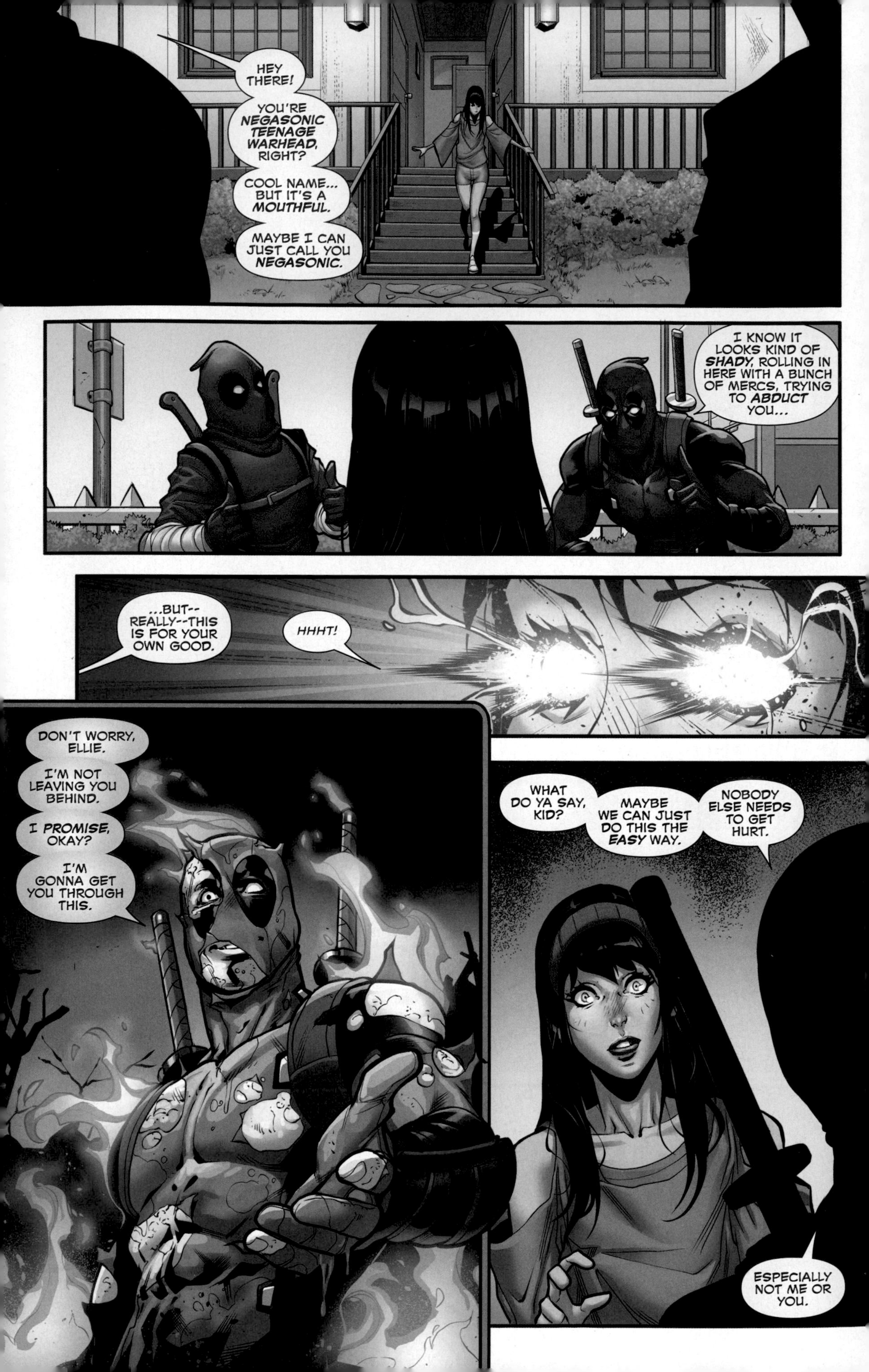
HEY THERE!
YOU'RE NEGASONIC TEENAGE WARHEAD, RIGHT?
COOL NAME... BUT IT'S A MOUTHFUL.
MAYBE I CAN JUST CALL YOU NEGASONIC.
I KNOW IT LOOKS KIND OF SHADY, ROLLING IN HERE WITH A BUNCH OF MERCS, TRYING TO ABDUCT YOU...
...BUT--REALLY--THIS IS FOR YOUR OWN GOOD.
HHHT!
DON'T WORRY, ELLIE.
I'M NOT LEAVING YOU BEHIND.
I PROMISE, OKAY?
I'M GONNA GET YOU THROUGH THIS.
WHAT DO YA SAY, KID?
MAYBE WE CAN JUST DO THIS THE EASY WAY.
NOBODY ELSE NEEDS TO GET HURT.
ESPECIALLY NOT ME OR YOU.

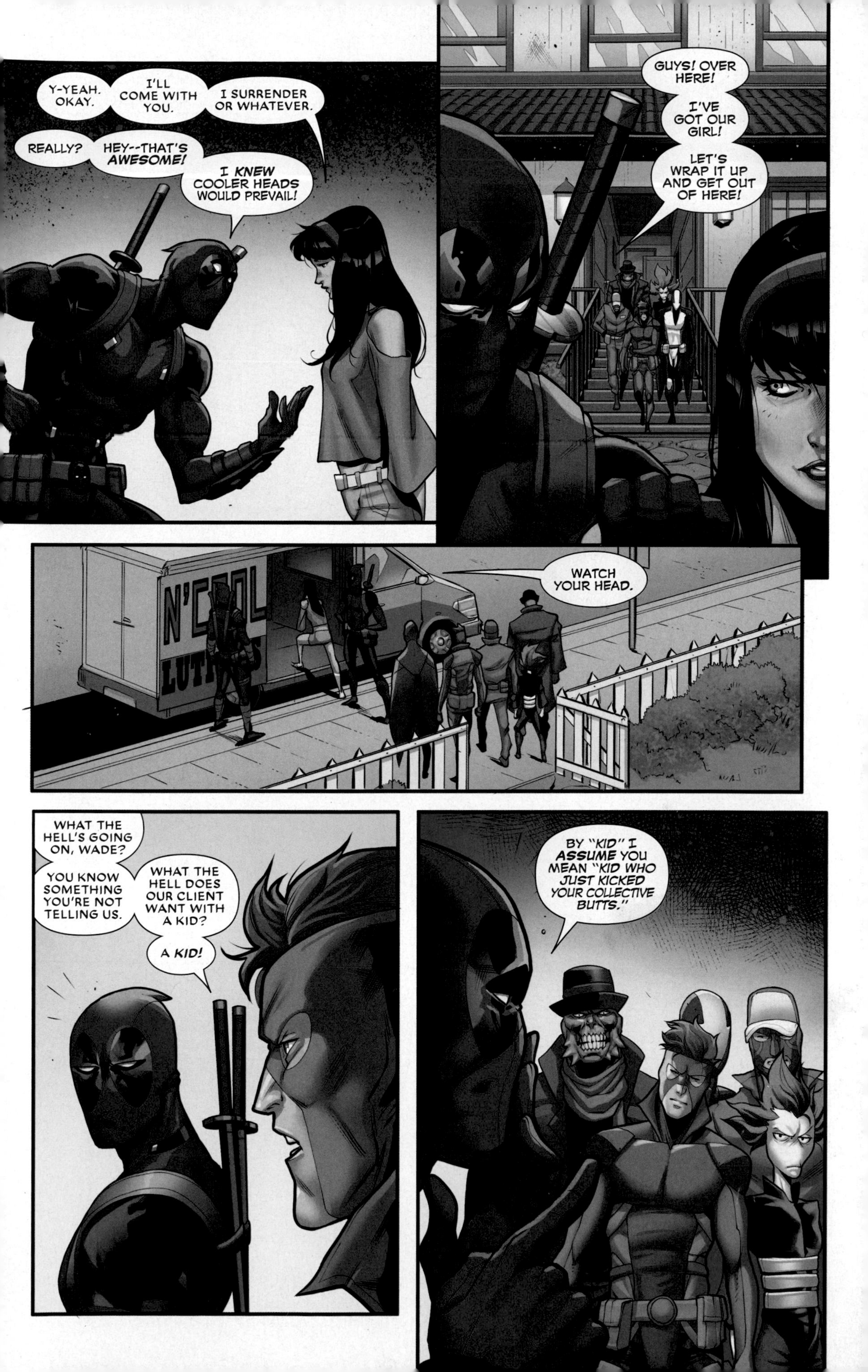
Y-YEAH. OKAY.
I'LL COME WITH YOU.
I SURRENDER OR WHATEVER.
REALLY?
HEY--THAT'S AWESOME!
I KNEW COOLER HEADS WOULD PREVAIL!
GUYS! OVER HERE!
I'VE GOT OUR GIRL!
LET'S WRAP IT UP AND GET OUT OF HERE!
WATCH YOUR HEAD.
WHAT THE HELL'S GOING ON, WADE?
YOU KNOW SOMETHING YOU'RE NOT TELLING US.
WHAT THE HELL DOES OUR CLIENT WANT WITH A KID?
A KID!
BY "KID" I ASSUME YOU MEAN "KID WHO JUST KICKED YOUR COLLECTIVE BUTTS."

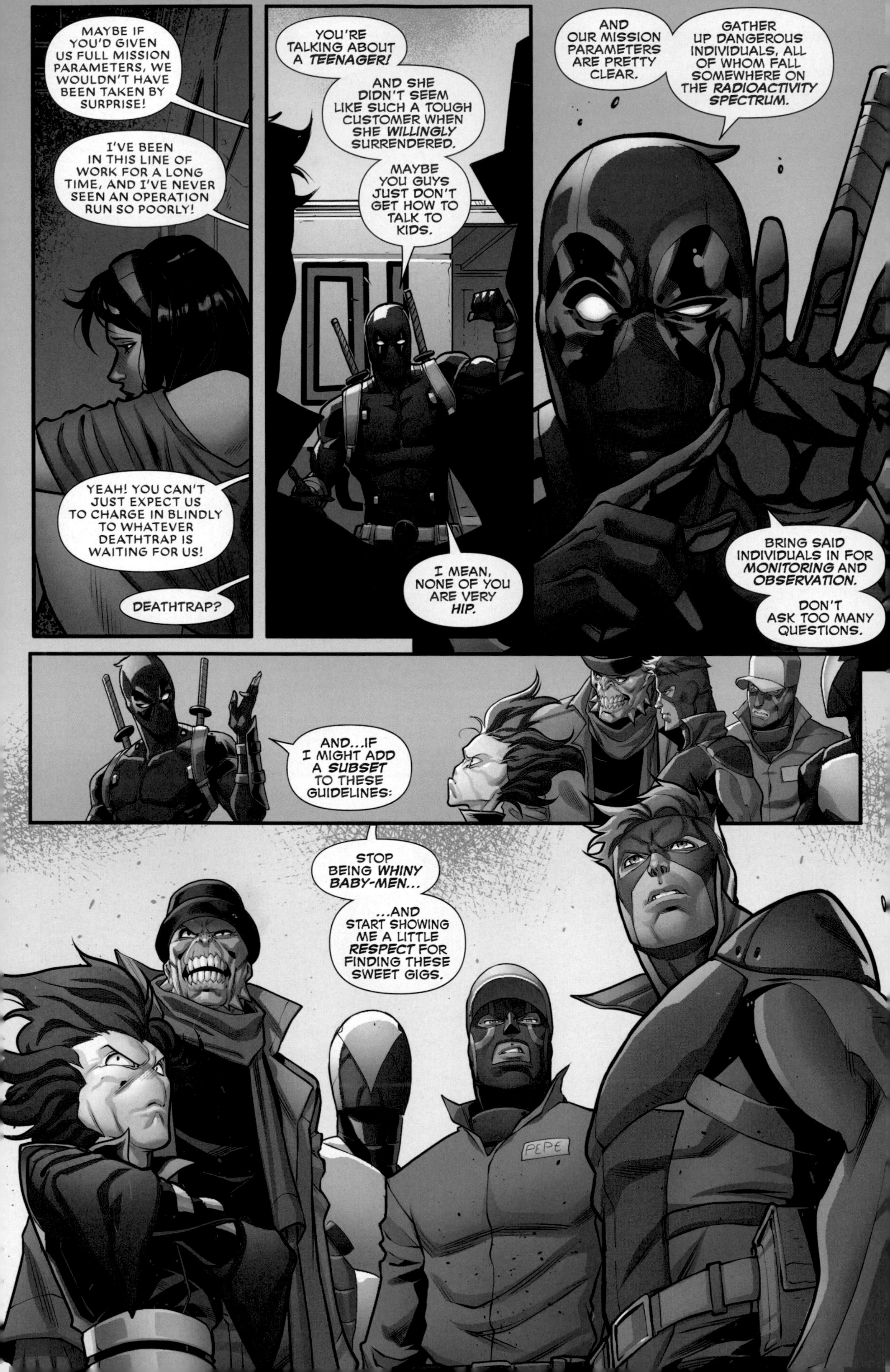
MAYBE IF YOU'D GIVEN US FULL MISSION PARAMETERS, WE WOULDN'T HAVE BEEN TAKEN BY SURPRISE!
I'VE BEEN IN THIS LINE OF WORK FOR A LONG TIME, AND I'VE NEVER SEEN AN OPERATION RUN SO POORLY!
YEAH! YOU CAN'T JUST EXPECT US TO CHARGE IN BLINDLY TO WHATEVER DEATHTRAP IS WAITING FOR US!
DEATHTRAP?
YOU'RE TALKING ABOUT A *TEENAGER!*
AND SHE DIDN'T SEEM LIKE SUCH A TOUGH CUSTOMER WHEN SHE *WILLINGLY* SURRENDERED.
MAYBE YOU GUYS JUST DON'T GET HOW TO TALK TO KIDS.
I MEAN, NONE OF YOU ARE VERY *HIP.*
AND OUR MISSION PARAMETERS ARE PRETTY CLEAR.
GATHER UP DANGEROUS INDIVIDUALS, ALL OF WHOM FALL SOMEWHERE ON THE *RADIOACTIVITY SPECTRUM.*
BRING SAID INDIVIDUALS IN FOR *MONITORING* AND *OBSERVATION.*
DON'T ASK TOO MANY QUESTIONS.
AND...IF I MIGHT ADD A *SUBSET* TO THESE GUIDELINES:
STOP BEING *WHINY BABY-MEN...*
...AND START SHOWING ME A LITTLE *RESPECT* FOR FINDING THESE SWEET GIGS.
PEPE

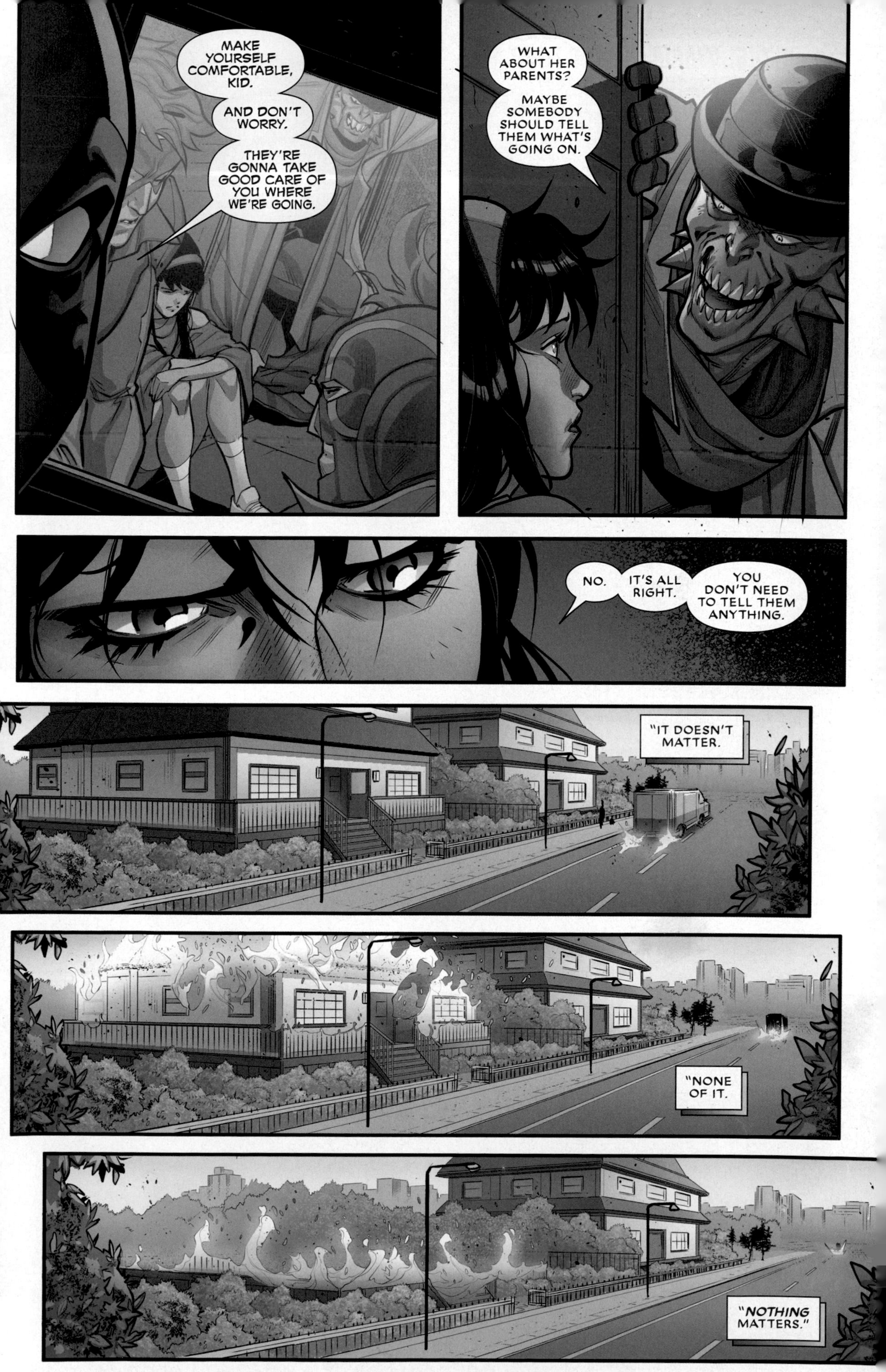
MAKE YOURSELF COMFORTABLE, KID.
AND DON'T WORRY.
THEY'RE GONNA TAKE GOOD CARE OF YOU WHERE WE'RE GOING.
WHAT ABOUT HER PARENTS?
MAYBE SOMEBODY SHOULD TELL THEM WHAT'S GOING ON.
NO.
IT'S ALL RIGHT.
YOU DON'T NEED TO TELL THEM ANYTHING.
"IT DOESN'T MATTER.
"NONE OF IT.
"NOTHING MATTERS."

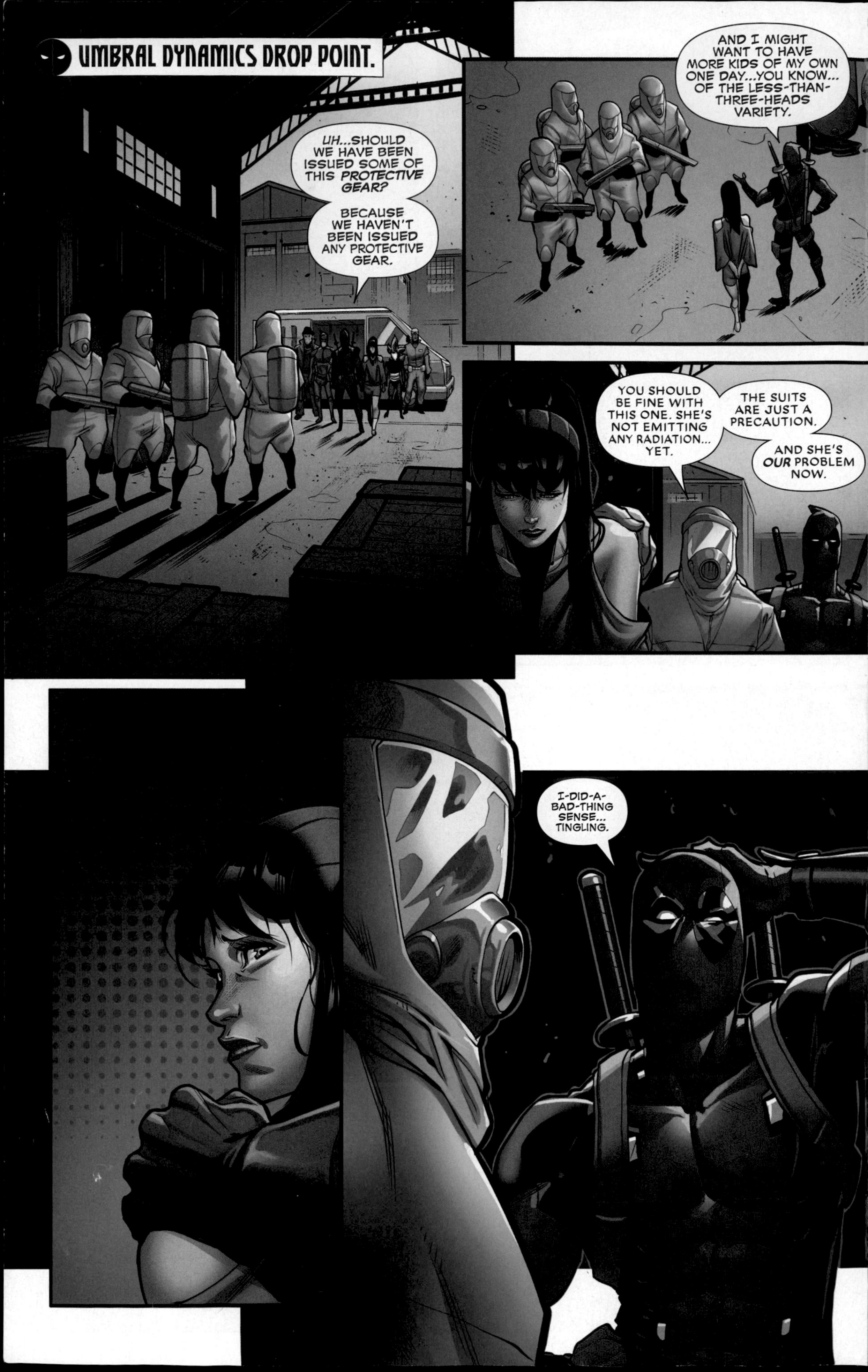
UMBRAL DYNAMICS DROP POINT.
UH...SHOULD WE HAVE BEEN ISSUED SOME OF THIS PROTECTIVE GEAR?
BECAUSE WE HAVEN'T BEEN ISSUED ANY PROTECTIVE GEAR.
AND I MIGHT WANT TO HAVE MORE KIDS OF MY OWN ONE DAY...YOU KNOW... OF THE LESS-THAN-THREE-HEADS VARIETY.
YOU SHOULD BE FINE WITH THIS ONE. SHE'S NOT EMITTING ANY RADIATION... YET.
THE SUITS ARE JUST A PRECAUTION.
AND SHE'S OUR PROBLEM NOW.
I-DID-A-BAD-THING SENSE... TINGLING.

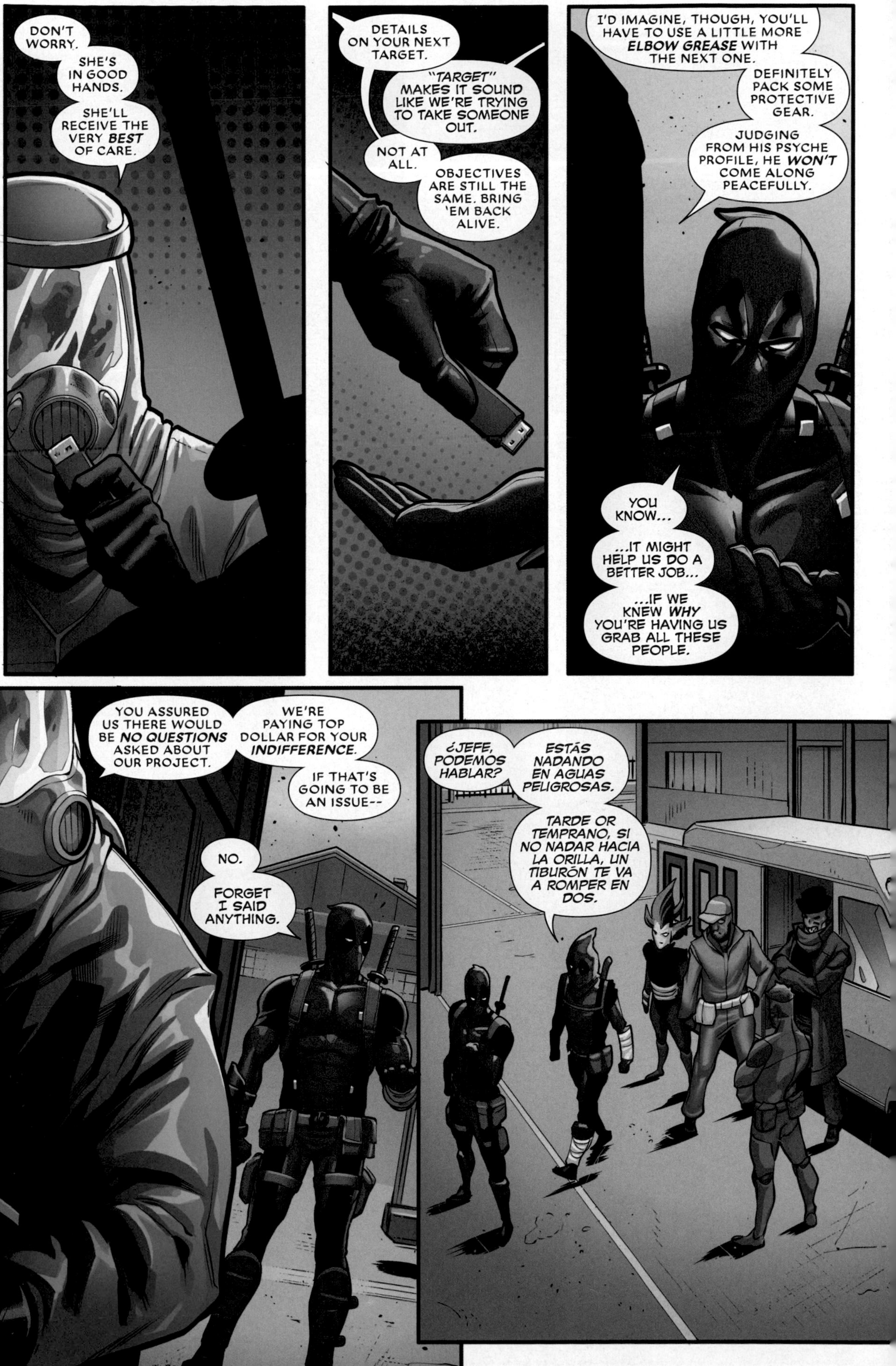

DON'T WORRY.
SHE'S IN GOOD HANDS.
SHE'LL RECEIVE THE VERY BEST OF CARE.
DETAILS ON YOUR NEXT TARGET.
"TARGET" MAKES IT SOUND LIKE WE'RE TRYING TO TAKE SOMEONE OUT.
NOT AT ALL.
OBJECTIVES ARE STILL THE SAME. BRING 'EM BACK ALIVE.
I'D IMAGINE, THOUGH, YOU'LL HAVE TO USE A LITTLE MORE ELBOW GREASE WITH THE NEXT ONE.
DEFINITELY PACK SOME PROTECTIVE GEAR.
JUDGING FROM HIS PSYCHE PROFILE, HE WON'T COME ALONG PEACEFULLY.
YOU KNOW...
...IT MIGHT HELP US DO A BETTER JOB...
...IF WE KNEW WHY YOU'RE HAVING US GRAB ALL THESE PEOPLE.
YOU ASSURED US THERE WOULD BE NO QUESTIONS ASKED ABOUT OUR PROJECT.
WE'RE PAYING TOP DOLLAR FOR YOUR INDIFFERENCE.
IF THAT'S GOING TO BE AN ISSUE--
NO.
FORGET I SAID ANYTHING.
¿JEFE, PODEMOS HABLAR?
ESTÁS NADANDO EN AGUAS PELIGROSAS.
TARDE OR TEMPRANO, SI NO NADAR HACIA LA ORILLA, UN TIBURÓN TE VA A ROMPER EN DOS.

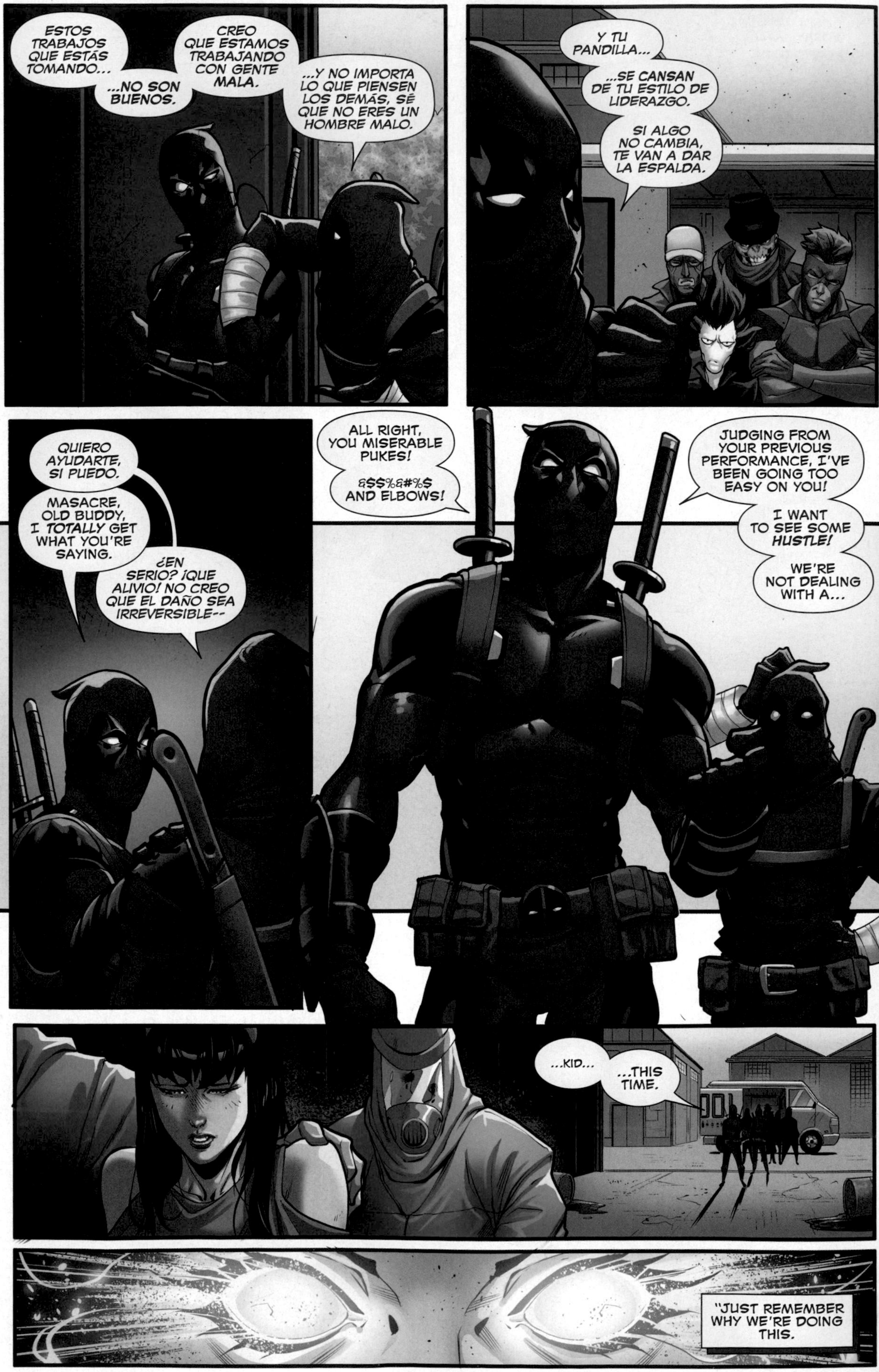
ESTOS TRABAJOS QUE ESTÁS TOMANDO...
...NO SON BUENOS.
CREO QUE ESTAMOS TRABAJANDO CON GENTE MALA.
...Y NO IMPORTA LO QUE PIENSEN LOS DEMÁS, SÉ QUE NO ERES UN HOMBRE MALO.
Y TU PANDILLA...
...SE CANSAN DE TU ESTILO DE LIDERAZGO.
SI ALGO NO CAMBIA, TE VAN A DAR LA ESPALDA.
QUIERO AYUDARTE, SI PUEDO.
MASACRE, OLD BUDDY, I TOTALLY GET WHAT YOU'RE SAYING.
¿EN SERIO? ¡QUE ALIVIO! NO CREO QUE EL DAÑO SEA IRREVERSIBLE--
ALL RIGHT, YOU MISERABLE PUKES!
&$$%&#%$ AND ELBOWS!
JUDGING FROM YOUR PREVIOUS PERFORMANCE, I'VE BEEN GOING TOO EASY ON YOU!
I WANT TO SEE SOME HUSTLE!
WE'RE NOT DEALING WITH A...
...KID...
...THIS TIME.
"JUST REMEMBER WHY WE'RE DOING THIS.

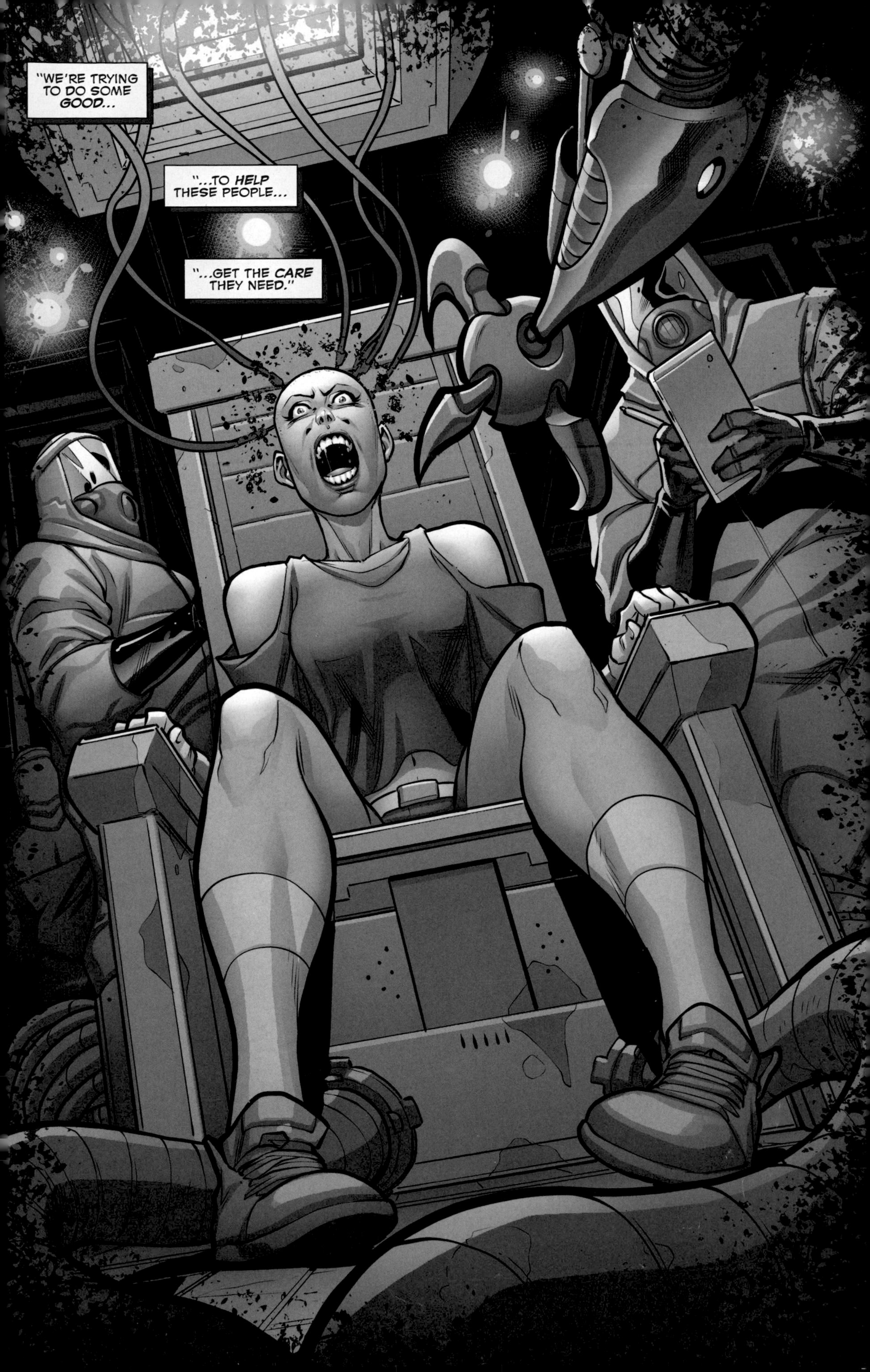
"WE'RE TRYING TO DO SOME GOOD...
"...TO HELP THESE PEOPLE...
"...GET THE CARE THEY NEED."

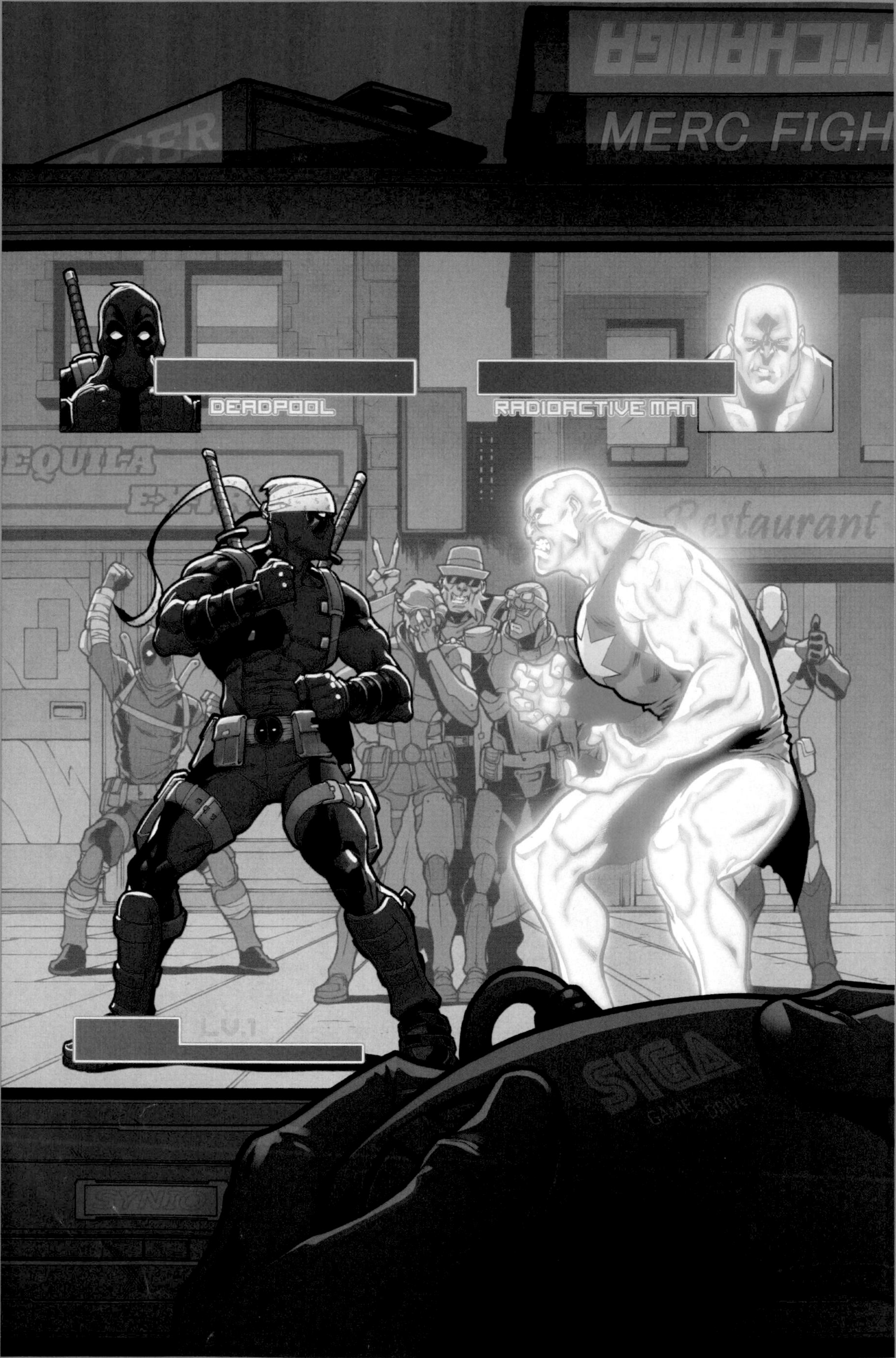

MERC FIGH
DEADPOOL
RADIOACTIVE MAN
EQUILA
Restaurant
LV.1
SIGA
GAME DRIVE

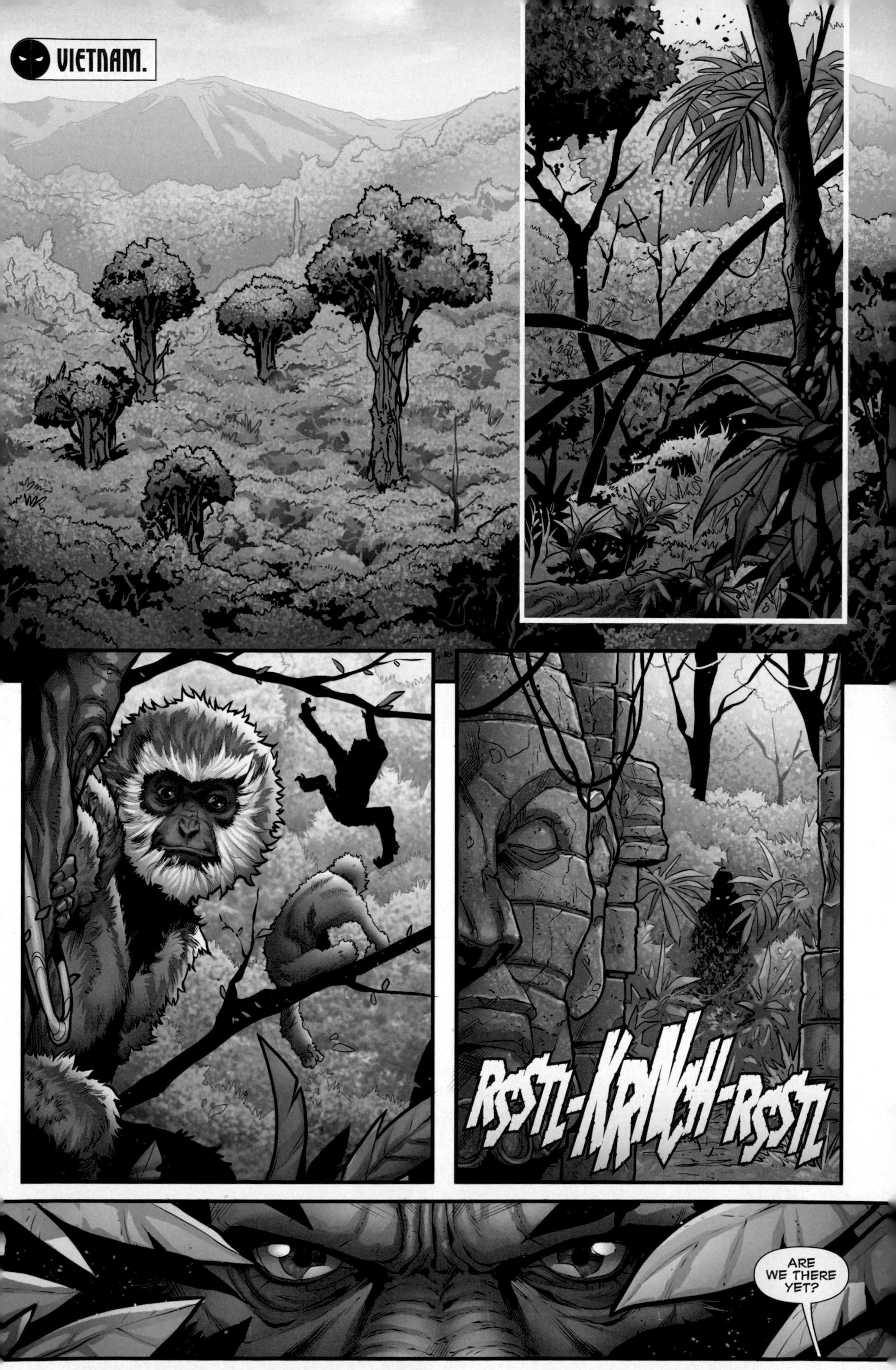
VIETNAM.
RSSTL-KRNCH-RSSTL
ARE WE THERE YET?

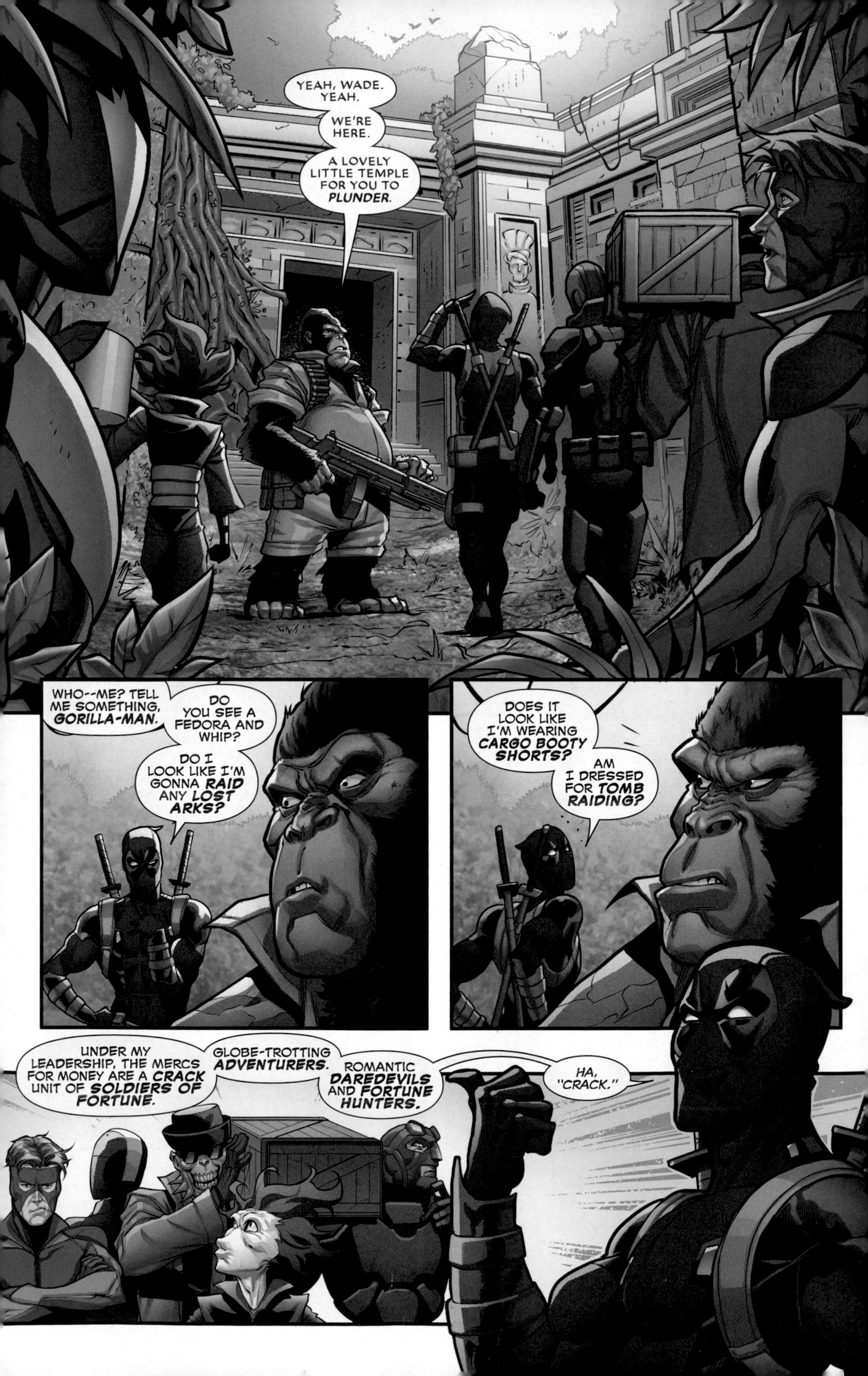
YEAH, WADE. YEAH.
WE'RE HERE.
A LOVELY LITTLE TEMPLE FOR YOU TO PLUNDER.
WHO--ME? TELL ME SOMETHING, GORILLA-MAN.
DO YOU SEE A FEDORA AND WHIP?
DO I LOOK LIKE I'M GONNA RAID ANY LOST ARKS?
DOES IT LOOK LIKE I'M WEARING CARGO BOOTY SHORTS?
AM I DRESSED FOR TOMB RAIDING?
UNDER MY LEADERSHIP, THE MERCS FOR MONEY ARE A CRACK UNIT OF SOLDIERS OF FORTUNE.
GLOBE-TROTTING ADVENTURERS.
ROMANTIC DAREDEVILS AND FORTUNE HUNTERS.
HA, "CRACK."

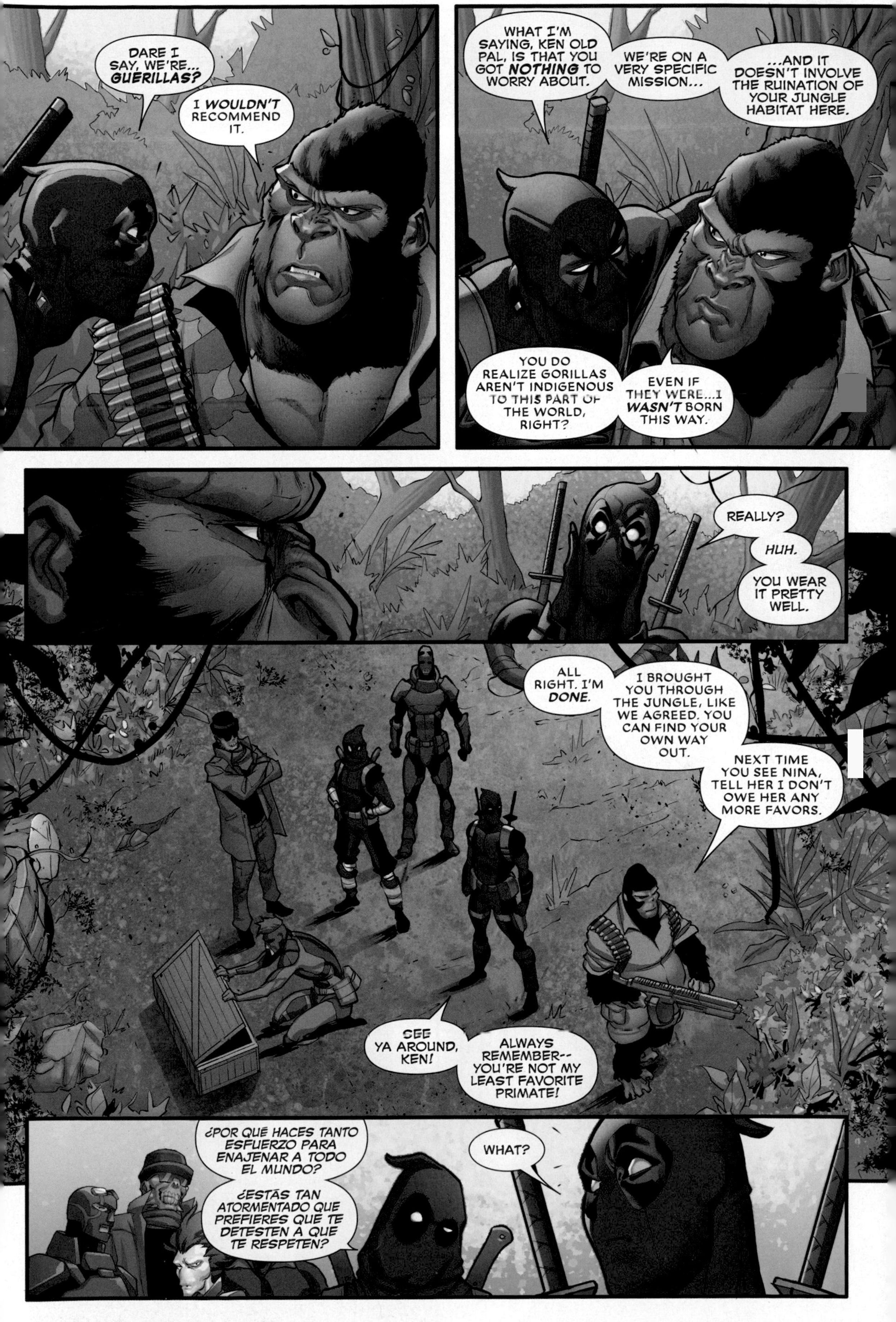
DARE I SAY, WE'RE... GUERILLAS?
I WOULDN'T RECOMMEND IT.
WHAT I'M SAYING, KEN OLD PAL, IS THAT YOU GOT NOTHING TO WORRY ABOUT.
WE'RE ON A VERY SPECIFIC MISSION...
...AND IT DOESN'T INVOLVE THE RUINATION OF YOUR JUNGLE HABITAT HERE.
YOU DO REALIZE GORILLAS AREN'T INDIGENOUS TO THIS PART OF THE WORLD, RIGHT?
EVEN IF THEY WERE...I WASN'T BORN THIS WAY.
REALLY?
HUH.
YOU WEAR IT PRETTY WELL.
ALL RIGHT. I'M DONE.
I BROUGHT YOU THROUGH THE JUNGLE, LIKE WE AGREED. YOU CAN FIND YOUR OWN WAY OUT.
NEXT TIME YOU SEE NINA, TELL HER I DON'T OWE HER ANY MORE FAVORS.
SEE YA AROUND, KEN!
ALWAYS REMEMBER-- YOU'RE NOT MY LEAST FAVORITE PRIMATE!
¿POR QUÉ HACES TANTO ESFUERZO PARA ENAJENAR A TODO EL MUNDO?
¿ESTÁS TAN ATORMENTADO QUE PREFIERES QUE TE DETESTEN A QUE TE RESPETEN?
WHAT?

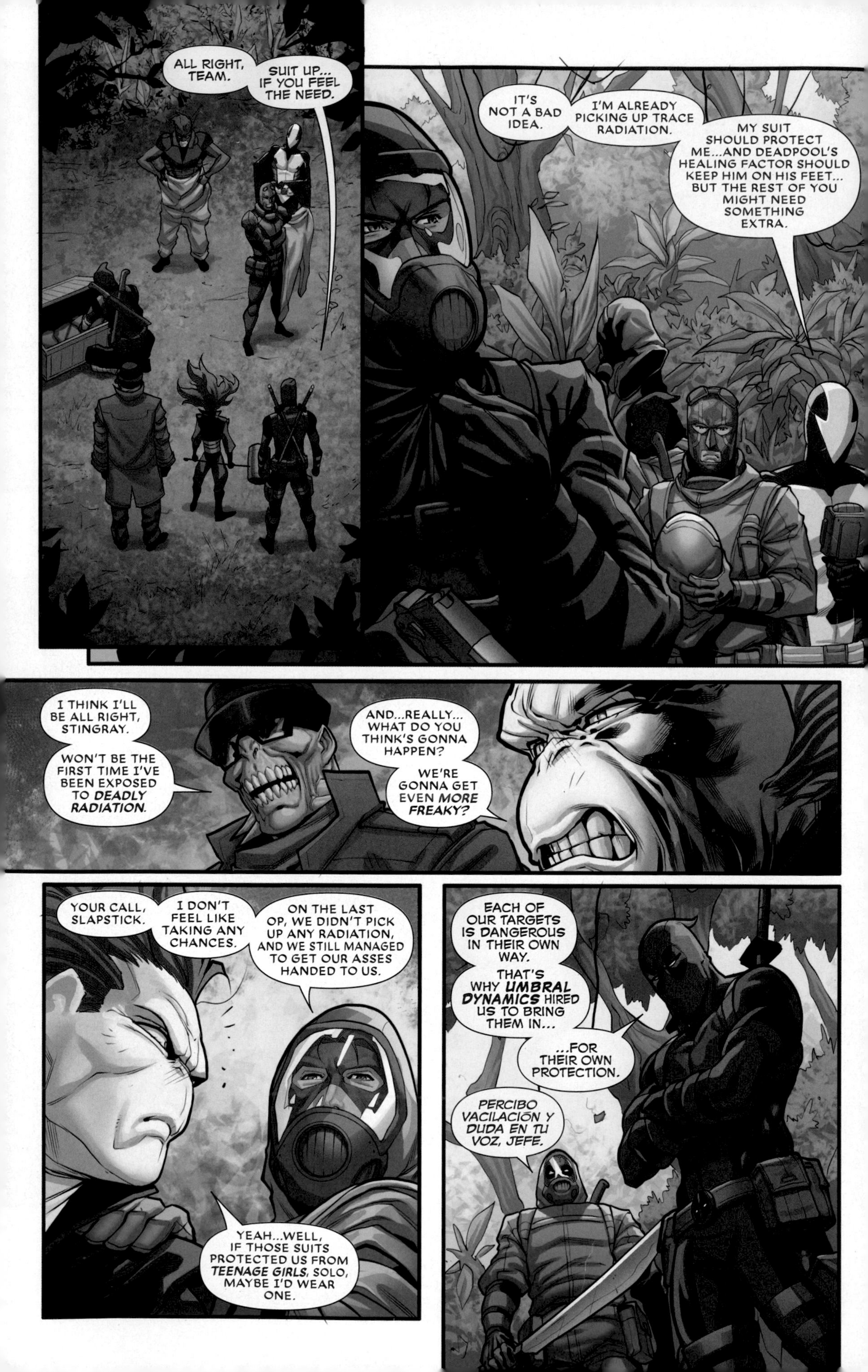
ALL RIGHT, TEAM.
SUIT UP... IF YOU FEEL THE NEED.
IT'S NOT A BAD IDEA.
I'M ALREADY PICKING UP TRACE RADIATION.
MY SUIT SHOULD PROTECT ME...AND DEADPOOL'S HEALING FACTOR SHOULD KEEP HIM ON HIS FEET... BUT THE REST OF YOU MIGHT NEED SOMETHING EXTRA.
I THINK I'LL BE ALL RIGHT, STINGRAY.
WON'T BE THE FIRST TIME I'VE BEEN EXPOSED TO *DEADLY RADIATION*.
AND...REALLY... WHAT DO YOU THINK'S GONNA HAPPEN?
WE'RE GONNA GET EVEN *MORE FREAKY?*
YOUR CALL, SLAPSTICK.
I DON'T FEEL LIKE TAKING ANY CHANCES.
ON THE LAST OP, WE DIDN'T PICK UP ANY RADIATION, AND WE STILL MANAGED TO GET OUR ASSES HANDED TO US.
YEAH...WELL, IF THOSE SUITS PROTECTED US FROM *TEENAGE GIRLS*, SOLO, MAYBE I'D WEAR ONE.
EACH OF OUR TARGETS IS DANGEROUS IN THEIR OWN WAY.
THAT'S WHY *UMBRAL DYNAMICS* HIRED US TO BRING THEM IN...
...FOR THEIR OWN PROTECTION.
PERCIBO VACILACIÓN Y DUDA EN TU VOZ, JEFE.

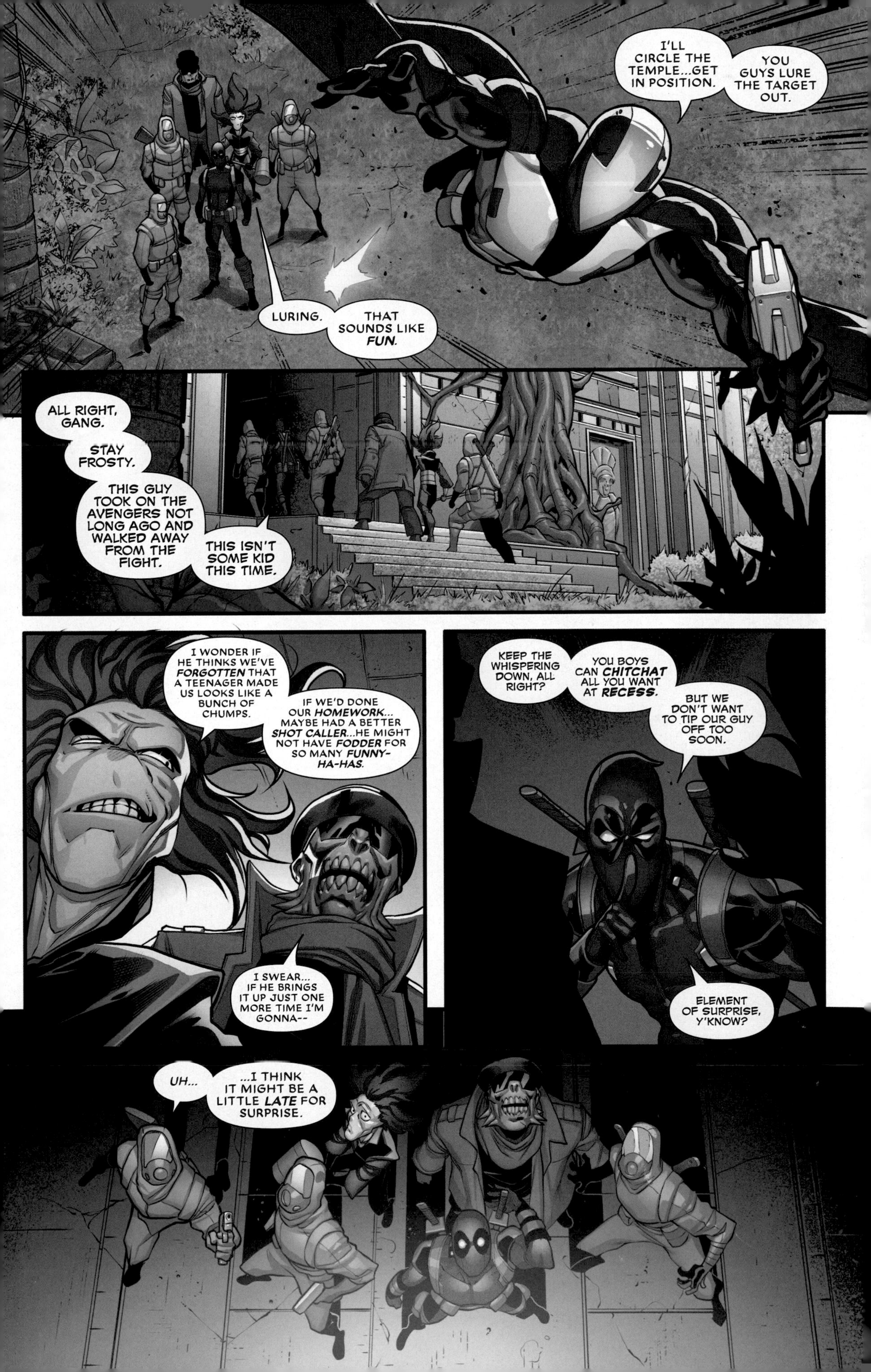
I'LL CIRCLE THE TEMPLE...GET IN POSITION.
YOU GUYS LURE THE TARGET OUT.
LURING.
THAT SOUNDS LIKE FUN.
ALL RIGHT, GANG.
STAY FROSTY.
THIS GUY TOOK ON THE AVENGERS NOT LONG AGO AND WALKED AWAY FROM THE FIGHT.
THIS ISN'T SOME KID THIS TIME.
I WONDER IF HE THINKS WE'VE FORGOTTEN THAT A TEENAGER MADE US LOOKS LIKE A BUNCH OF CHUMPS.
IF WE'D DONE OUR HOMEWORK... MAYBE HAD A BETTER SHOT CALLER...HE MIGHT NOT HAVE FODDER FOR SO MANY FUNNY-HA-HAS.
I SWEAR... IF HE BRINGS IT UP JUST ONE MORE TIME I'M GONNA--
KEEP THE WHISPERING DOWN, ALL RIGHT?
YOU BOYS CAN CHITCHAT ALL YOU WANT AT RECESS.
BUT WE DON'T WANT TO TIP OUR GUY OFF TOO SOON.
ELEMENT OF SURPRISE, Y'KNOW?
UH...
...I THINK IT MIGHT BE A LITTLE LATE FOR SURPRISE.

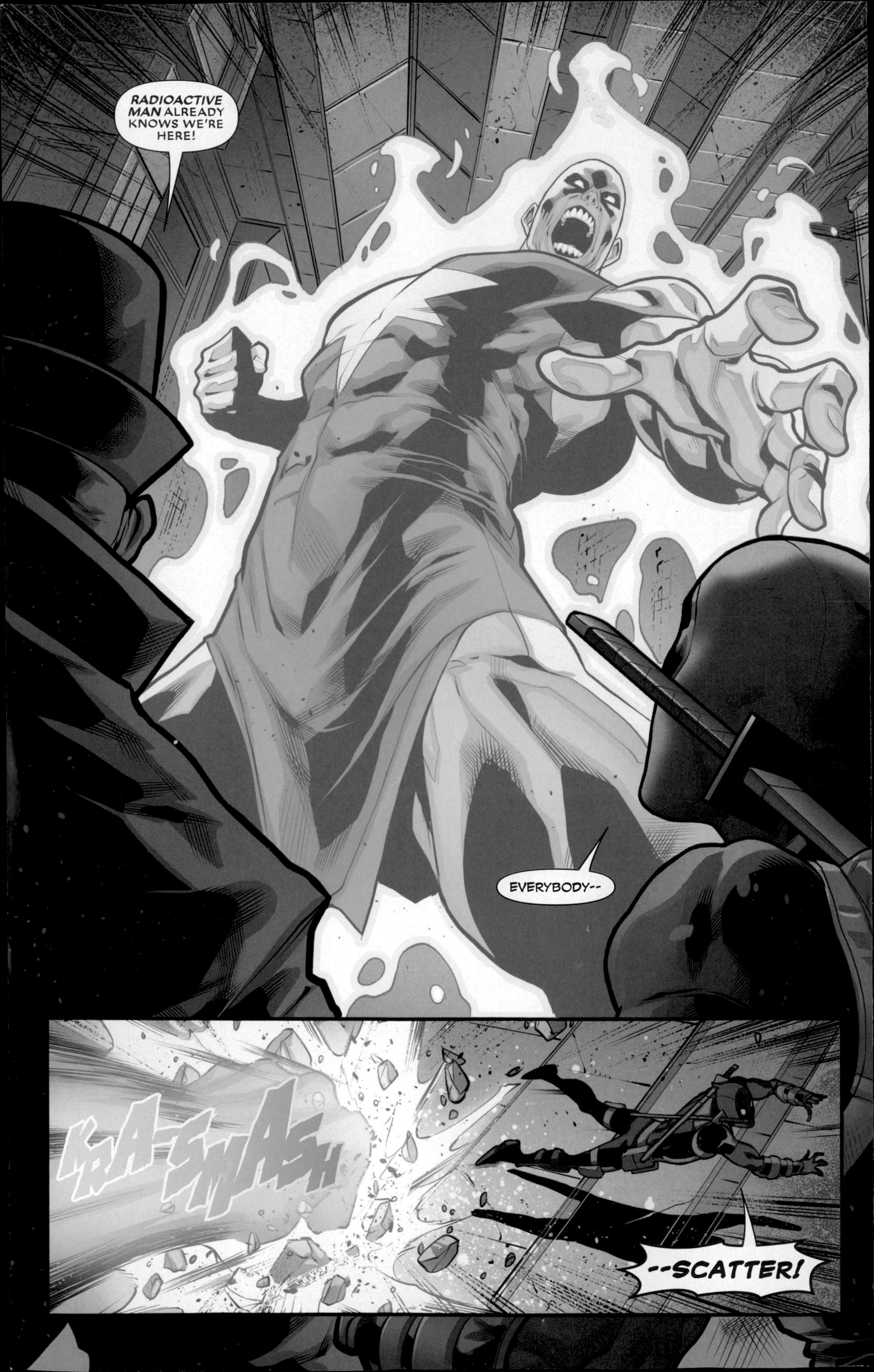
RADIOACTIVE MAN ALREADY KNOWS WE'RE HERE!
EVERYBODY--
KRA-SMASH
--SCATTER!

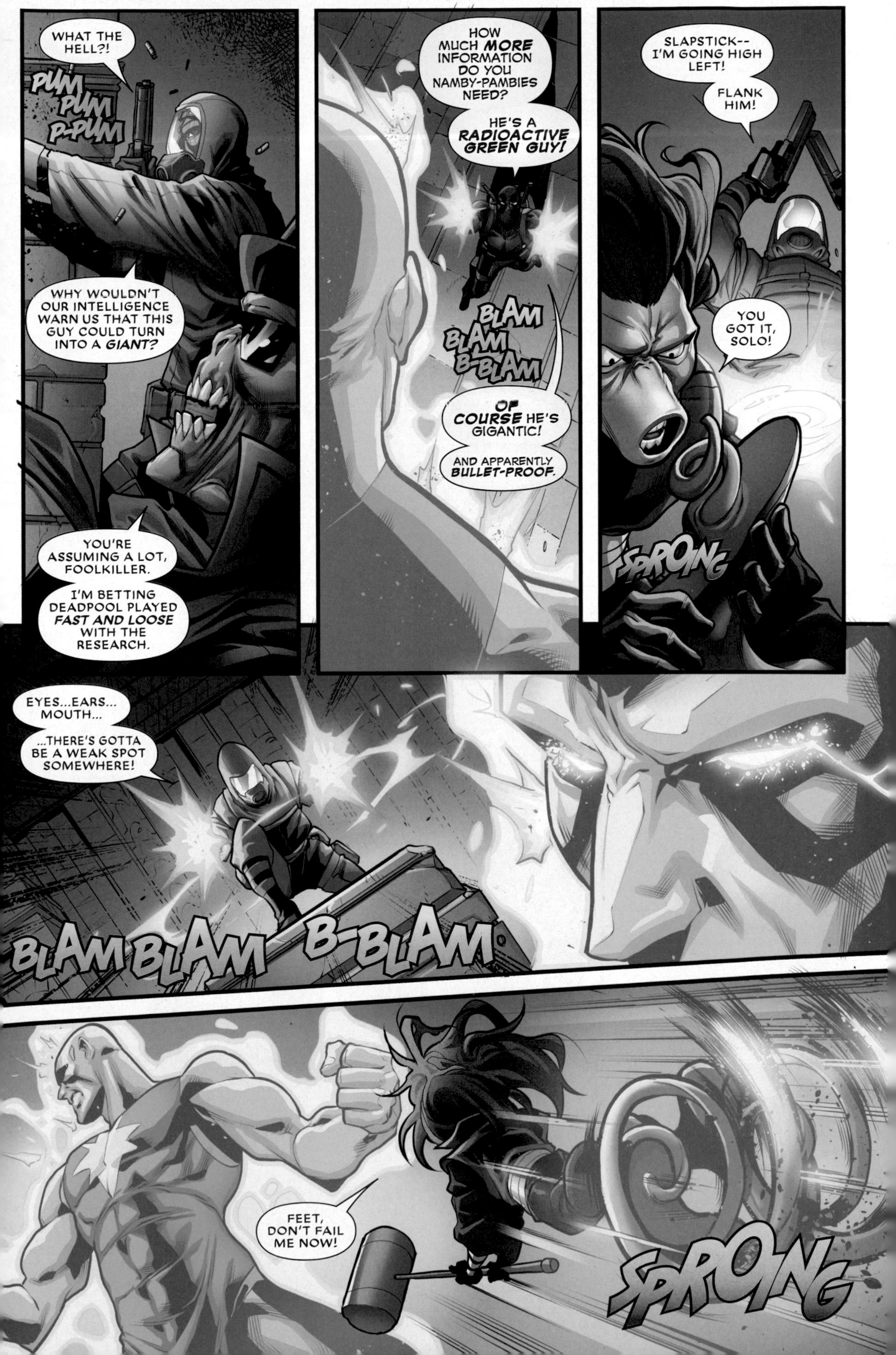
WHAT THE HELL?!
PUM PUM P-PUM
WHY WOULDN'T OUR INTELLIGENCE WARN US THAT THIS GUY COULD TURN INTO A GIANT?
YOU'RE ASSUMING A LOT, FOOLKILLER.
I'M BETTING DEADPOOL PLAYED FAST AND LOOSE WITH THE RESEARCH.
HOW MUCH MORE INFORMATION DO YOU NAMBY-PAMBIES NEED?
HE'S A RADIOACTIVE GREEN GUY!
BLAM BLAM B-BLAM
OF COURSE HE'S GIGANTIC!
AND APPARENTLY BULLET-PROOF.
SLAPSTICK-- I'M GOING HIGH LEFT!
FLANK HIM!
YOU GOT IT, SOLO!
SPROING
EYES...EARS... MOUTH...
...THERE'S GOTTA BE A WEAK SPOT SOMEWHERE!
BLAM BLAM B-BLAM
FEET, DON'T FAIL ME NOW!
SPROING

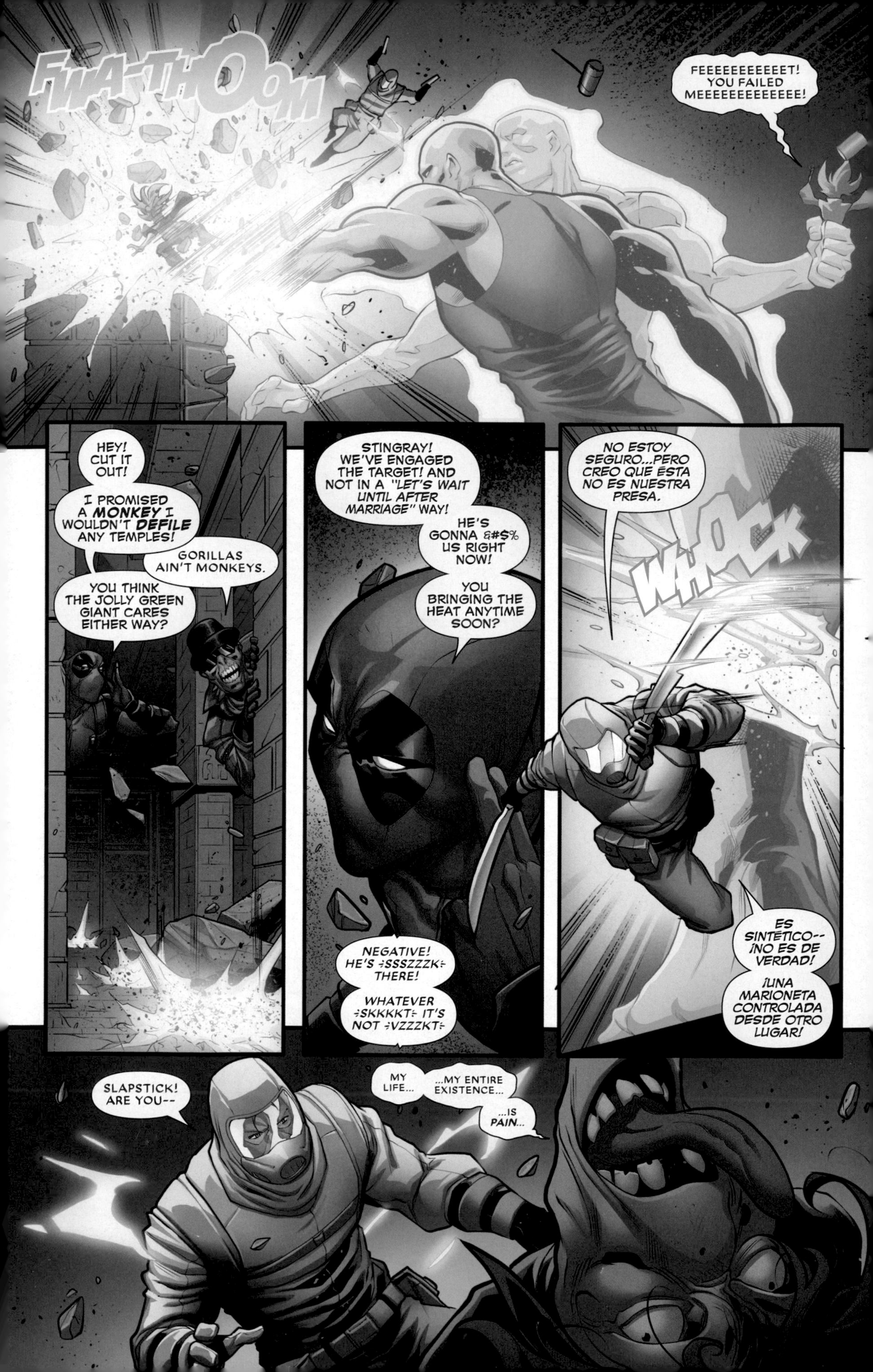
FWA-THOOM
FEEEEEEEEEEEET! YOU FAILED MEEEEEEEEEEEEE!
HEY! CUT IT OUT!
I PROMISED A MONKEY I WOULDN'T DEFILE ANY TEMPLES!
GORILLAS AIN'T MONKEYS.
YOU THINK THE JOLLY GREEN GIANT CARES EITHER WAY?
STINGRAY! WE'VE ENGAGED THE TARGET! AND NOT IN A "LET'S WAIT UNTIL AFTER MARRIAGE" WAY!
HE'S GONNA &#$% US RIGHT NOW!
YOU BRINGING THE HEAT ANYTIME SOON?
NEGATIVE! HE'S ÷SSSZZZK÷ THERE!
WHATEVER ÷SKKKKT÷ IT'S NOT ÷VZZZKT÷
NO ESTOY SEGURO...PERO CREO QUE ÉSTA NO ES NUESTRA PRESA.
WHOCK
ES SINTÉTICO-- ¡NO ES DE VERDAD!
¡UNA MARIONETA CONTROLADA DESDE OTRO LUGAR!
SLAPSTICK! ARE YOU--
MY LIFE...
...MY ENTIRE EXISTENCE...
...IS PAIN...

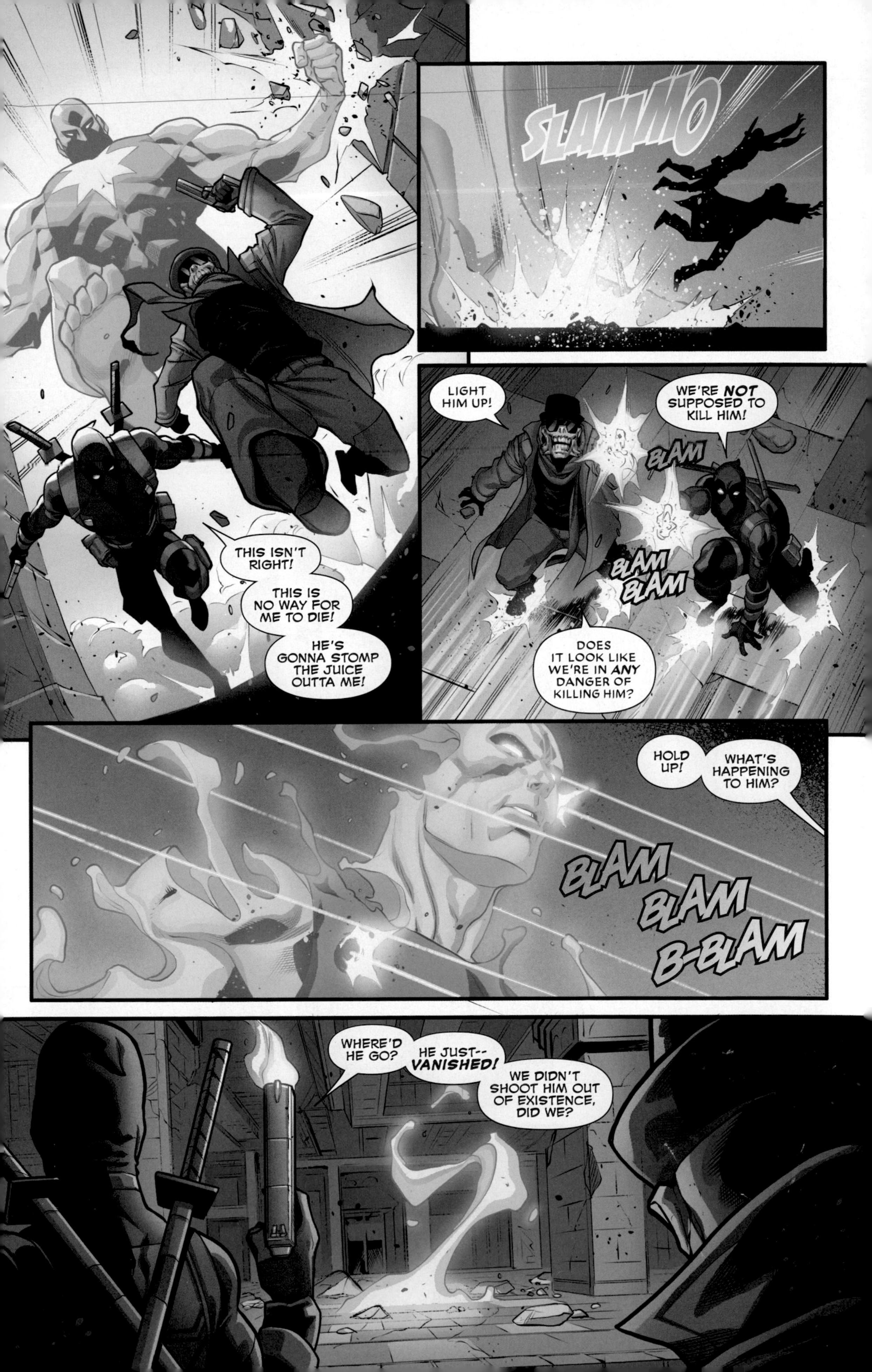

SLAMMO
THIS ISN'T RIGHT!
THIS IS NO WAY FOR ME TO DIE!
HE'S GONNA STOMP THE JUICE OUTTA ME!
LIGHT HIM UP!
WE'RE NOT SUPPOSED TO KILL HIM!
BLAM
BLAM BLAM
DOES IT LOOK LIKE WE'RE IN ANY DANGER OF KILLING HIM?
HOLD UP!
WHAT'S HAPPENING TO HIM?
BLAM BLAM B-BLAM
WHERE'D HE GO?
HE JUST-- VANISHED!
WE DIDN'T SHOOT HIM OUT OF EXISTENCE, DID WE?

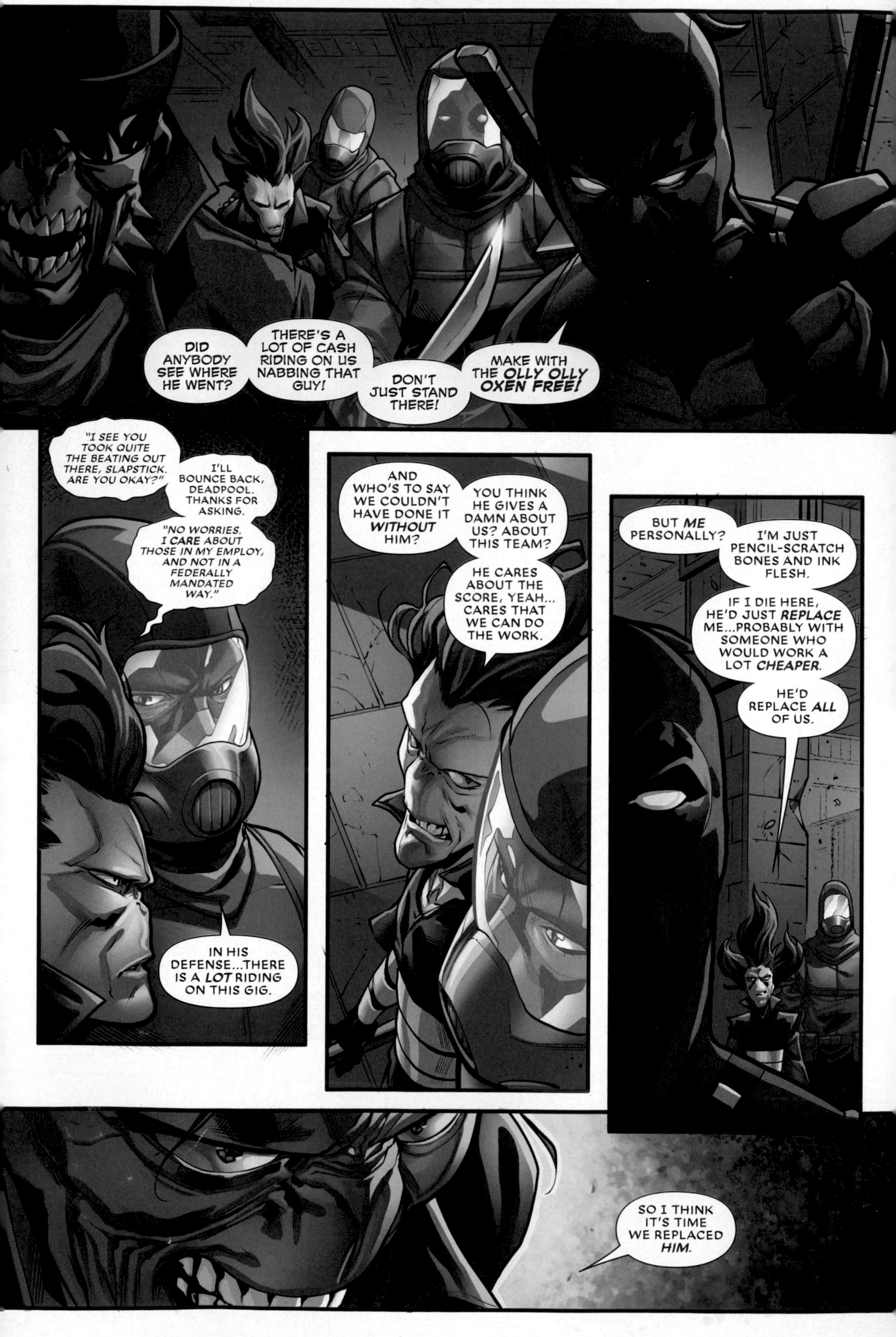
DID ANYBODY SEE WHERE HE WENT?
THERE'S A LOT OF CASH RIDING ON US NABBING THAT GUY!
DON'T JUST STAND THERE!
MAKE WITH THE OLLY OLLY OXEN FREE!
"I SEE YOU TOOK QUITE THE BEATING OUT THERE, SLAPSTICK. ARE YOU OKAY?"
I'LL BOUNCE BACK, DEADPOOL. THANKS FOR ASKING.
"NO WORRIES. I CARE ABOUT THOSE IN MY EMPLOY, AND NOT IN A FEDERALLY MANDATED WAY."
IN HIS DEFENSE...THERE IS A LOT RIDING ON THIS GIG.
AND WHO'S TO SAY WE COULDN'T HAVE DONE IT WITHOUT HIM?
YOU THINK HE GIVES A DAMN ABOUT US? ABOUT THIS TEAM?
HE CARES ABOUT THE SCORE, YEAH... CARES THAT WE CAN DO THE WORK.
BUT ME PERSONALLY?
I'M JUST PENCIL-SCRATCH BONES AND INK FLESH.
IF I DIE HERE, HE'D JUST REPLACE ME...PROBABLY WITH SOMEONE WHO WOULD WORK A LOT CHEAPER.
HE'D REPLACE ALL OF US.
SO I THINK IT'S TIME WE REPLACED HIM.

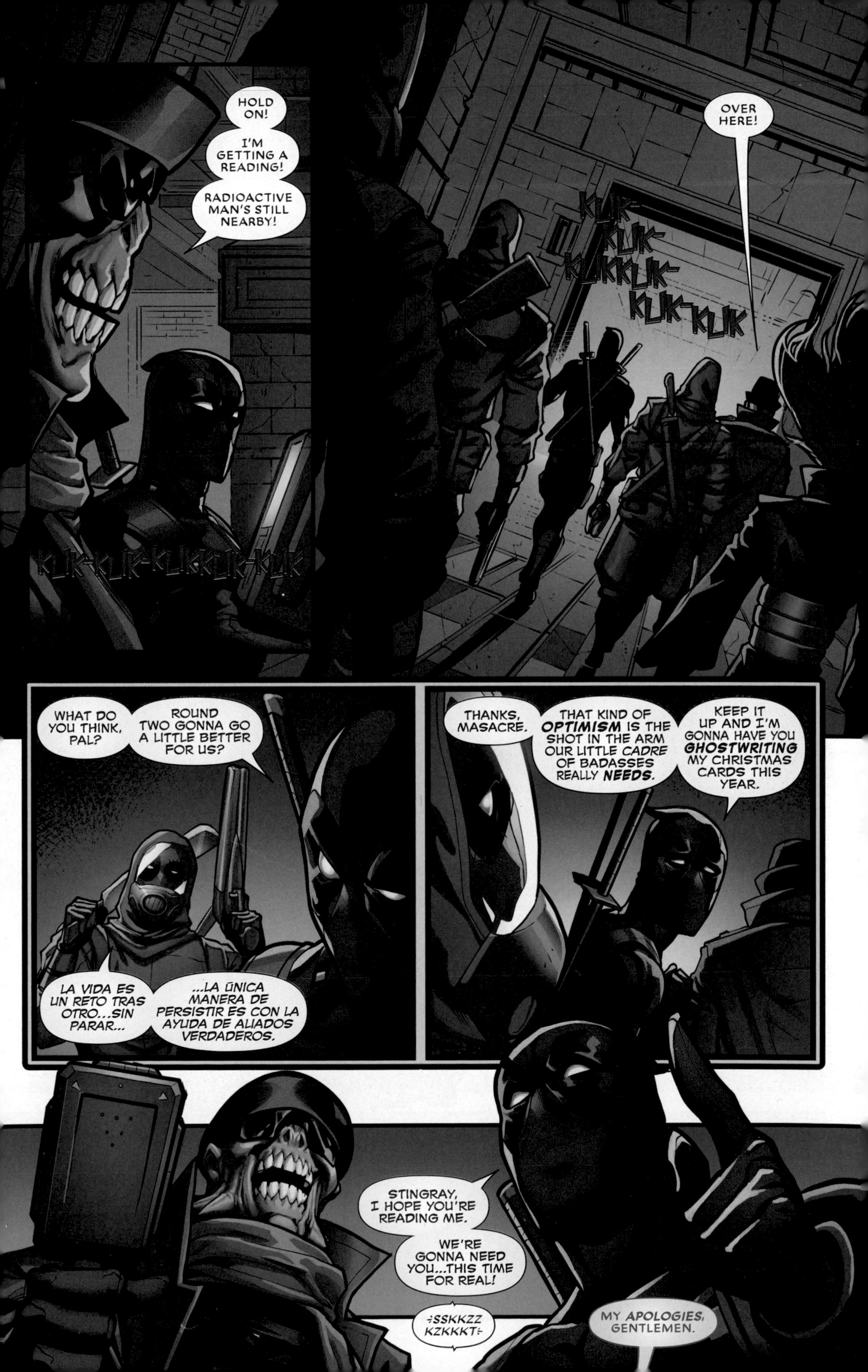
HOLD ON!
I'M GETTING A READING!
RADIOACTIVE MAN'S STILL NEARBY!
KLIK-KLIK-KLIKKLIK-KLIK
OVER HERE!
KLIK-KLIK-KLIKKLIK-KLIK-KLIK
WHAT DO YOU THINK, PAL?
ROUND TWO GONNA GO A LITTLE BETTER FOR US?
LA VIDA ES UN RETO TRAS OTRO...SIN PARAR...
...LA ÚNICA MANERA DE PERSISTIR ES CON LA AYUDA DE ALIADOS VERDADEROS.
THANKS, MASACRE.
THAT KIND OF OPTIMISM IS THE SHOT IN THE ARM OUR LITTLE CADRE OF BADASSES REALLY NEEDS.
KEEP IT UP AND I'M GONNA HAVE YOU GHOSTWRITING MY CHRISTMAS CARDS THIS YEAR.
STINGRAY, I HOPE YOU'RE READING ME.
WE'RE GONNA NEED YOU...THIS TIME FOR REAL!
SSKKZZ KZKKKT
MY APOLOGIES, GENTLEMEN.

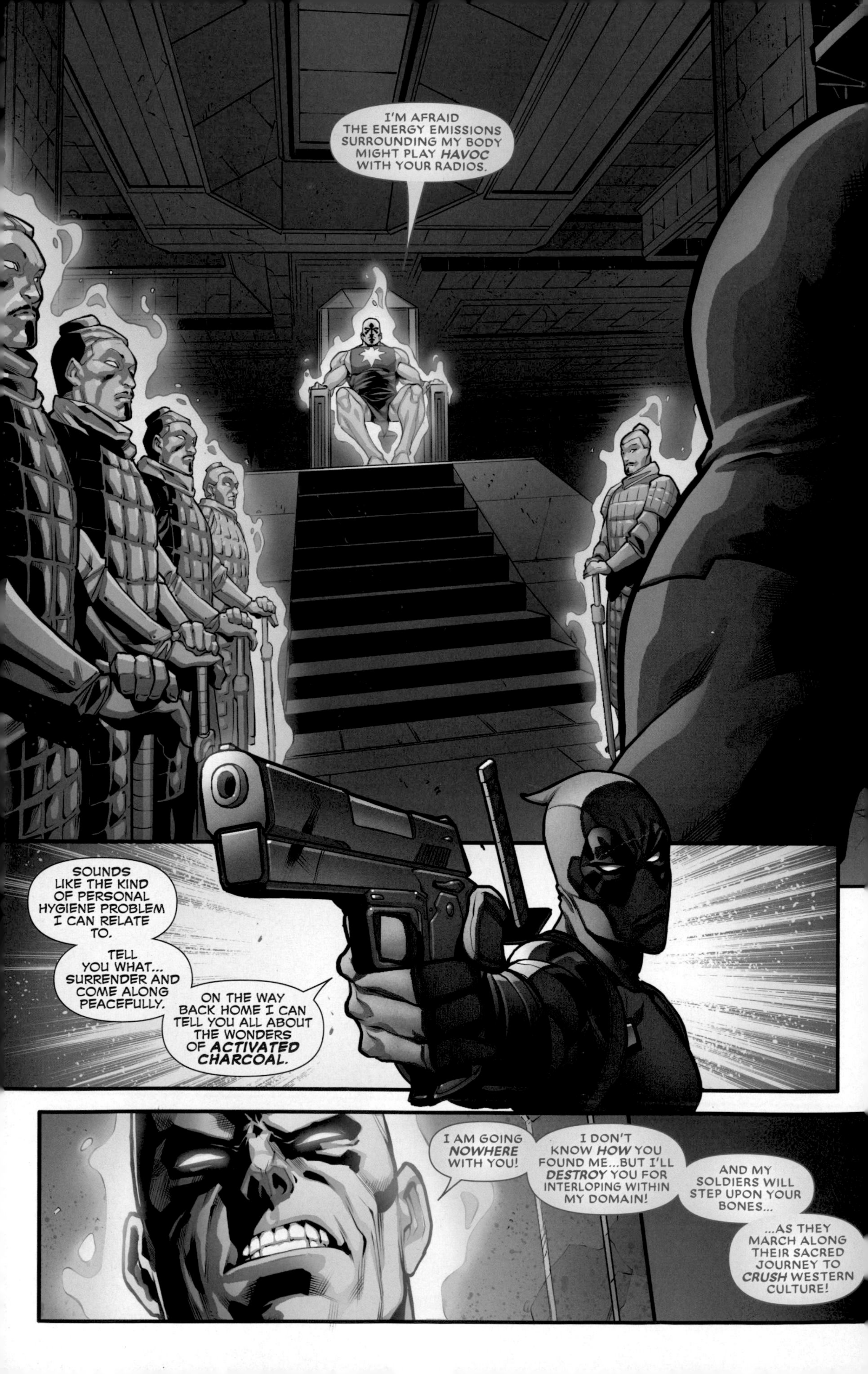
I'M AFRAID THE ENERGY EMISSIONS SURROUNDING MY BODY MIGHT PLAY *HAVOC* WITH YOUR RADIOS.
SOUNDS LIKE THE KIND OF PERSONAL HYGIENE PROBLEM I CAN RELATE TO.
TELL YOU WHAT... SURRENDER AND COME ALONG PEACEFULLY.
ON THE WAY BACK HOME I CAN TELL YOU ALL ABOUT THE WONDERS OF ***ACTIVATED CHARCOAL.***
I AM GOING *NOWHERE* WITH YOU!
I DON'T KNOW *HOW* YOU FOUND ME...BUT I'LL *DESTROY* YOU FOR INTERLOPING WITHIN MY DOMAIN!
AND MY SOLDIERS WILL STEP UPON YOUR BONES...
...AS THEY MARCH ALONG THEIR SACRED JOURNEY TO *CRUSH* WESTERN CULTURE!

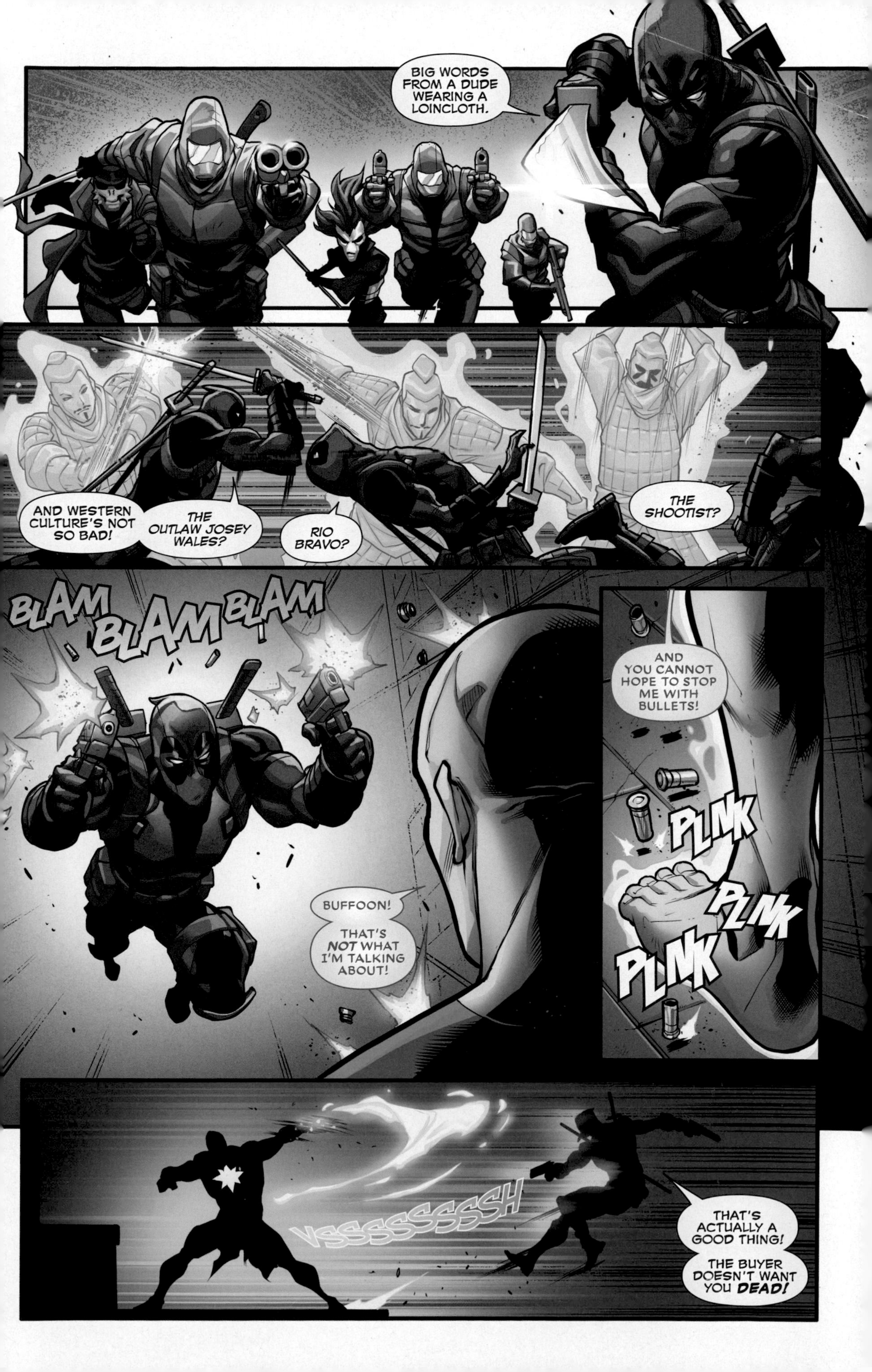
BIG WORDS FROM A DUDE WEARING A LOINCLOTH.
AND WESTERN CULTURE'S NOT SO BAD!
THE OUTLAW JOSEY WALES?
RIO BRAVO?
THE SHOOTIST?
BLAM BLAM BLAM
BUFFOON!
THAT'S NOT WHAT I'M TALKING ABOUT!
AND YOU CANNOT HOPE TO STOP ME WITH BULLETS!
PLINK
PLINK
PLINK
VSSSSSSSSSH
THAT'S ACTUALLY A GOOD THING!
THE BUYER DOESN'T WANT YOU DEAD!

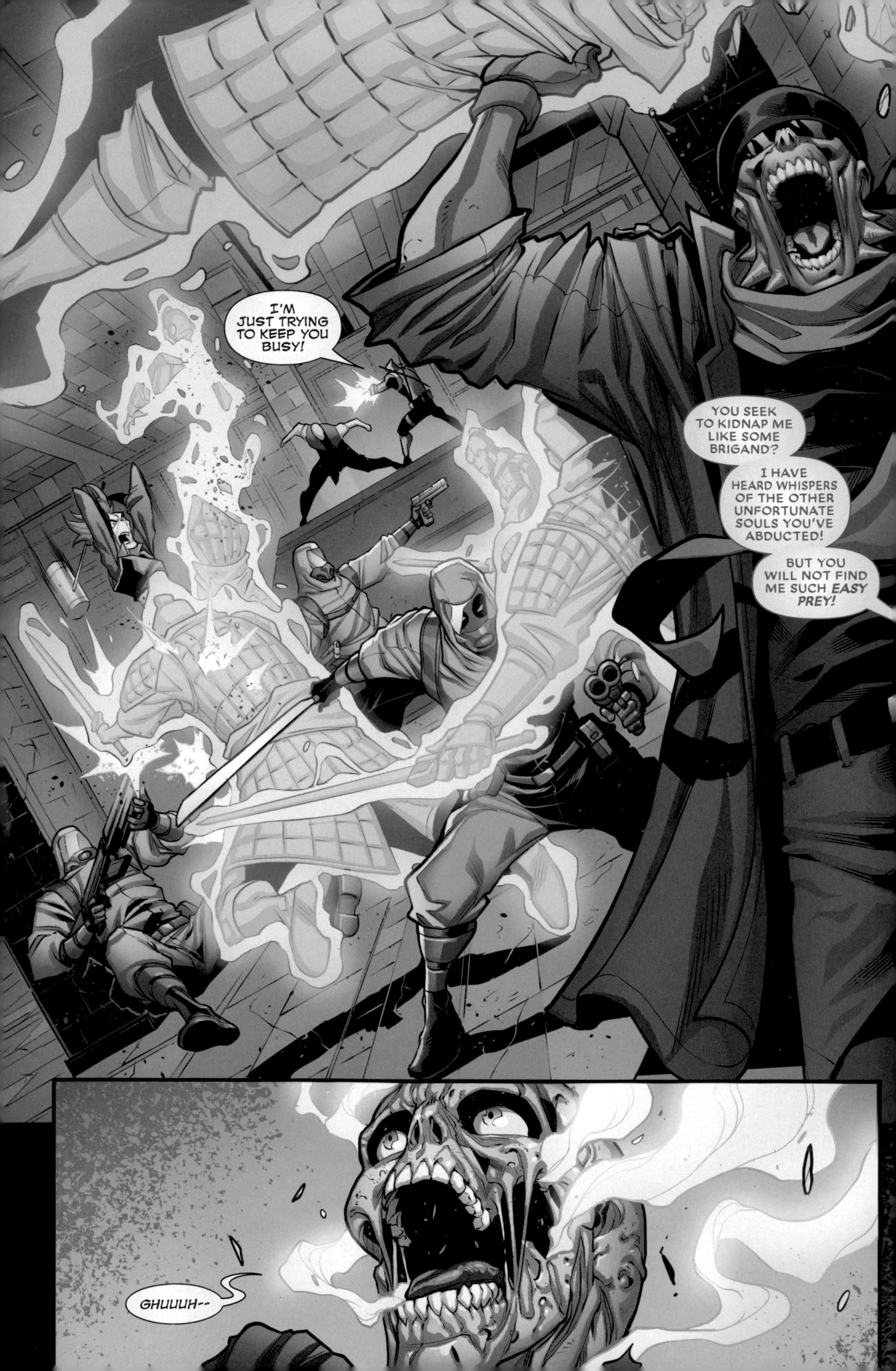
I'M JUST TRYING TO KEEP YOU BUSY!
YOU SEEK TO KIDNAP ME LIKE SOME BRIGAND?
I HAVE HEARD WHISPERS OF THE OTHER UNFORTUNATE SOULS YOU'VE ABDUCTED!
BUT YOU WILL NOT FIND ME SUCH *EASY PREY!*
GHUUUH--

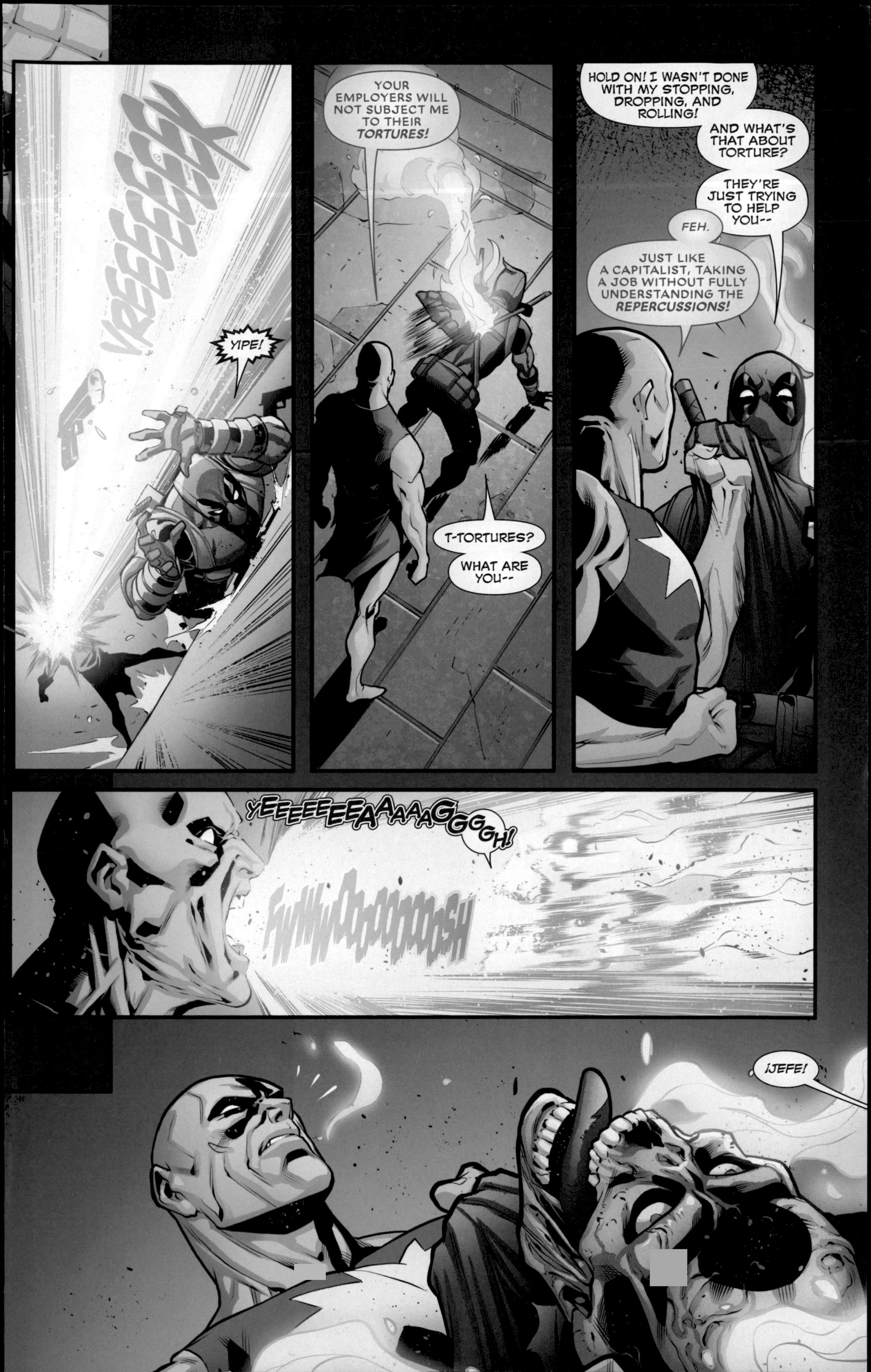
VREEEEEEEK
YIPE!
YOUR EMPLOYERS WILL NOT SUBJECT ME TO THEIR *TORTURES!*
T-TORTURES?
WHAT ARE YOU--
HOLD ON! I WASN'T DONE WITH MY STOPPING, DROPPING, AND ROLLING!
AND WHAT'S THAT ABOUT TORTURE?
THEY'RE JUST TRYING TO HELP YOU--
FEH.
JUST LIKE A CAPITALIST, TAKING A JOB WITHOUT FULLY UNDERSTANDING THE *REPERCUSSIONS!*
YEEEEEEEAAAAAGGGGH!
FWWWOOOOOOOOOSH
¡JEFE!

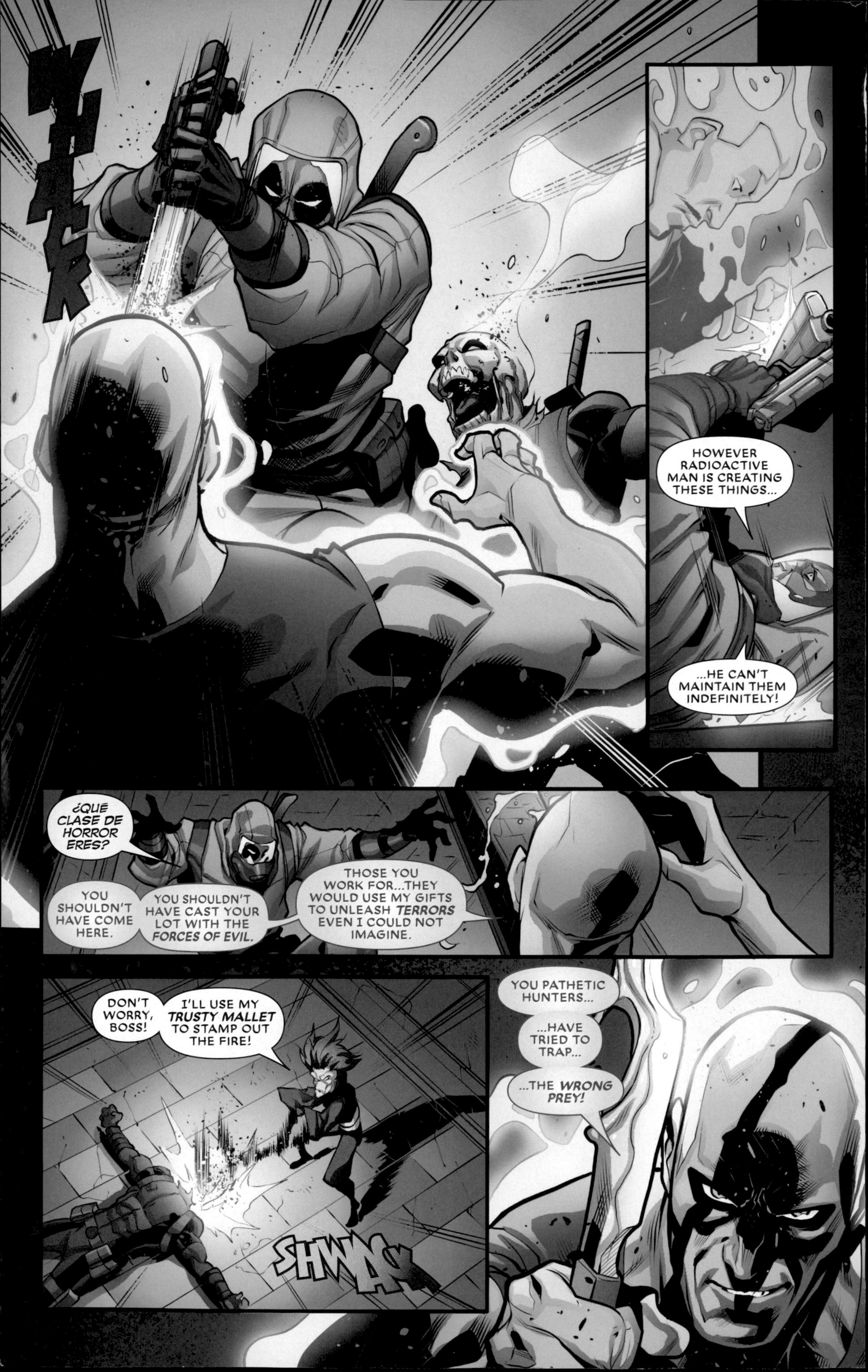

WHAK
HOWEVER RADIOACTIVE MAN IS CREATING THESE THINGS...
...HE CAN'T MAINTAIN THEM INDEFINITELY!
¿QUÉ CLASE DE HORROR ERES?
YOU SHOULDN'T HAVE COME HERE.
YOU SHOULDN'T HAVE CAST YOUR LOT WITH THE *FORCES OF EVIL.*
THOSE YOU WORK FOR...THEY WOULD USE MY GIFTS TO UNLEASH *TERRORS* EVEN I COULD NOT IMAGINE.
DON'T WORRY, BOSS!
I'LL USE MY *TRUSTY MALLET* TO STAMP OUT THE FIRE!
SHWAK
YOU PATHETIC HUNTERS...
...HAVE TRIED TO TRAP...
...THE *WRONG PREY!*

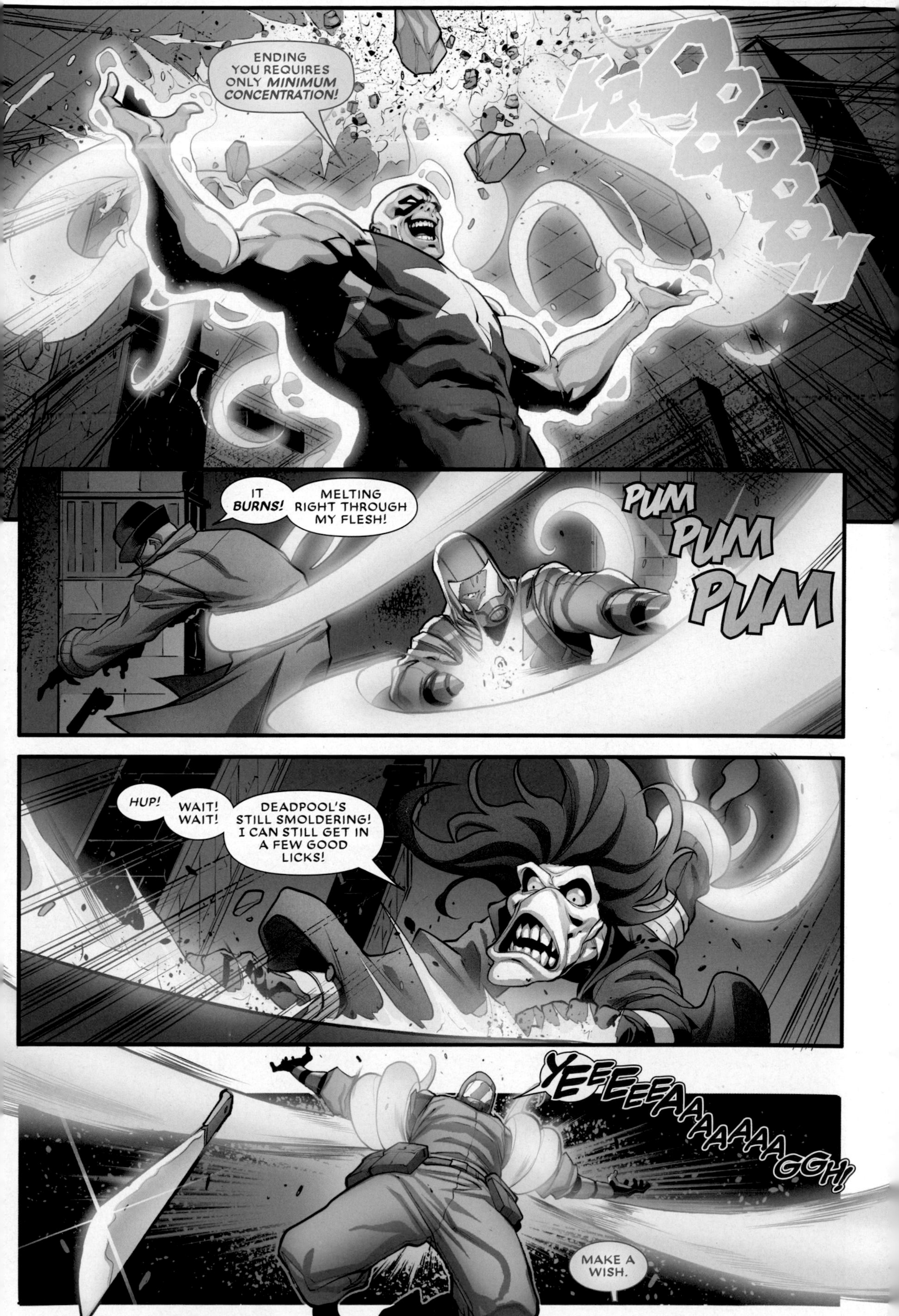
ENDING YOU REQUIRES ONLY MINIMUM CONCENTRATION!
KRAKOOOOOM
IT BURNS!
MELTING RIGHT THROUGH MY FLESH!
PUM PUM PUM
HUP!
WAIT! WAIT!
DEADPOOL'S STILL SMOLDERING! I CAN STILL GET IN A FEW GOOD LICKS!
YEEEEEAAAAAAAGGH!
MAKE A WISH.

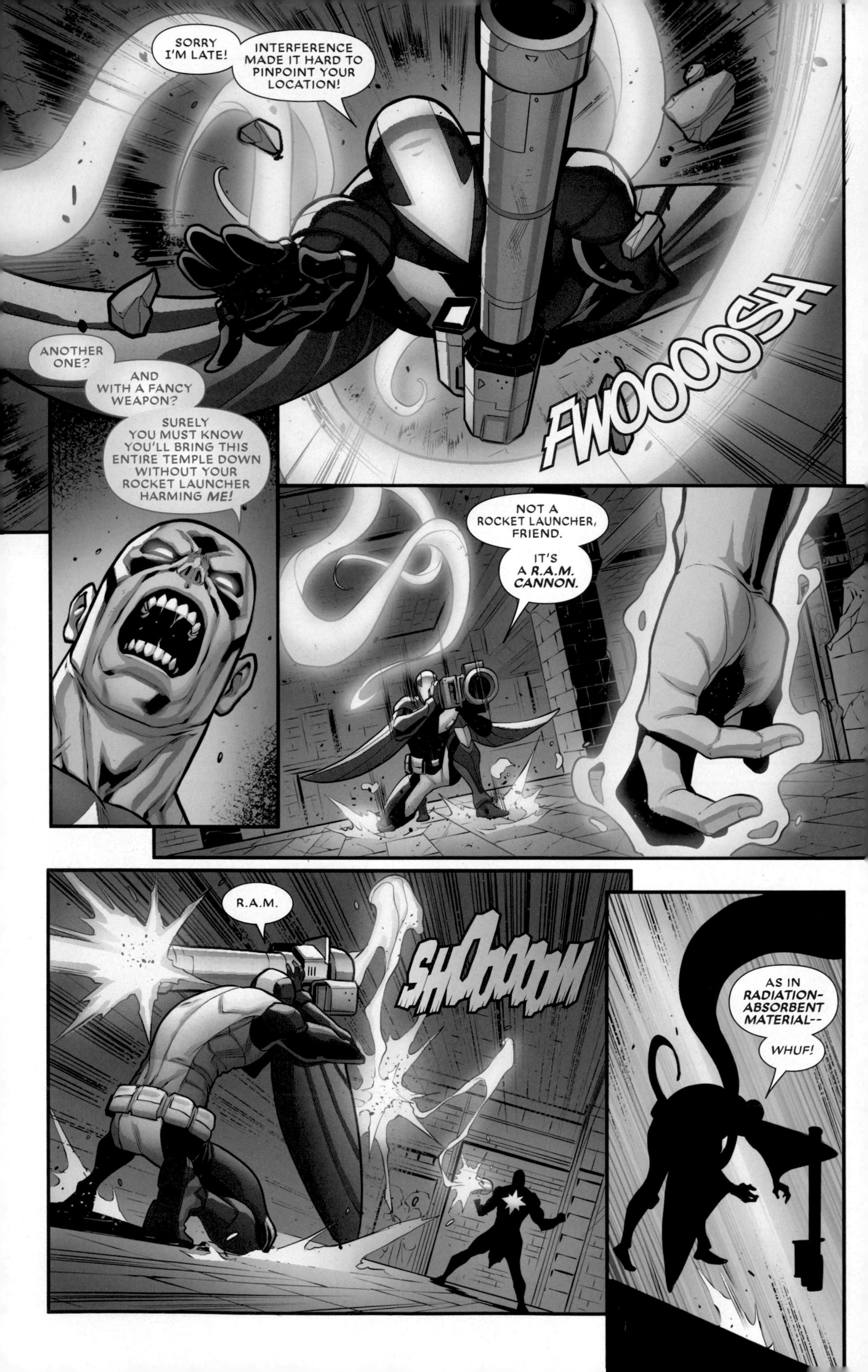
SORRY I'M LATE!
INTERFERENCE MADE IT HARD TO PINPOINT YOUR LOCATION!
FWOOOOSH
ANOTHER ONE?
AND WITH A FANCY WEAPON?
SURELY YOU MUST KNOW YOU'LL BRING THIS ENTIRE TEMPLE DOWN WITHOUT YOUR ROCKET LAUNCHER HARMING *ME!*
NOT A ROCKET LAUNCHER, FRIEND.
IT'S A **R.A.M. CANNON.**
R.A.M.
SHOOOOM
AS IN ***RADIATION-ABSORBENT MATERIAL***--
WHUF!

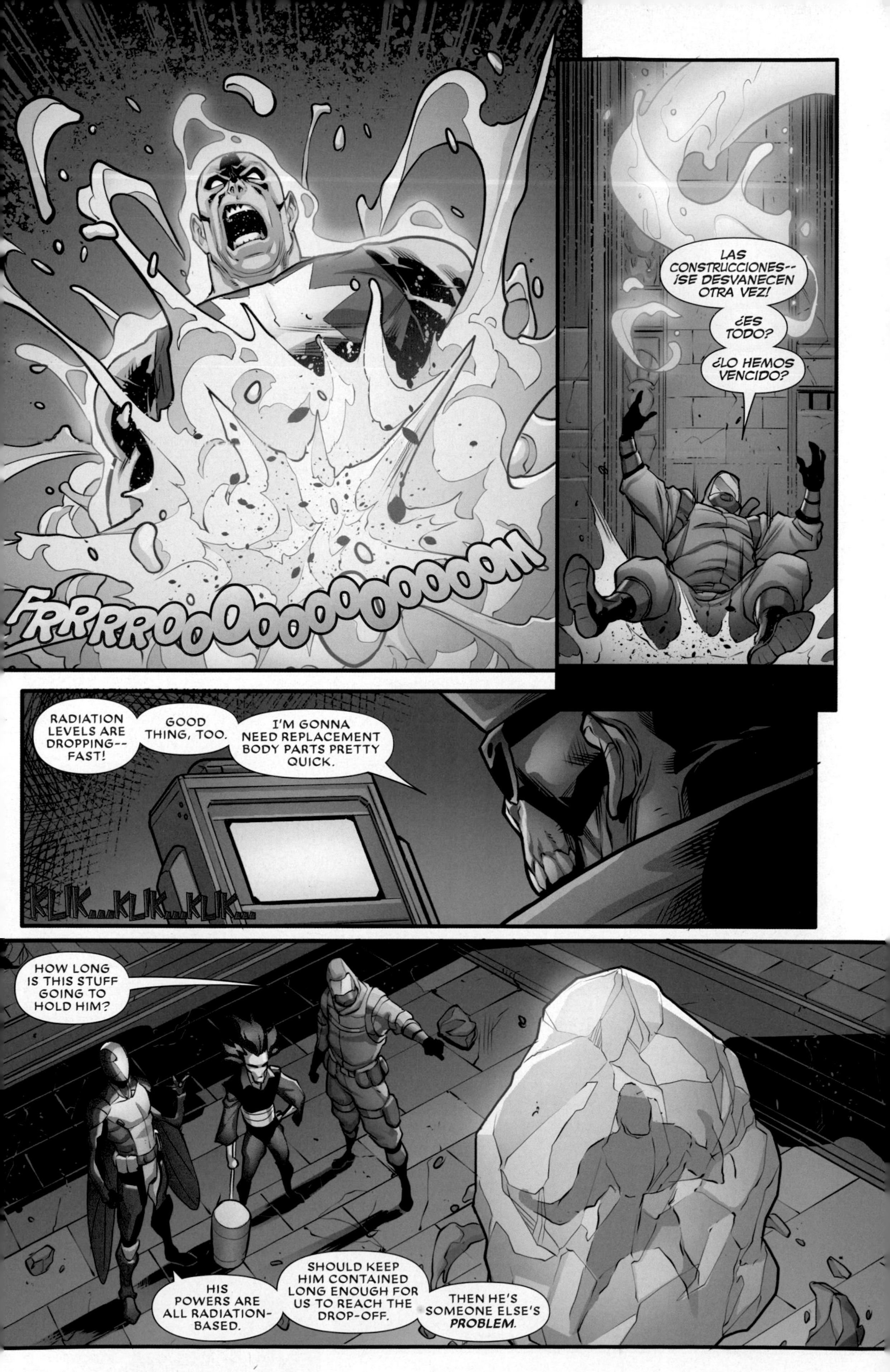
FRRRROOOOOOOOOOOOOOM
LAS CONSTRUCCIONES-- ¡SE DESVANECEN OTRA VEZ!
¿ES TODO?
¿LO HEMOS VENCIDO?
RADIATION LEVELS ARE DROPPING-- FAST!
GOOD THING, TOO.
I'M GONNA NEED REPLACEMENT BODY PARTS PRETTY QUICK.
KLIK...KLIK...KLIK...
HOW LONG IS THIS STUFF GOING TO HOLD HIM?
HIS POWERS ARE ALL RADIATION-BASED.
SHOULD KEEP HIM CONTAINED LONG ENOUGH FOR US TO REACH THE DROP-OFF.
THEN HE'S SOMEONE ELSE'S *PROBLEM*.

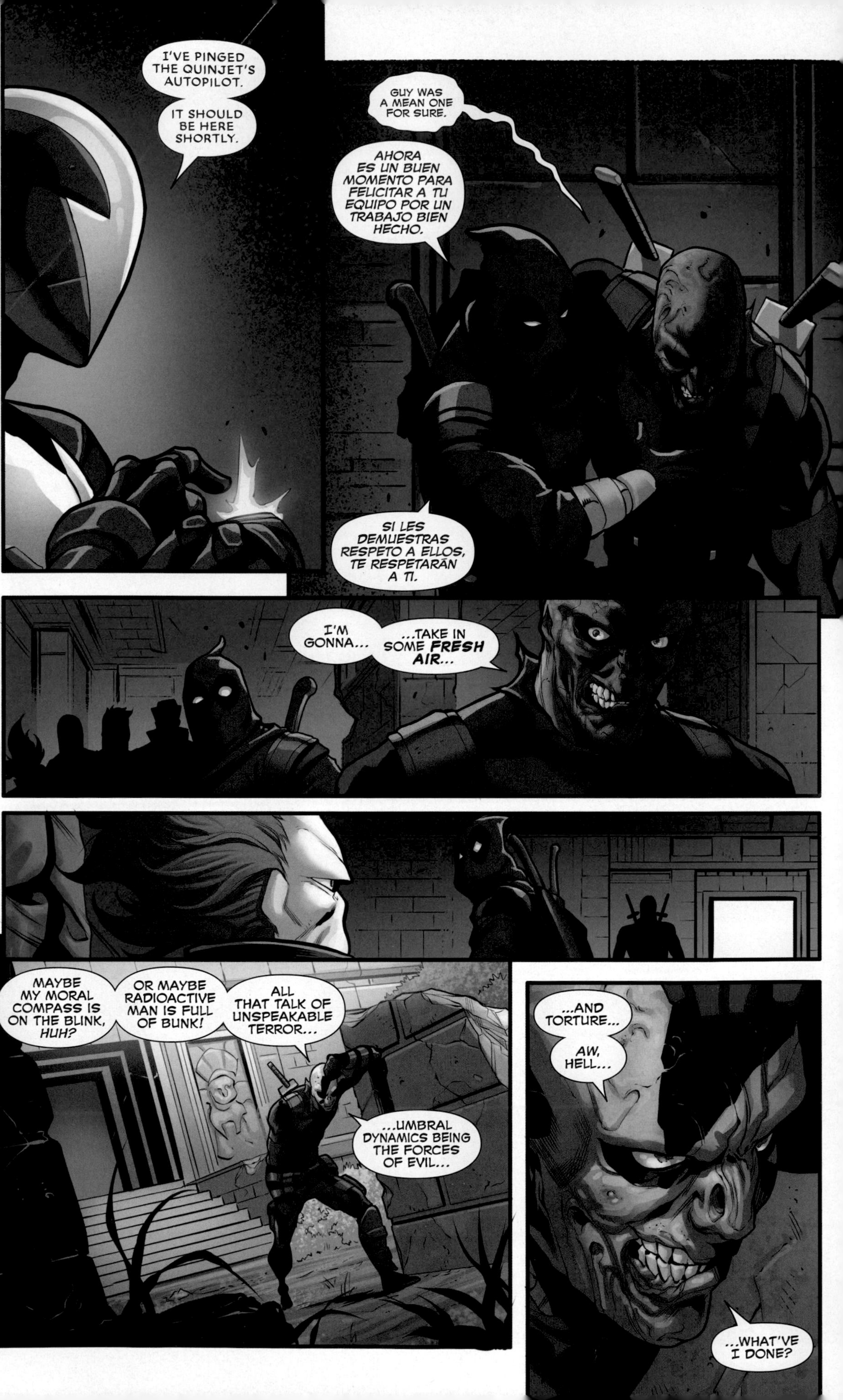

I'VE PINGED THE QUINJET'S AUTOPILOT.
IT SHOULD BE HERE SHORTLY.
GUY WAS A MEAN ONE FOR SURE.
AHORA ES UN BUEN MOMENTO PARA FELICITAR A TU EQUIPO POR UN TRABAJO BIEN HECHO.
SI LES DEMUESTRAS RESPETO A ELLOS, TE RESPETARÁN A TI.
I'M GONNA...
...TAKE IN SOME FRESH AIR...
MAYBE MY MORAL COMPASS IS ON THE BLINK, HUH?
OR MAYBE RADIOACTIVE MAN IS FULL OF BUNK!
ALL THAT TALK OF UNSPEAKABLE TERROR...
...UMBRAL DYNAMICS BEING THE FORCES OF EVIL...
...AND TORTURE...
AW, HELL...
...WHAT'VE I DONE?

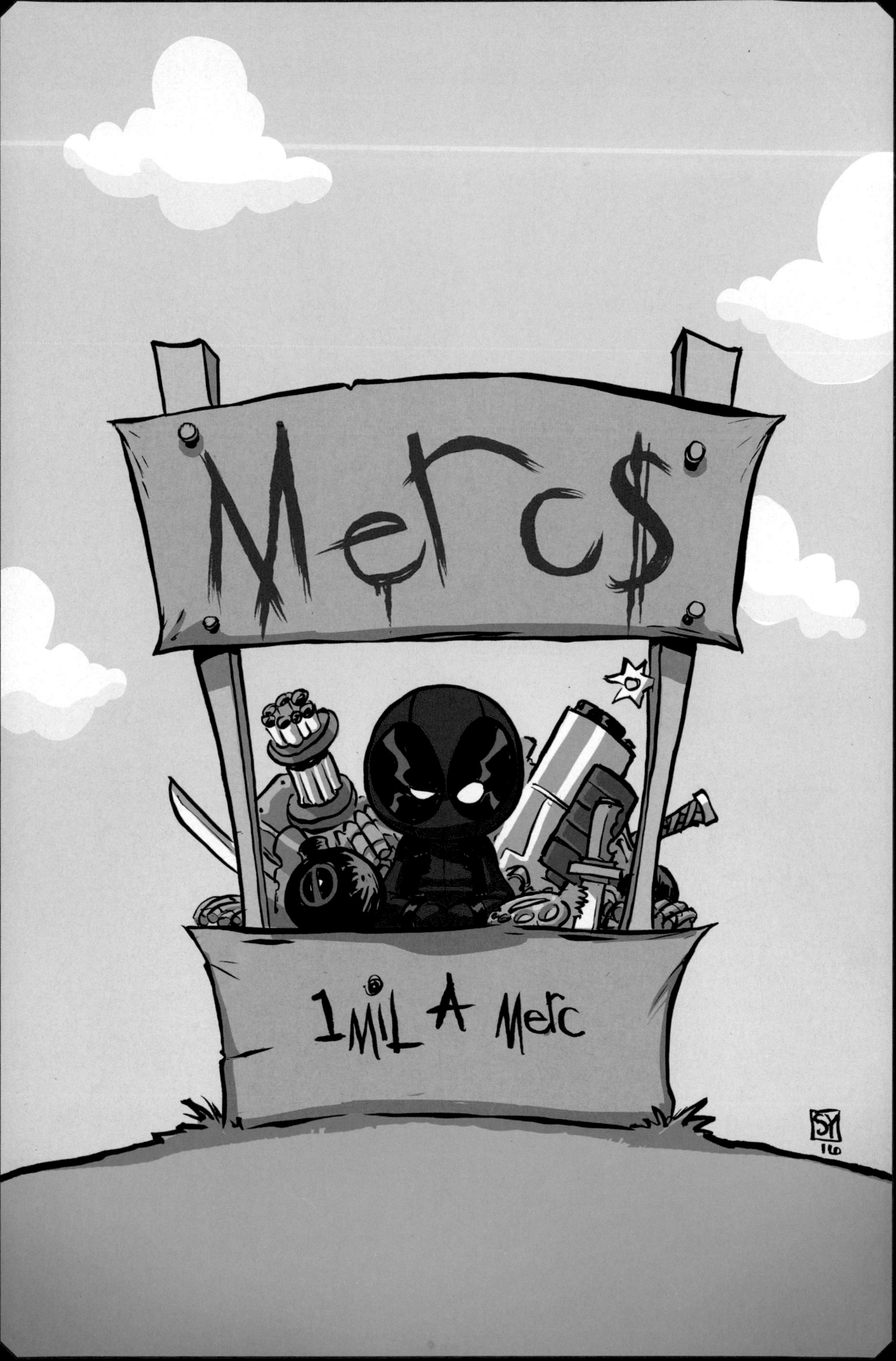
Merc$
1 MIL A Merc
SY 16

SKOTTIE YOUNG

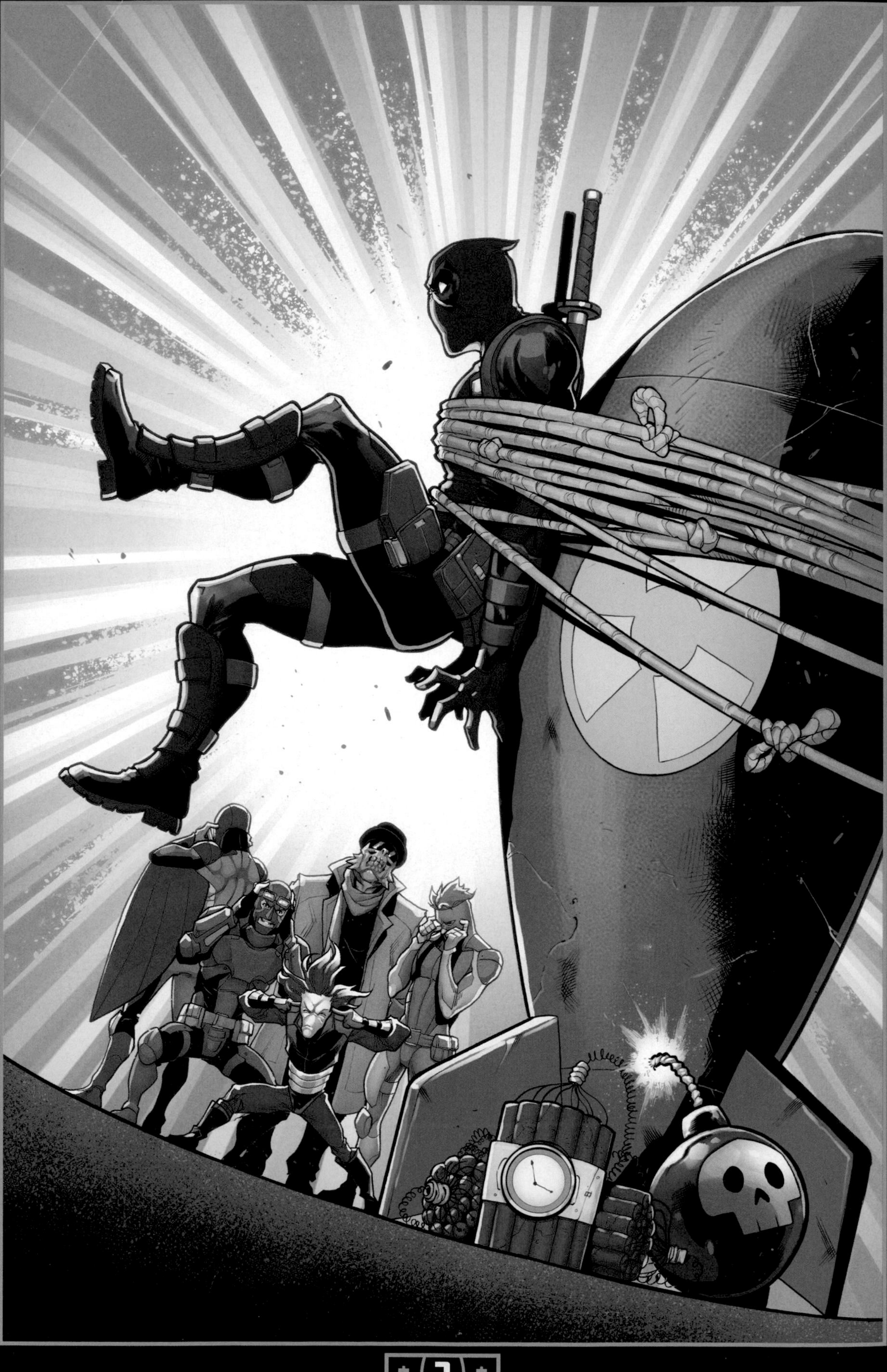

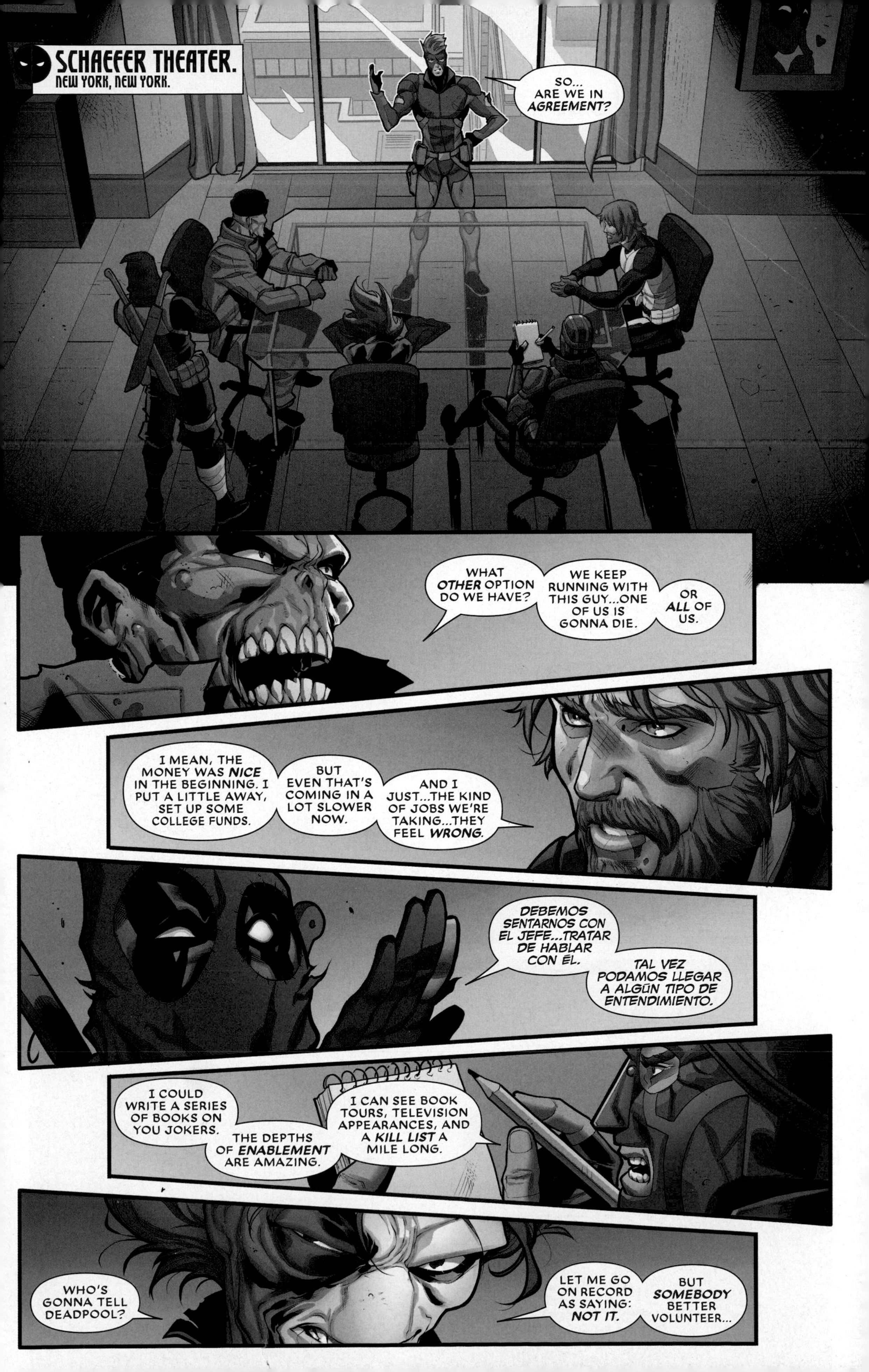
SCHAEFER THEATER.
NEW YORK, NEW YORK.
SO... ARE WE IN AGREEMENT?
WHAT OTHER OPTION DO WE HAVE?
WE KEEP RUNNING WITH THIS GUY...ONE OF US IS GONNA DIE.
OR ALL OF US.
I MEAN, THE MONEY WAS NICE IN THE BEGINNING. I PUT A LITTLE AWAY, SET UP SOME COLLEGE FUNDS.
BUT EVEN THAT'S COMING IN A LOT SLOWER NOW.
AND I JUST...THE KIND OF JOBS WE'RE TAKING...THEY FEEL WRONG.
DEBEMOS SENTARNOS CON EL JEFE...TRATAR DE HABLAR CON ÉL.
TAL VEZ PODAMOS LLEGAR A ALGŪN TIPO DE ENTENDIMIENTO.
I COULD WRITE A SERIES OF BOOKS ON YOU JOKERS.
THE DEPTHS OF ENABLEMENT ARE AMAZING.
I CAN SEE BOOK TOURS, TELEVISION APPEARANCES, AND A KILL LIST A MILE LONG.
WHO'S GONNA TELL DEADPOOL?
LET ME GO ON RECORD AS SAYING: NOT IT.
BUT SOMEBODY BETTER VOLUNTEER...

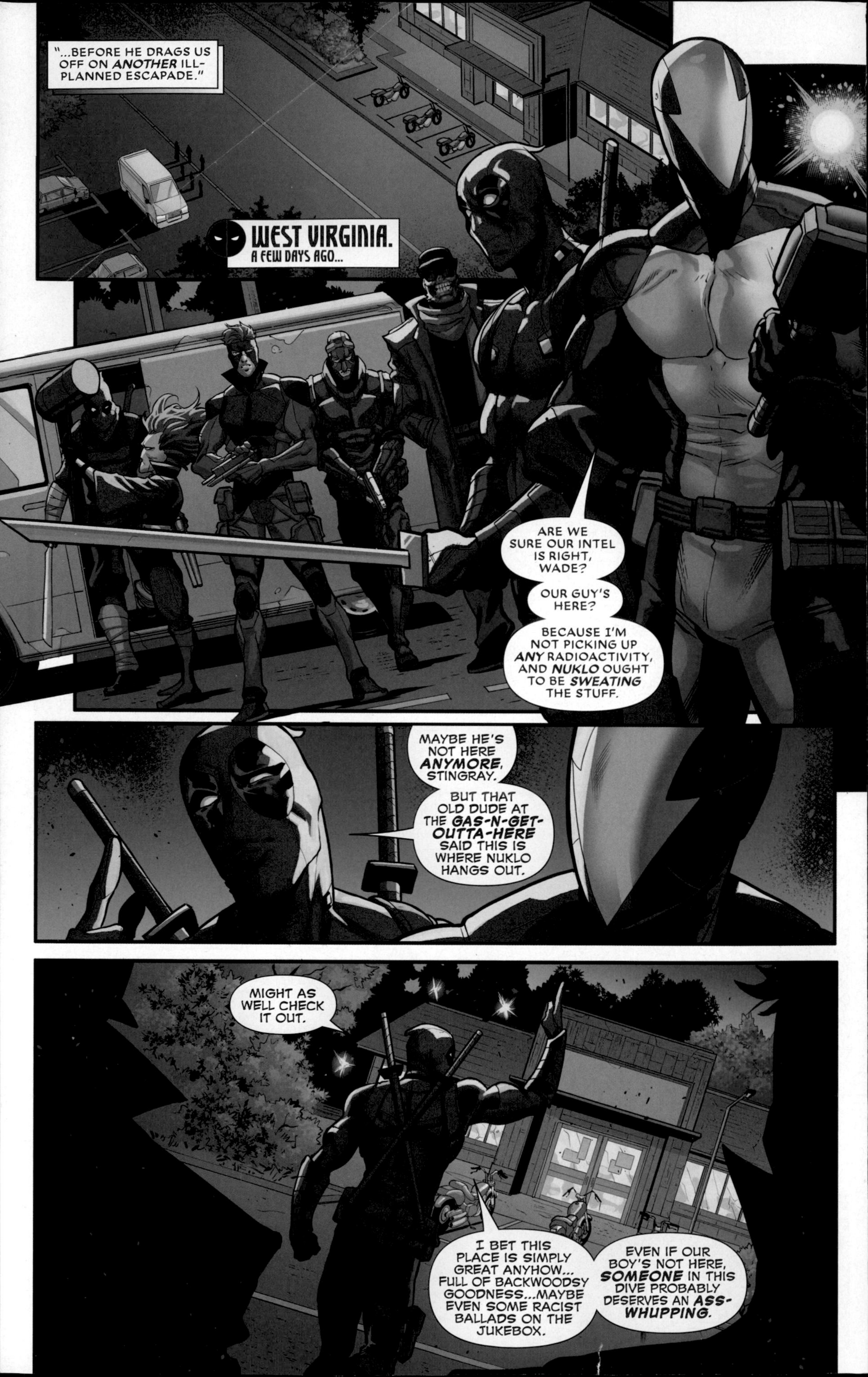
"...BEFORE HE DRAGS US OFF ON ANOTHER ILL-PLANNED ESCAPADE."
WEST VIRGINIA. A FEW DAYS AGO...
ARE WE SURE OUR INTEL IS RIGHT, WADE?
OUR GUY'S HERE?
BECAUSE I'M NOT PICKING UP ANY RADIOACTIVITY, AND NUKLO OUGHT TO BE SWEATING THE STUFF.
MAYBE HE'S NOT HERE ANYMORE, STINGRAY.
BUT THAT OLD DUDE AT THE GAS-N-GET-OUTTA-HERE SAID THIS IS WHERE NUKLO HANGS OUT.
MIGHT AS WELL CHECK IT OUT.
I BET THIS PLACE IS SIMPLY GREAT ANYHOW... FULL OF BACKWOODSY GOODNESS...MAYBE EVEN SOME RACIST BALLADS ON THE JUKEBOX.
EVEN IF OUR BOY'S NOT HERE, SOMEONE IN THIS DIVE PROBABLY DESERVES AN ASS-WHUPPING.

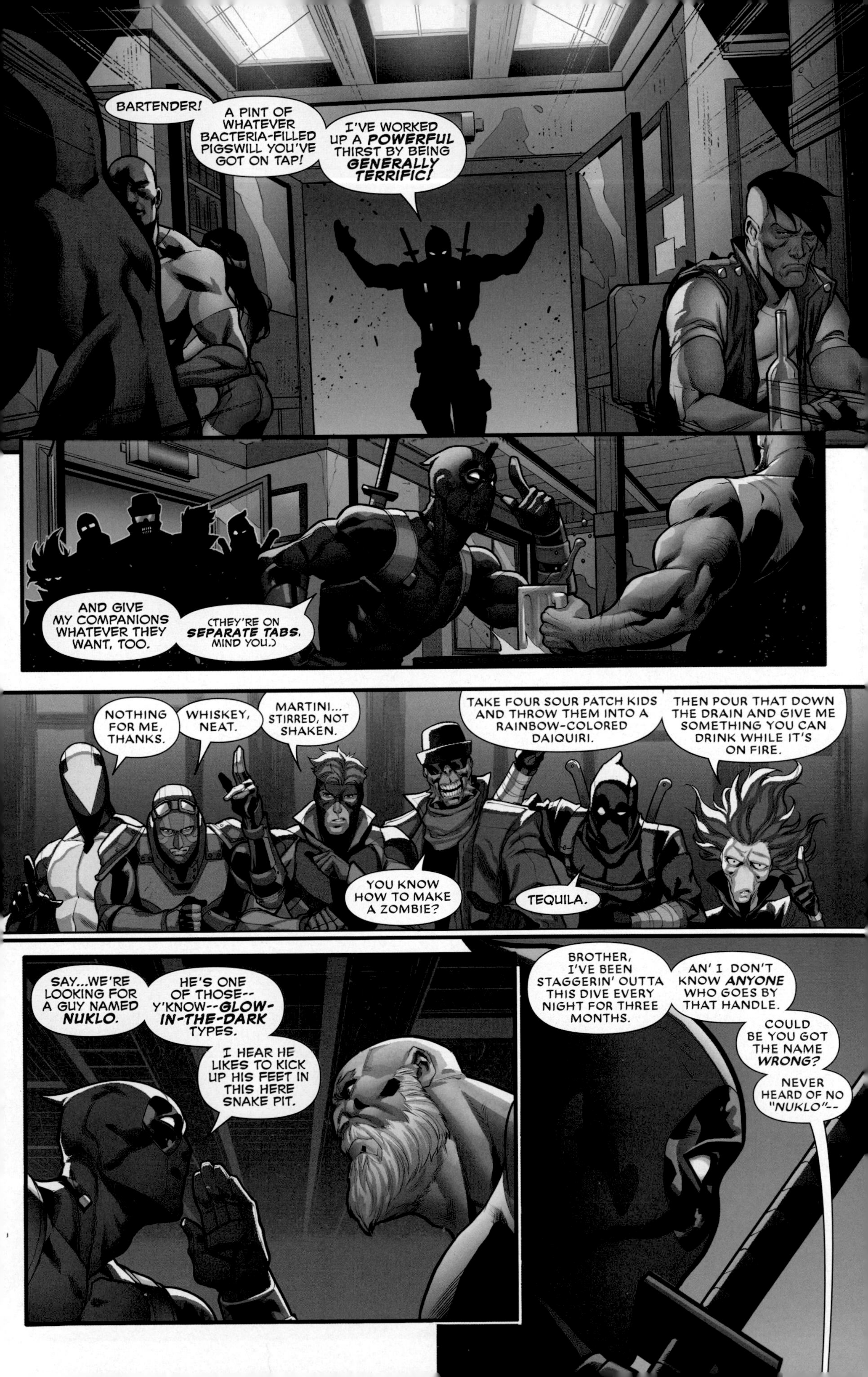
BARTENDER!
A PINT OF WHATEVER BACTERIA-FILLED PIGSWILL YOU'VE GOT ON TAP!
I'VE WORKED UP A POWERFUL THIRST BY BEING GENERALLY TERRIFIC!
AND GIVE MY COMPANIONS WHATEVER THEY WANT, TOO.
(THEY'RE ON SEPARATE TABS, MIND YOU.)
NOTHING FOR ME, THANKS.
WHISKEY, NEAT.
MARTINI... STIRRED, NOT SHAKEN.
YOU KNOW HOW TO MAKE A ZOMBIE?
TAKE FOUR SOUR PATCH KIDS AND THROW THEM INTO A RAINBOW-COLORED DAIQUIRI.
TEQUILA.
THEN POUR THAT DOWN THE DRAIN AND GIVE ME SOMETHING YOU CAN DRINK WHILE IT'S ON FIRE.
SAY...WE'RE LOOKING FOR A GUY NAMED NUKLO.
HE'S ONE OF THOSE--Y'KNOW--GLOW-IN-THE-DARK TYPES.
I HEAR HE LIKES TO KICK UP HIS FEET IN THIS HERE SNAKE PIT.
BROTHER, I'VE BEEN STAGGERIN' OUTTA THIS DIVE EVERY NIGHT FOR THREE MONTHS.
AN' I DON'T KNOW ANYONE WHO GOES BY THAT HANDLE.
COULD BE YOU GOT THE NAME WRONG?
NEVER HEARD OF NO "NUKLO"--

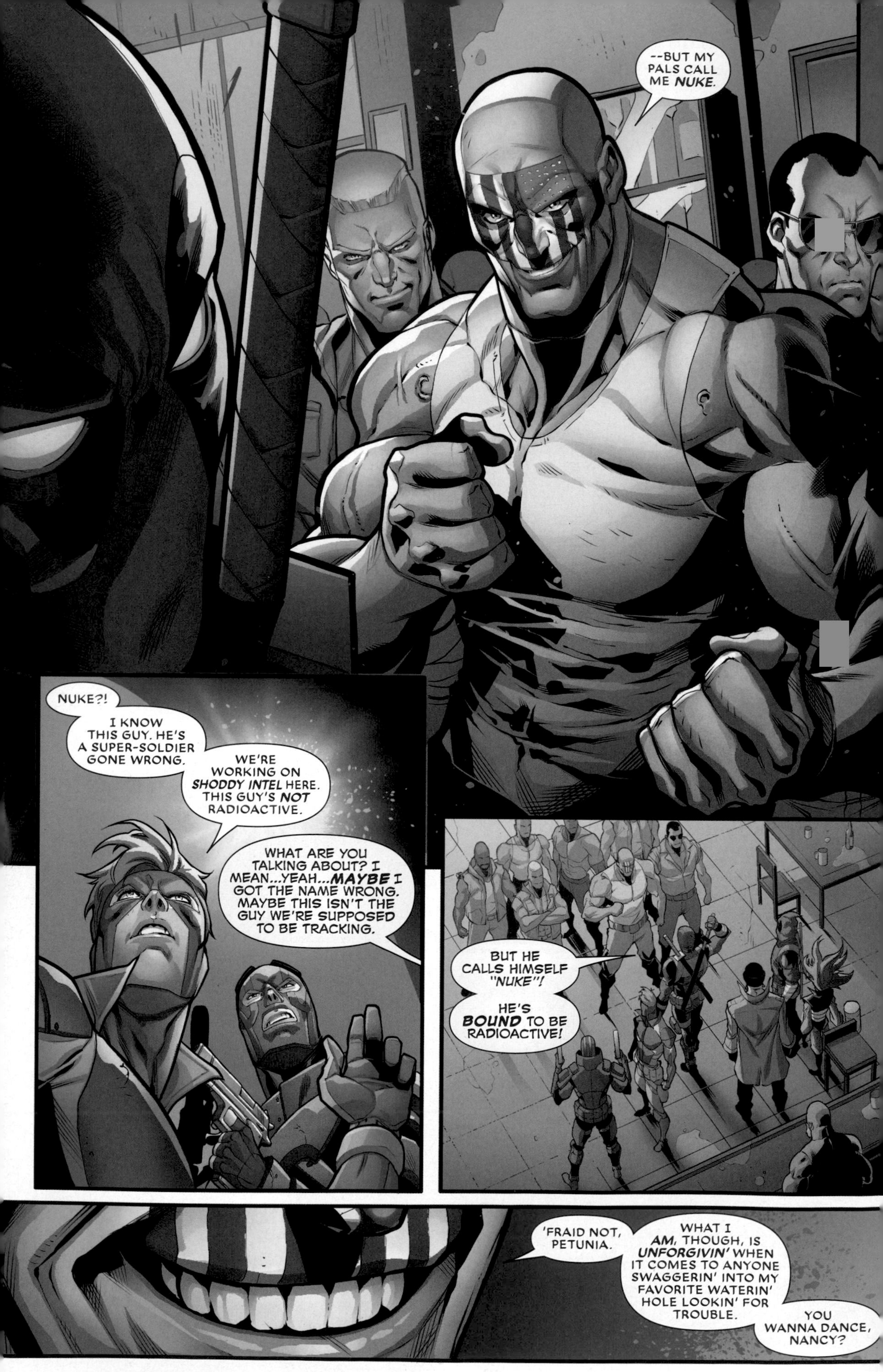
--BUT MY PALS CALL ME NUKE.
NUKE?!
I KNOW THIS GUY. HE'S A SUPER-SOLDIER GONE WRONG.
WE'RE WORKING ON SHODDY INTEL HERE. THIS GUY'S NOT RADIOACTIVE.
WHAT ARE YOU TALKING ABOUT? I MEAN...YEAH...MAYBE I GOT THE NAME WRONG. MAYBE THIS ISN'T THE GUY WE'RE SUPPOSED TO BE TRACKING.
BUT HE CALLS HIMSELF "NUKE"!
HE'S BOUND TO BE RADIOACTIVE!
'FRAID NOT, PETUNIA.
WHAT I AM, THOUGH, IS UNFORGIVIN' WHEN IT COMES TO ANYONE SWAGGERIN' INTO MY FAVORITE WATERIN' HOLE LOOKIN' FOR TROUBLE.
YOU WANNA DANCE, NANCY?

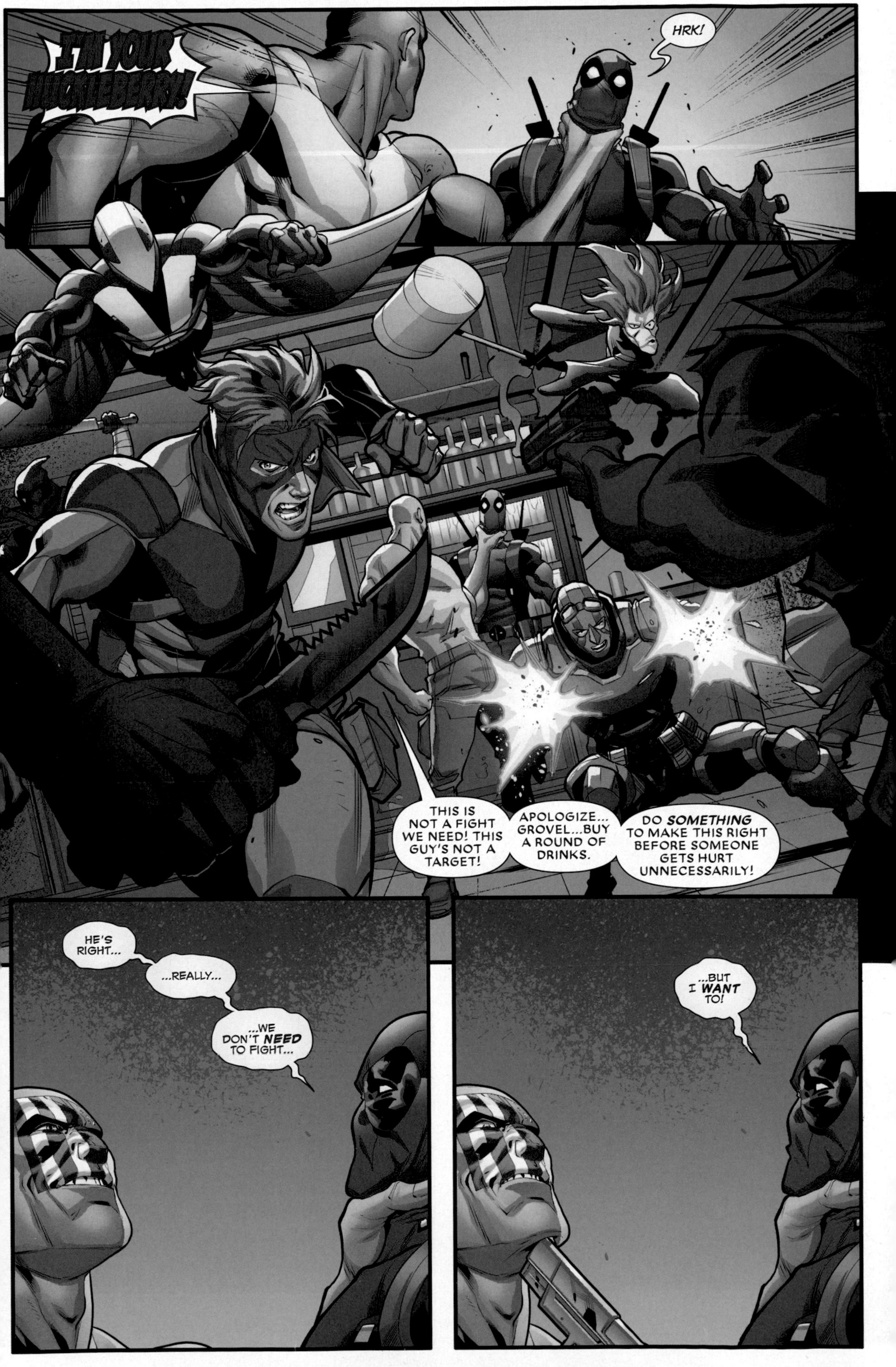
I'M YOUR HUCKLEBERRY!
HRK!
THIS IS NOT A FIGHT WE NEED! THIS GUY'S NOT A TARGET!
APOLOGIZE... GROVEL...BUY A ROUND OF DRINKS.
DO SOMETHING TO MAKE THIS RIGHT BEFORE SOMEONE GETS HURT UNNECESSARILY!
HE'S RIGHT...
...REALLY...
...WE DON'T NEED TO FIGHT...
...BUT I WANT TO!

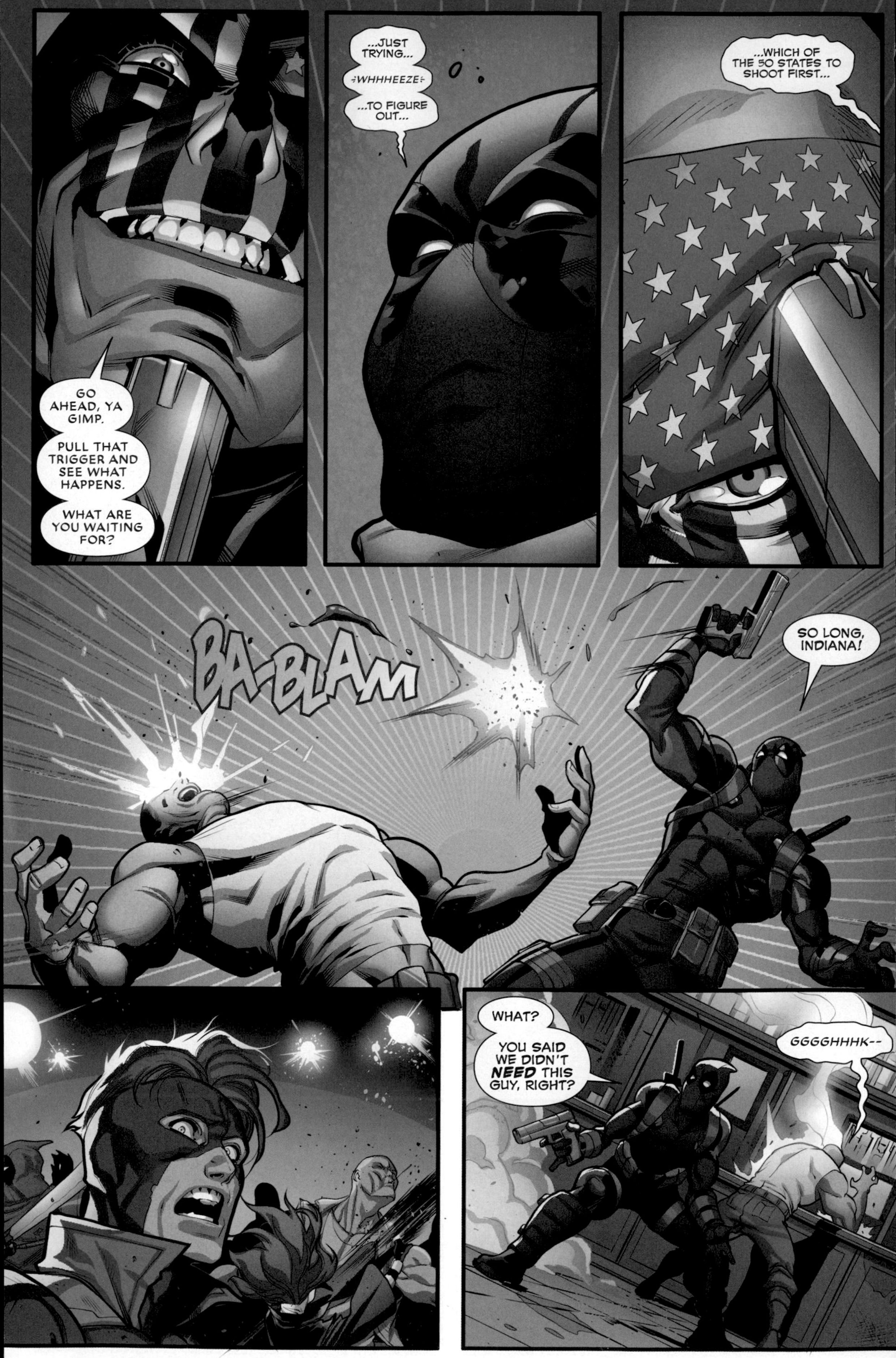
GO AHEAD, YA GIMP.
PULL THAT TRIGGER AND SEE WHAT HAPPENS.
WHAT ARE YOU WAITING FOR?
...JUST TRYING...
WHHHEEZE
...TO FIGURE OUT...
...WHICH OF THE 50 STATES TO SHOOT FIRST...
BA-BLAM
SO LONG, INDIANA!
WHAT?
YOU SAID WE DIDN'T NEED THIS GUY, RIGHT?
GGGGHHHK--

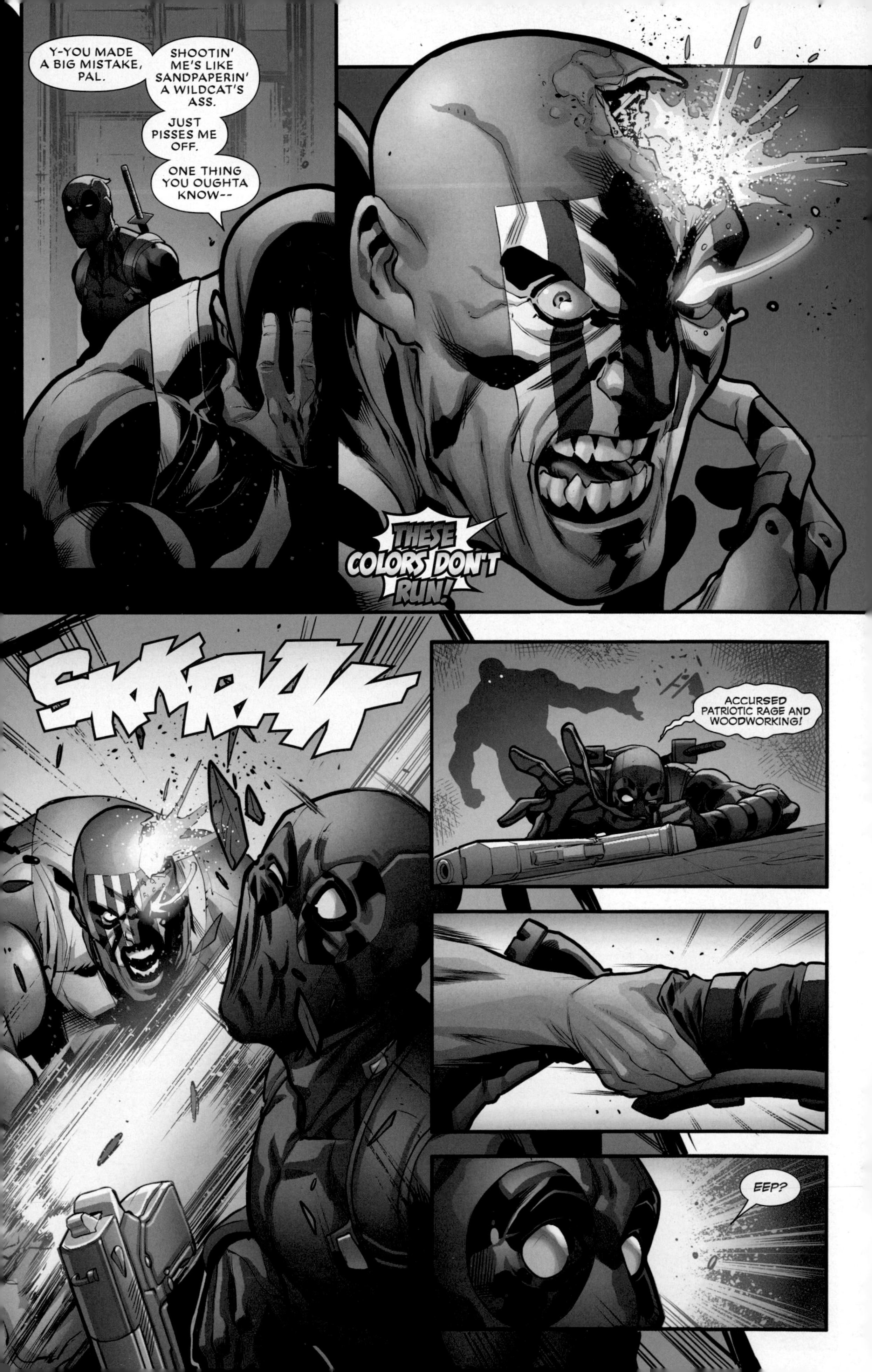
Y-YOU MADE A BIG MISTAKE, PAL.
SHOOTIN' ME'S LIKE SANDPAPERIN' A WILDCAT'S ASS.
JUST PISSES ME OFF.
ONE THING YOU OUGHTA KNOW--
THESE COLORS DON'T RUN!
SKRAK
ACCURSED PATRIOTIC RAGE AND WOODWORKING!
EEP?

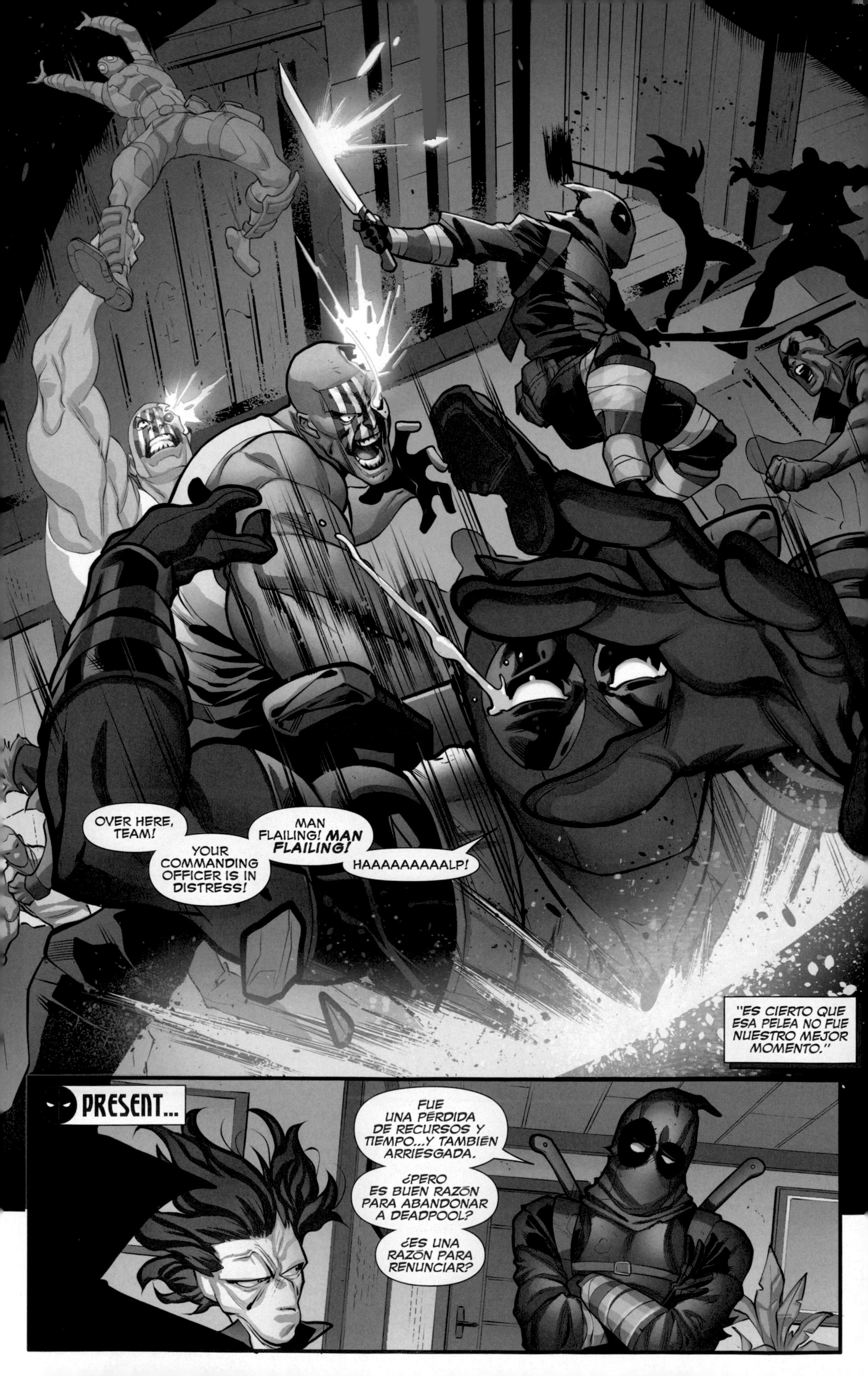
OVER HERE, TEAM!
YOUR COMMANDING OFFICER IS IN DISTRESS!
MAN FLAILING! MAN FLAILING!
HAAAAAAAAAALP!
"ES CIERTO QUE ESA PELEA NO FUE NUESTRO MEJOR MOMENTO."
PRESENT...
FUE UNA PÉRDIDA DE RECURSOS Y TIEMPO...Y TAMBIÉN ARRIESGADA.
¿PERO ES BUEN RAZÓN PARA ABANDONAR A DEADPOOL?
¿ES UNA RAZÓN PARA RENUNCIAR?

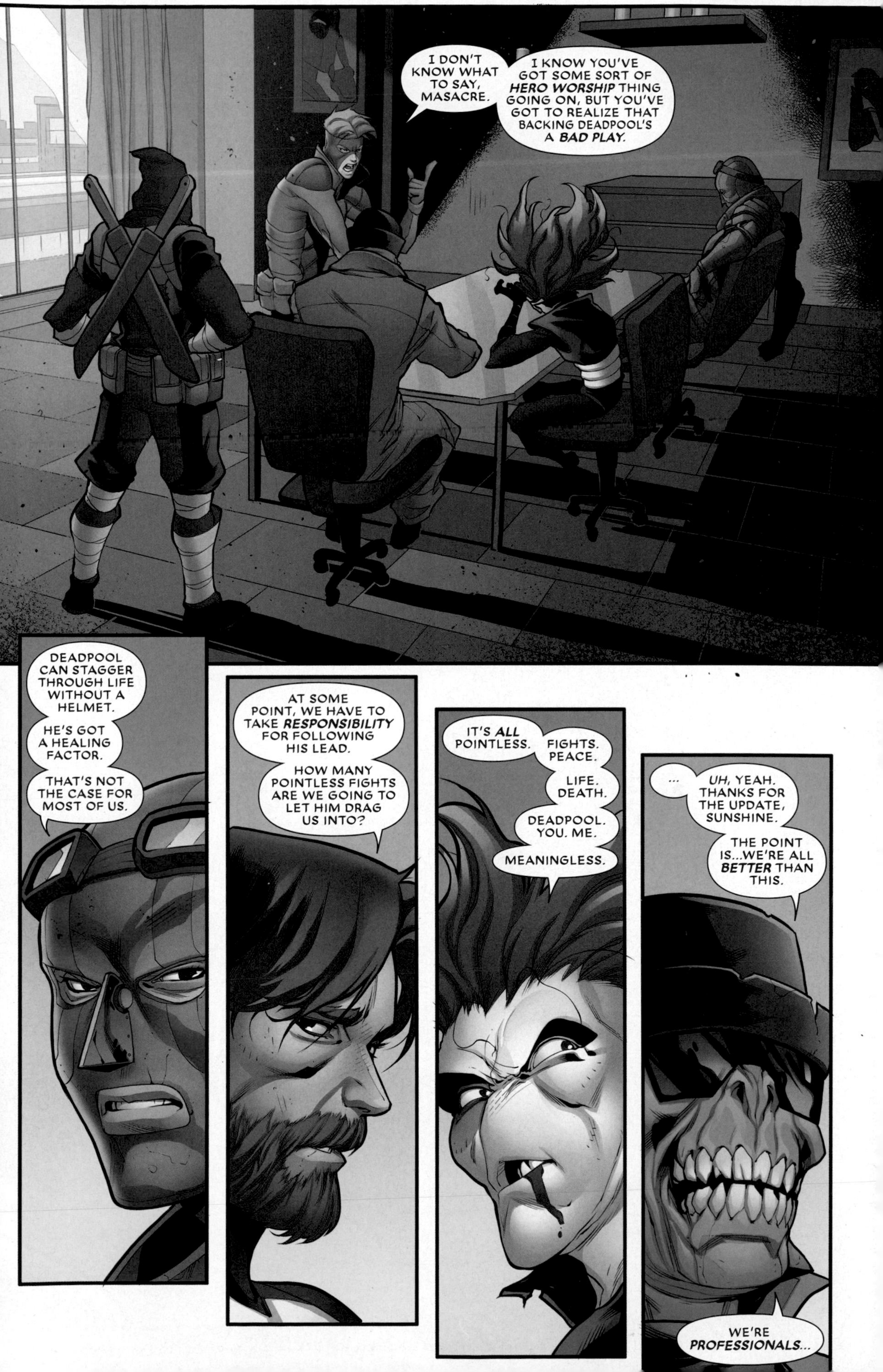

I DON'T KNOW WHAT TO SAY, MASACRE.
I KNOW YOU'VE GOT SOME SORT OF ***HERO WORSHIP*** THING GOING ON, BUT YOU'VE GOT TO REALIZE THAT BACKING DEADPOOL'S A ***BAD PLAY.***
DEADPOOL CAN STAGGER THROUGH LIFE WITHOUT A HELMET.
HE'S GOT A HEALING FACTOR.
THAT'S NOT THE CASE FOR MOST OF US.
AT SOME POINT, WE HAVE TO TAKE ***RESPONSIBILITY*** FOR FOLLOWING HIS LEAD.
HOW MANY POINTLESS FIGHTS ARE WE GOING TO LET HIM DRAG US INTO?
IT'S ***ALL*** POINTLESS.
FIGHTS. PEACE.
LIFE. DEATH.
DEADPOOL. YOU. ME.
MEANINGLESS.
...
UH, YEAH. THANKS FOR THE UPDATE, SUNSHINE.
THE POINT IS...WE'RE ALL ***BETTER*** THAN THIS.
WE'RE ***PROFESSIONALS...***

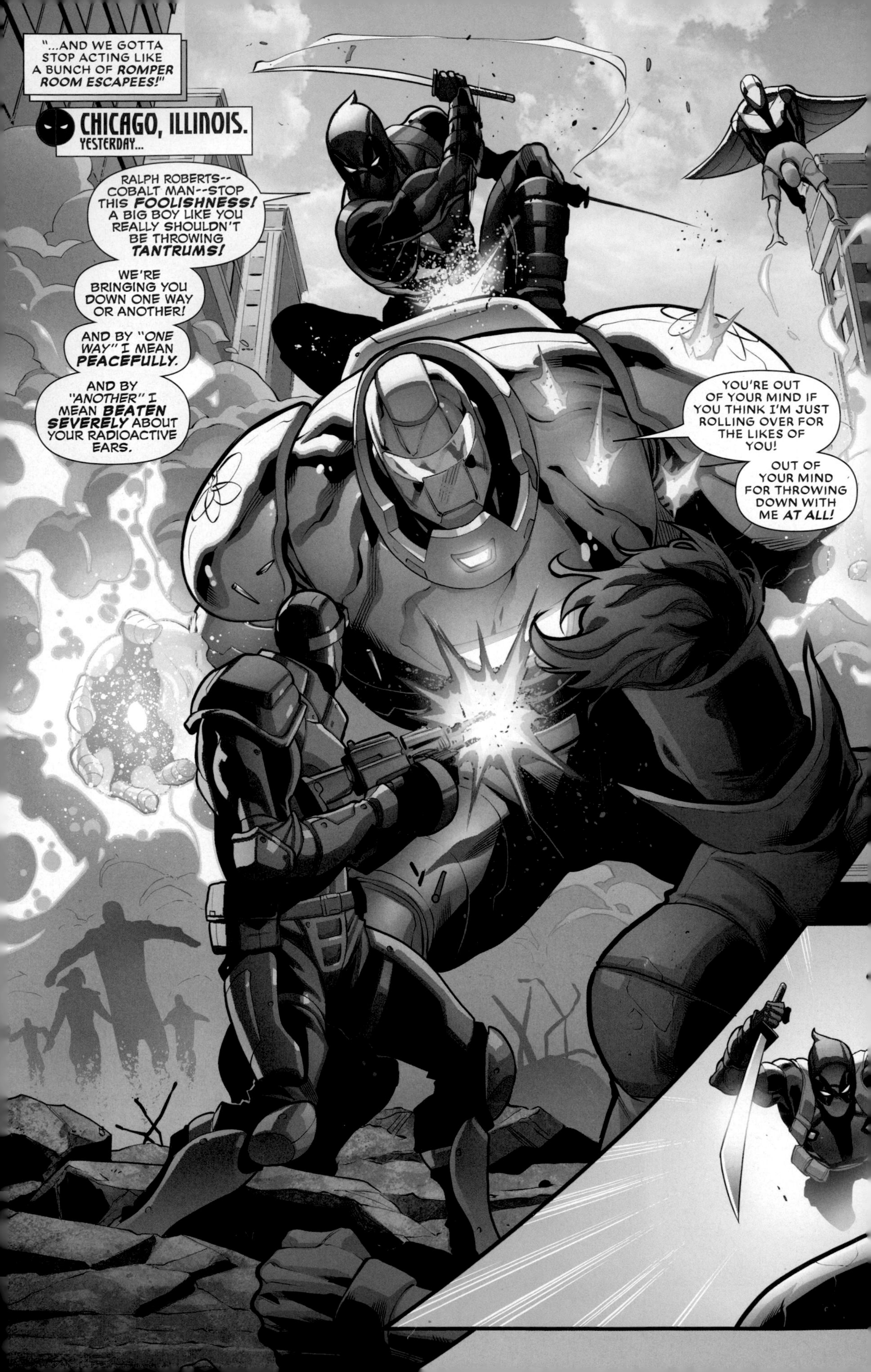
"...AND WE GOTTA STOP ACTING LIKE A BUNCH OF ROMPER ROOM ESCAPEES!"
CHICAGO, ILLINOIS. YESTERDAY...
RALPH ROBERTS--COBALT MAN--STOP THIS FOOLISHNESS! A BIG BOY LIKE YOU REALLY SHOULDN'T BE THROWING TANTRUMS!
WE'RE BRINGING YOU DOWN ONE WAY OR ANOTHER!
AND BY "ONE WAY" I MEAN PEACEFULLY.
AND BY "ANOTHER" I MEAN BEATEN SEVERELY ABOUT YOUR RADIOACTIVE EARS.
YOU'RE OUT OF YOUR MIND IF YOU THINK I'M JUST ROLLING OVER FOR THE LIKES OF YOU!
OUT OF YOUR MIND FOR THROWING DOWN WITH ME AT ALL!

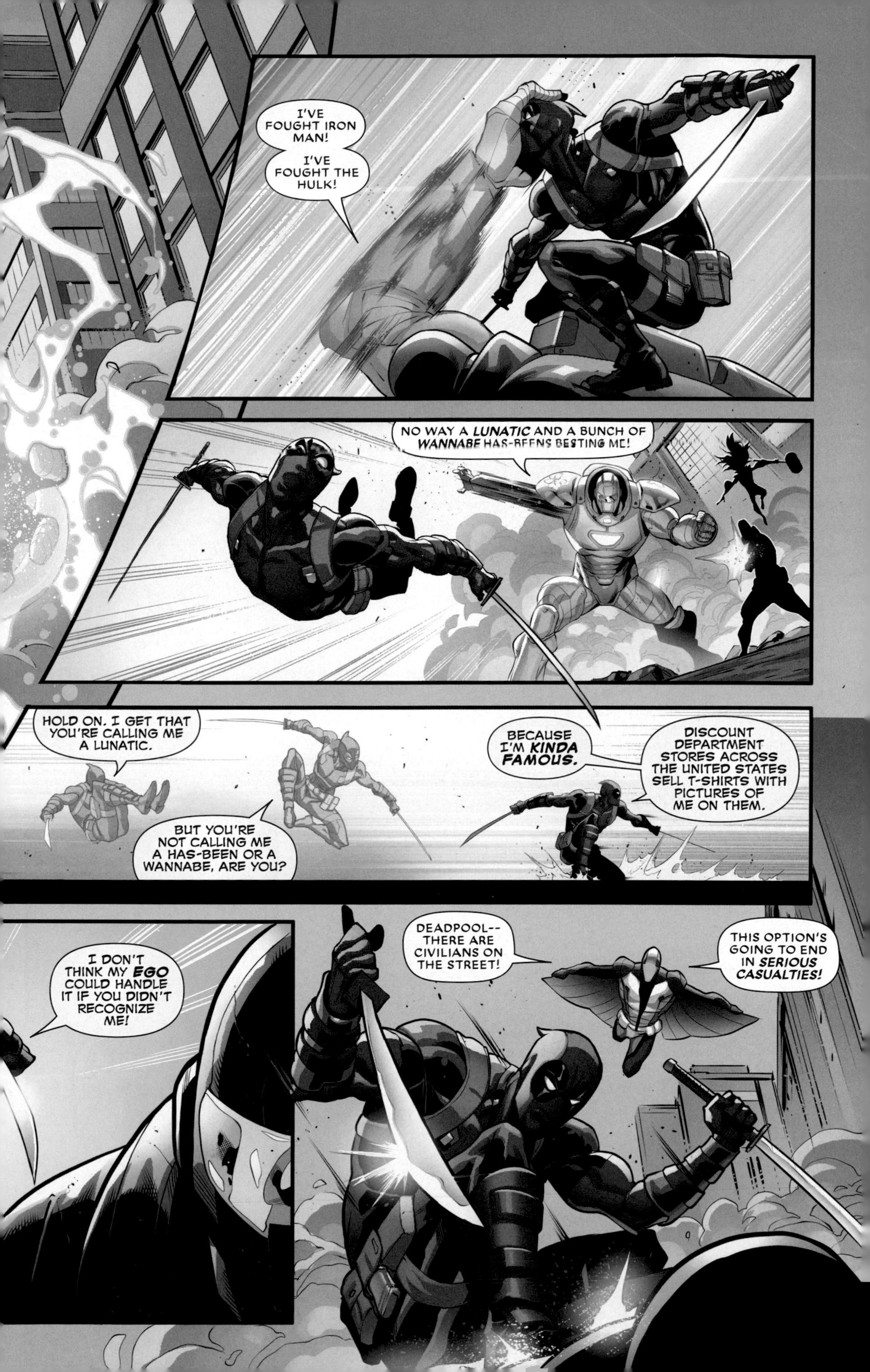
I'VE FOUGHT IRON MAN!
I'VE FOUGHT THE HULK!
NO WAY A LUNATIC AND A BUNCH OF WANNABE HAS-BEENS BESTING ME!
HOLD ON. I GET THAT YOU'RE CALLING ME A LUNATIC.
BUT YOU'RE NOT CALLING ME A HAS-BEEN OR A WANNABE, ARE YOU?
BECAUSE I'M KINDA FAMOUS.
DISCOUNT DEPARTMENT STORES ACROSS THE UNITED STATES SELL T-SHIRTS WITH PICTURES OF ME ON THEM.
I DON'T THINK MY EGO COULD HANDLE IT IF YOU DIDN'T RECOGNIZE ME!
DEADPOOL-- THERE ARE CIVILIANS ON THE STREET!
THIS OPTION'S GOING TO END IN SERIOUS CASUALTIES!

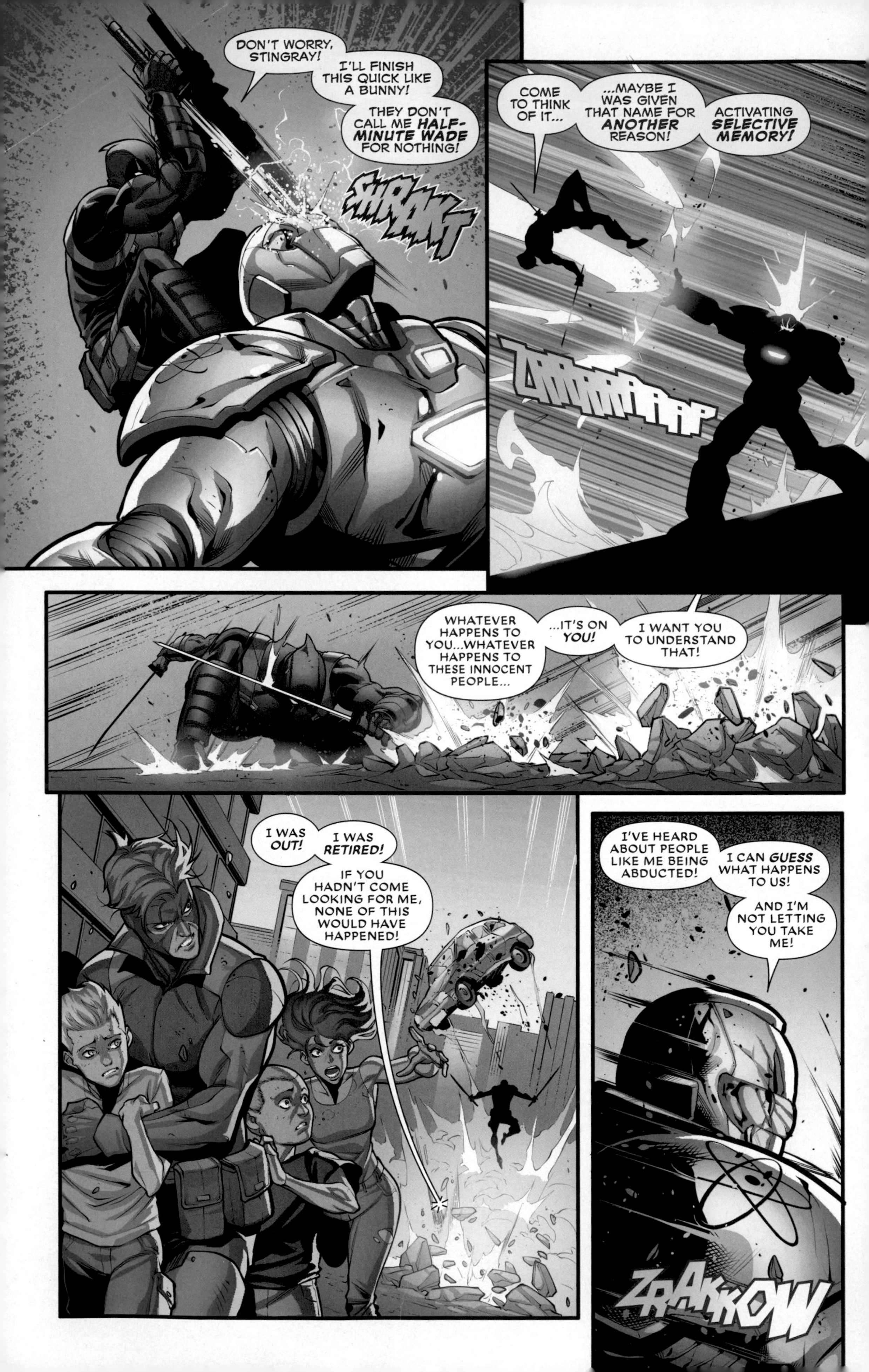
DON'T WORRY, STINGRAY!
I'LL FINISH THIS QUICK LIKE A BUNNY!
THEY DON'T CALL ME HALF-MINUTE WADE FOR NOTHING!
SHRAKT
COME TO THINK OF IT...
...MAYBE I WAS GIVEN THAT NAME FOR ANOTHER REASON!
ACTIVATING SELECTIVE MEMORY!
ZAAAAAAP
WHATEVER HAPPENS TO YOU...WHATEVER HAPPENS TO THESE INNOCENT PEOPLE...
...IT'S ON YOU!
I WANT YOU TO UNDERSTAND THAT!
I WAS OUT!
I WAS RETIRED!
IF YOU HADN'T COME LOOKING FOR ME, NONE OF THIS WOULD HAVE HAPPENED!
I'VE HEARD ABOUT PEOPLE LIKE ME BEING ABDUCTED!
I CAN GUESS WHAT HAPPENS TO US!
AND I'M NOT LETTING YOU TAKE ME!
ZRAKKOW

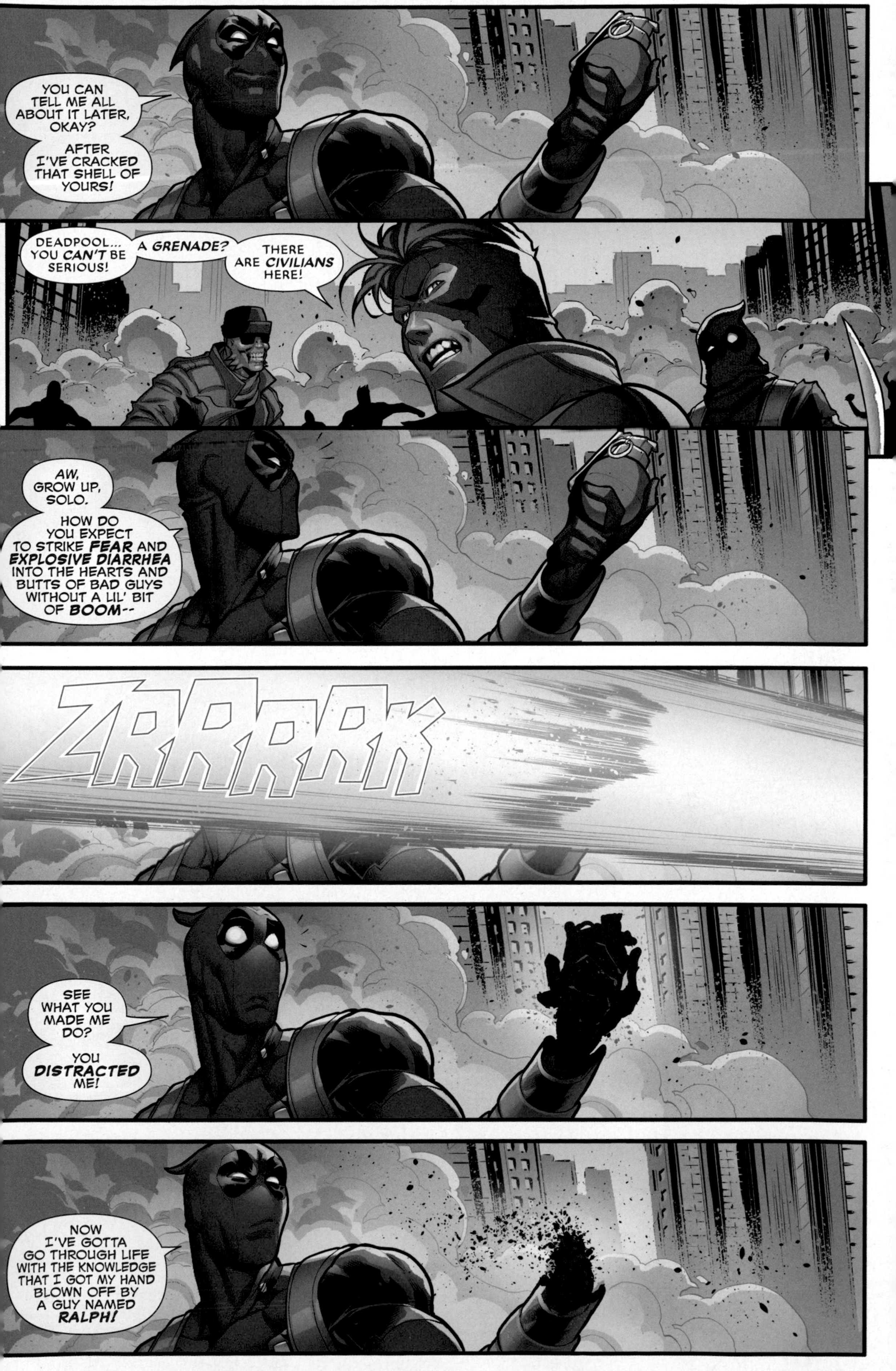

YOU CAN TELL ME ALL ABOUT IT LATER, OKAY?
AFTER I'VE CRACKED THAT SHELL OF YOURS!
DEADPOOL... YOU CAN'T BE SERIOUS!
A GRENADE?
THERE ARE CIVILIANS HERE!
AW, GROW UP, SOLO.
HOW DO YOU EXPECT TO STRIKE FEAR AND EXPLOSIVE DIARRHEA INTO THE HEARTS AND BUTTS OF BAD GUYS WITHOUT A LIL' BIT OF BOOM--
ZRRRRK
SEE WHAT YOU MADE ME DO?
YOU DISTRACTED ME!
NOW I'VE GOTTA GO THROUGH LIFE WITH THE KNOWLEDGE THAT I GOT MY HAND BLOWN OFF BY A GUY NAMED RALPH!

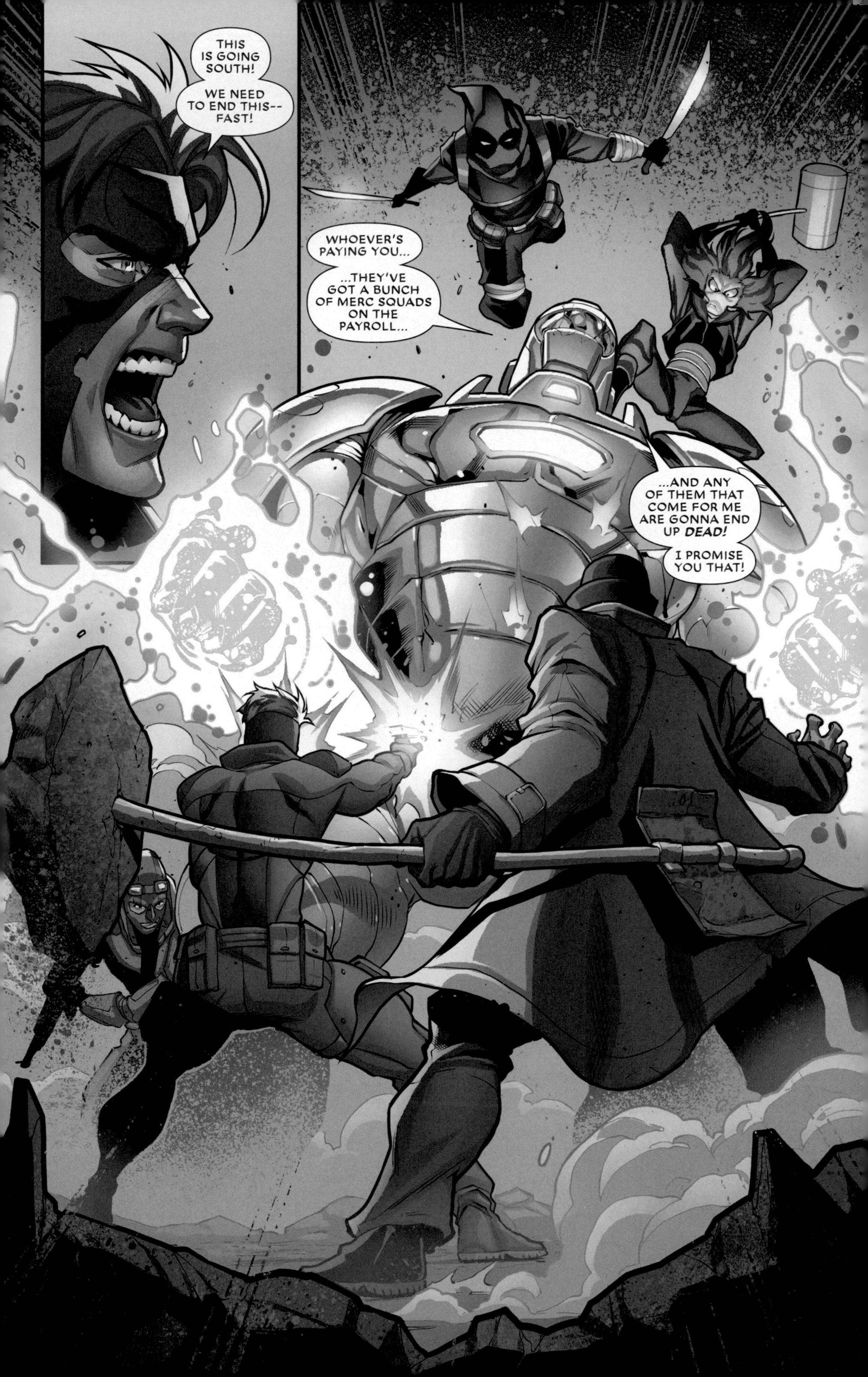
THIS IS GOING SOUTH!
WE NEED TO END THIS-- FAST!
WHOEVER'S PAYING YOU...
...THEY'VE GOT A BUNCH OF MERC SQUADS ON THE PAYROLL...
...AND ANY OF THEM THAT COME FOR ME ARE GONNA END UP DEAD!
I PROMISE YOU THAT!

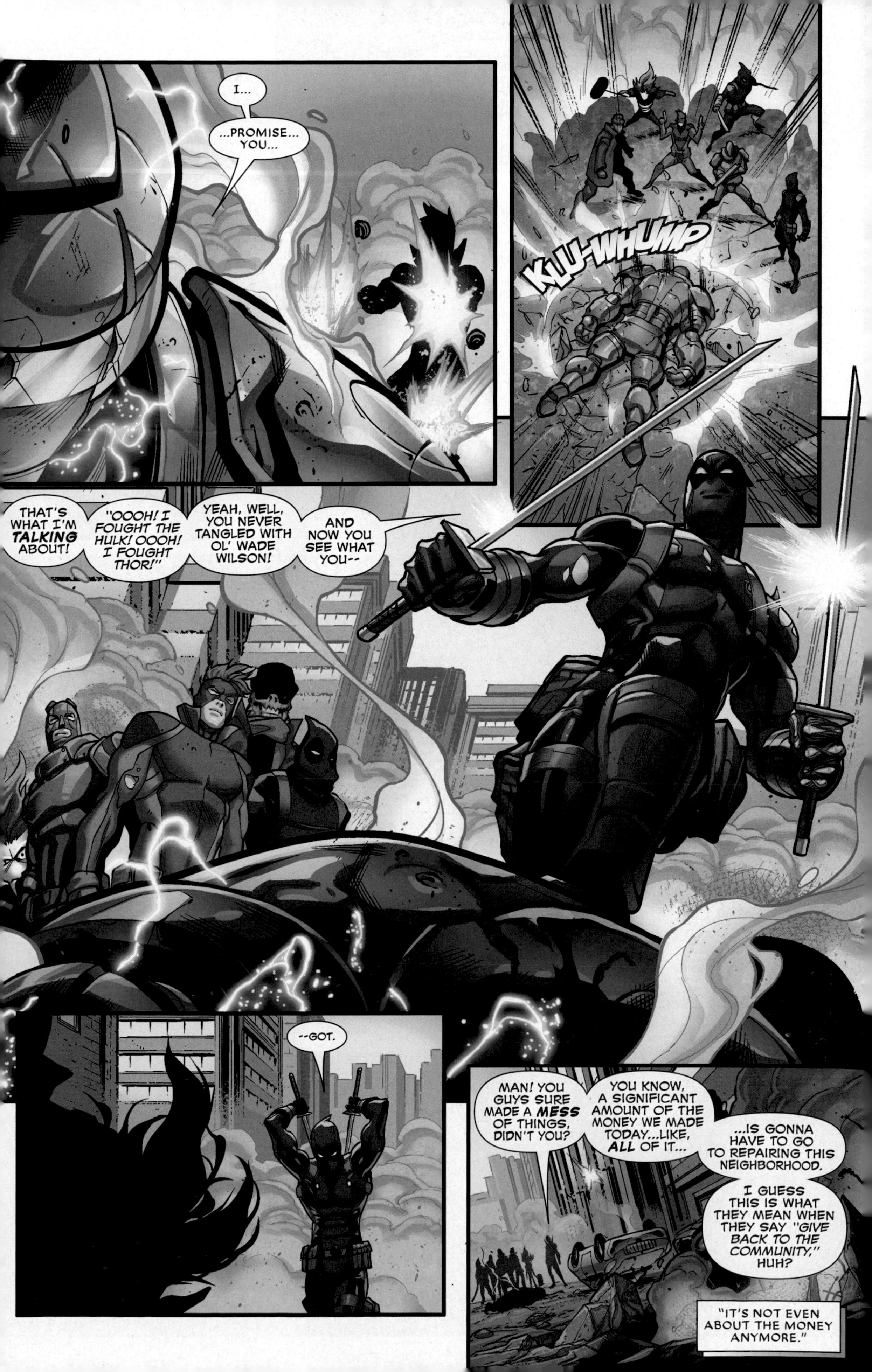
I...
...PROMISE... YOU...
KLU-WHUMP
THAT'S WHAT I'M **TALKING** ABOUT!
"OOOH! I FOUGHT THE HULK! OOOH! I FOUGHT THOR!"
YEAH, WELL, YOU NEVER TANGLED WITH OL' WADE WILSON!
AND NOW YOU SEE WHAT YOU--
--GOT.
MAN! YOU GUYS SURE MADE A **MESS** OF THINGS, DIDN'T YOU?
YOU KNOW, A SIGNIFICANT AMOUNT OF THE MONEY WE MADE TODAY...LIKE, **ALL** OF IT...
...IS GONNA HAVE TO GO TO REPAIRING THIS NEIGHBORHOOD.
I GUESS THIS IS WHAT THEY MEAN WHEN THEY SAY *"GIVE BACK TO THE COMMUNITY,"* HUH?
"IT'S NOT EVEN ABOUT THE MONEY ANYMORE."

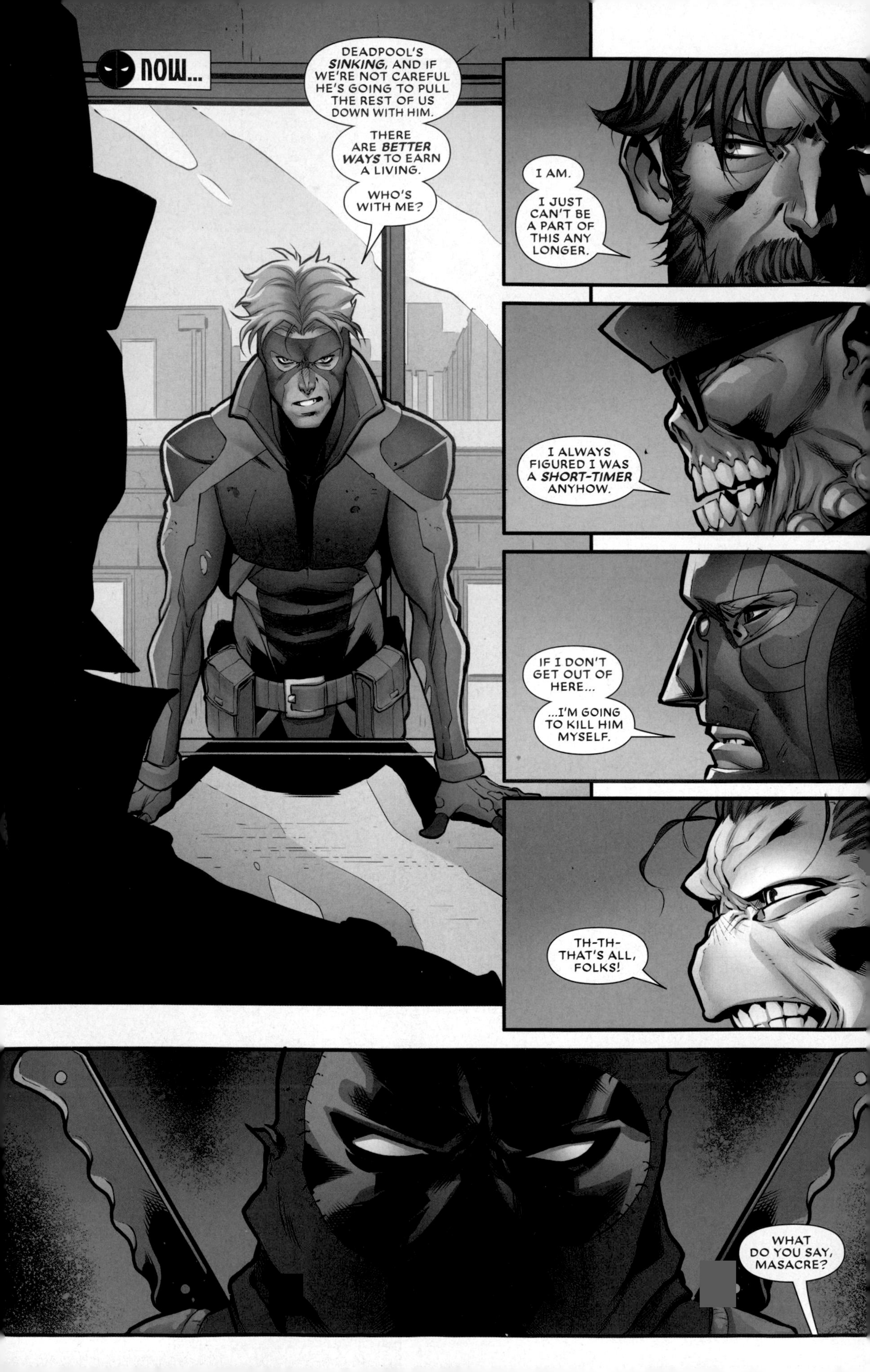
NOW...
DEADPOOL'S SINKING, AND IF WE'RE NOT CAREFUL HE'S GOING TO PULL THE REST OF US DOWN WITH HIM.
THERE ARE BETTER WAYS TO EARN A LIVING.
WHO'S WITH ME?
I AM.
I JUST CAN'T BE A PART OF THIS ANY LONGER.
I ALWAYS FIGURED I WAS A SHORT-TIMER ANYHOW.
IF I DON'T GET OUT OF HERE...
...I'M GOING TO KILL HIM MYSELF.
TH-TH-THAT'S ALL, FOLKS!
WHAT DO YOU SAY, MASACRE?

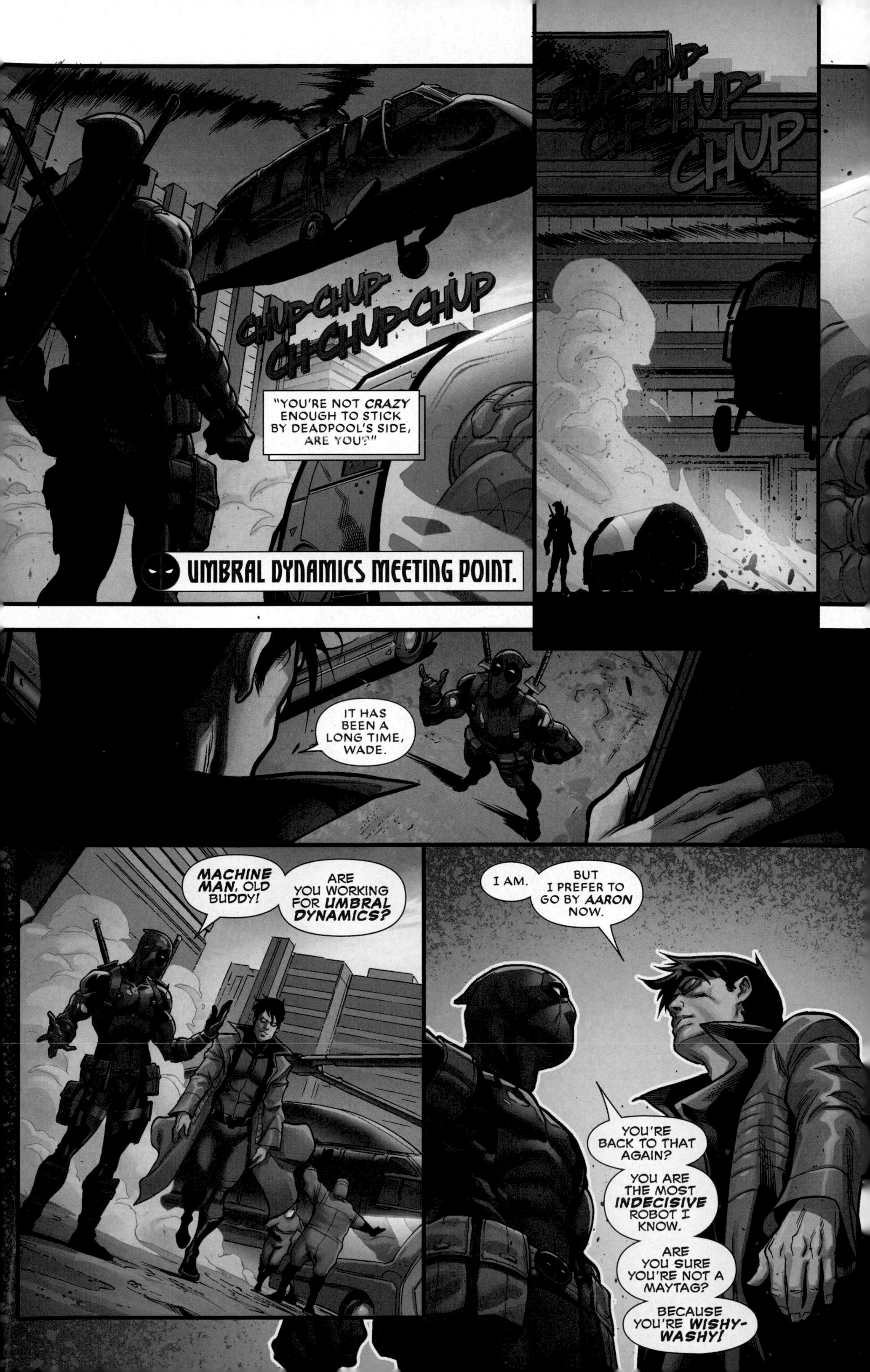
CHUP-CHUP
CH-CHUP-CHUP
"YOU'RE NOT CRAZY ENOUGH TO STICK BY DEADPOOL'S SIDE, ARE YOU?"
UMBRAL DYNAMICS MEETING POINT.
CHUP-CHUP
CH-CHUP
CHUP
IT HAS BEEN A LONG TIME, WADE.
MACHINE MAN, OLD BUDDY!
ARE YOU WORKING FOR UMBRAL DYNAMICS?
I AM.
BUT I PREFER TO GO BY AARON NOW.
YOU'RE BACK TO THAT AGAIN?
YOU ARE THE MOST INDECISIVE ROBOT I KNOW.
ARE YOU SURE YOU'RE NOT A MAYTAG?
BECAUSE YOU'RE WISHY-WASHY!

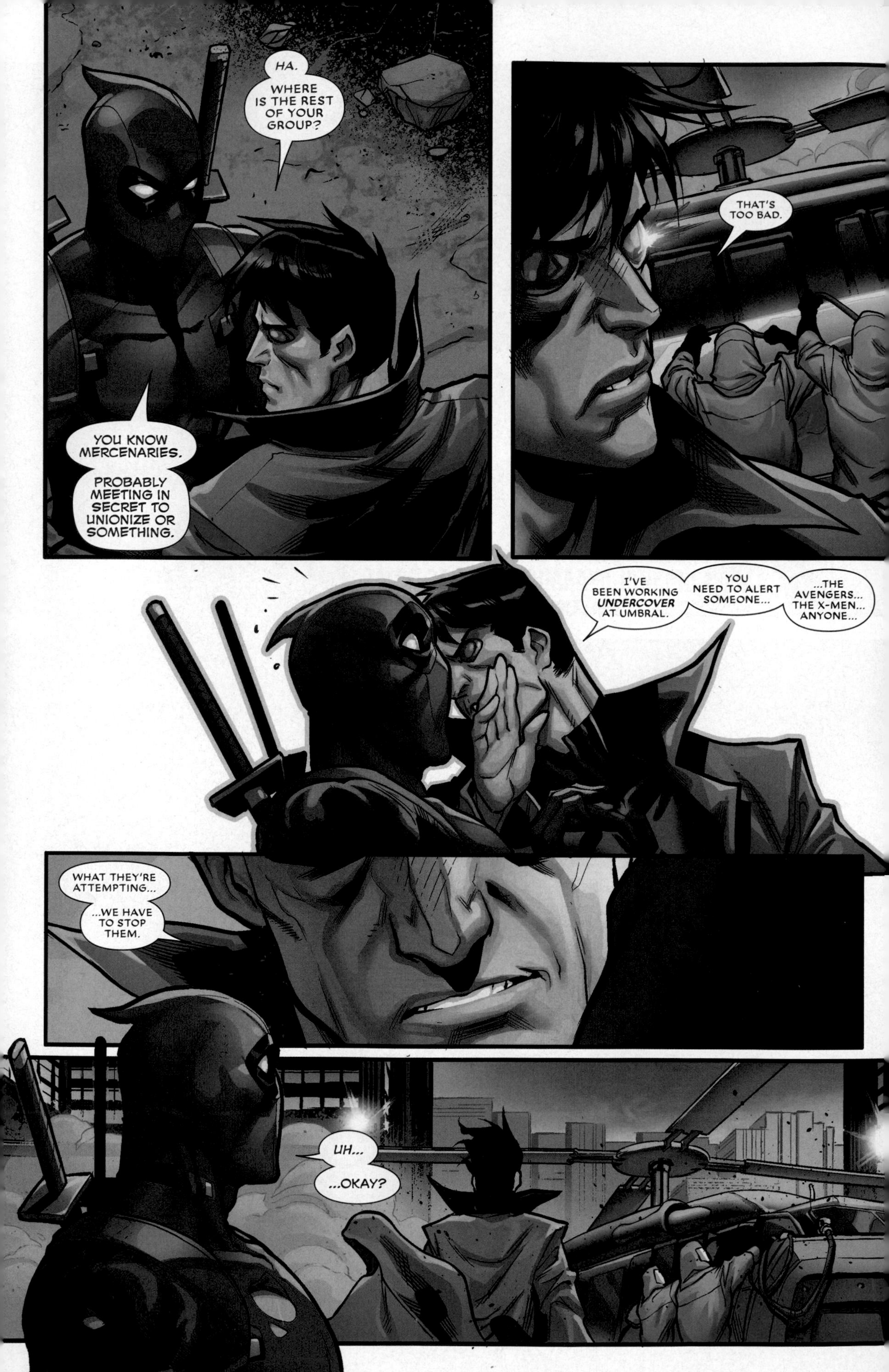
HA.
WHERE IS THE REST OF YOUR GROUP?
YOU KNOW MERCENARIES.
PROBABLY MEETING IN SECRET TO UNIONIZE OR SOMETHING.
THAT'S TOO BAD.
I'VE BEEN WORKING *UNDERCOVER* AT UMBRAL.
YOU NEED TO ALERT SOMEONE...
...THE AVENGERS... THE X-MEN... ANYONE...
WHAT THEY'RE ATTEMPTING...
...WE HAVE TO STOP THEM.
UH...
...OKAY?

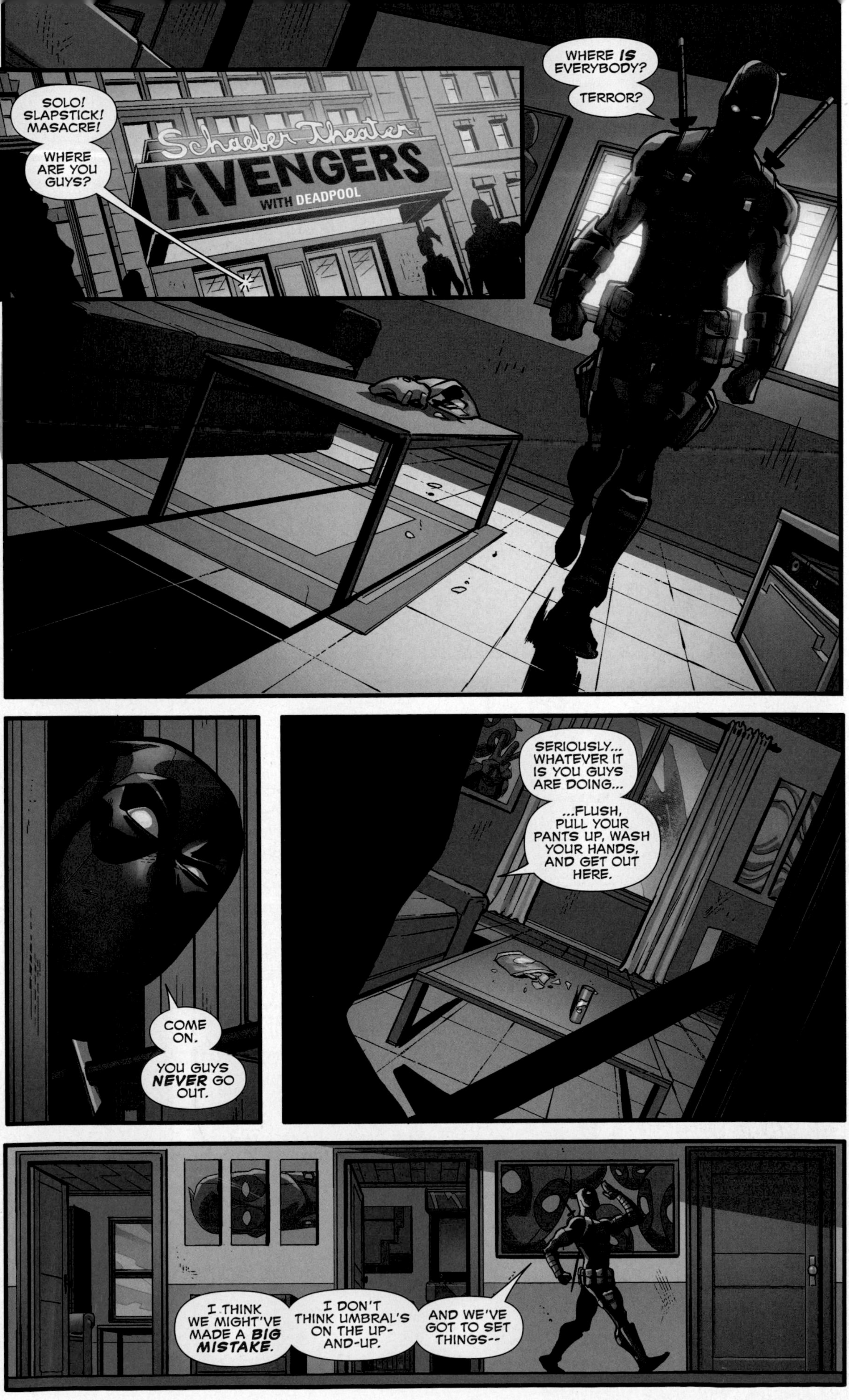
SOLO! SLAPSTICK! MASACRE!
WHERE ARE YOU GUYS?
Schaeber Theater
AVENGERS
WITH DEADPOOL
WHERE IS EVERYBODY?
TERROR?
COME ON.
YOU GUYS NEVER GO OUT.
SERIOUSLY... WHATEVER IT IS YOU GUYS ARE DOING...
...FLUSH, PULL YOUR PANTS UP, WASH YOUR HANDS, AND GET OUT HERE.
I THINK WE MIGHT'VE MADE A BIG MISTAKE.
I DON'T THINK UMBRAL'S ON THE UP-AND-UP.
AND WE'VE GOT TO SET THINGS--

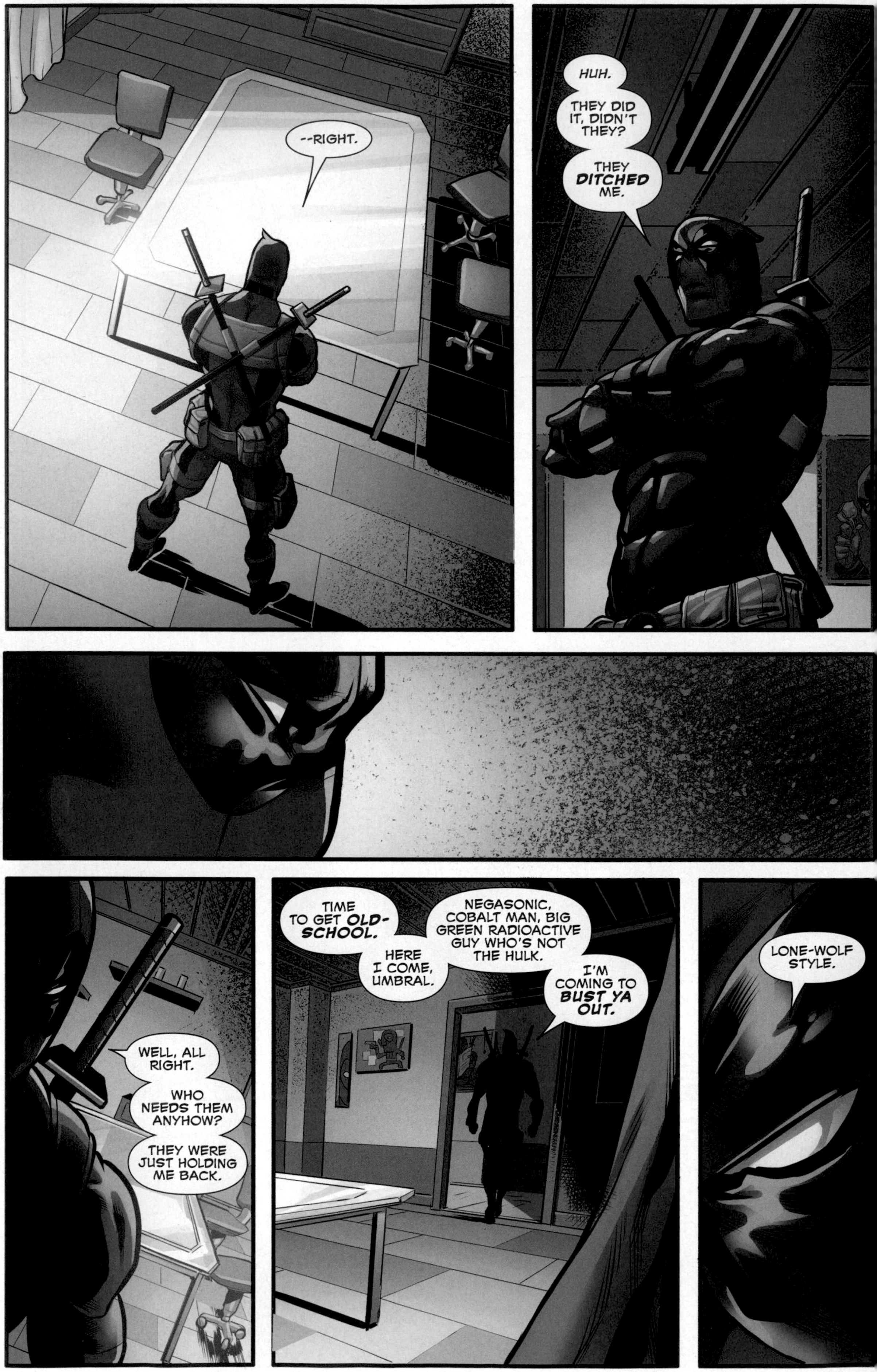
--RIGHT.
HUH.
THEY DID IT, DIDN'T THEY?
THEY DITCHED ME.
WELL, ALL RIGHT.
WHO NEEDS THEM ANYHOW?
THEY WERE JUST HOLDING ME BACK.
TIME TO GET OLD-SCHOOL.
HERE I COME, UMBRAL.
NEGASONIC, COBALT MAN, BIG GREEN RADIOACTIVE GUY WHO'S NOT THE HULK.
I'M COMING TO BUST YA OUT.
LONE-WOLF STYLE.

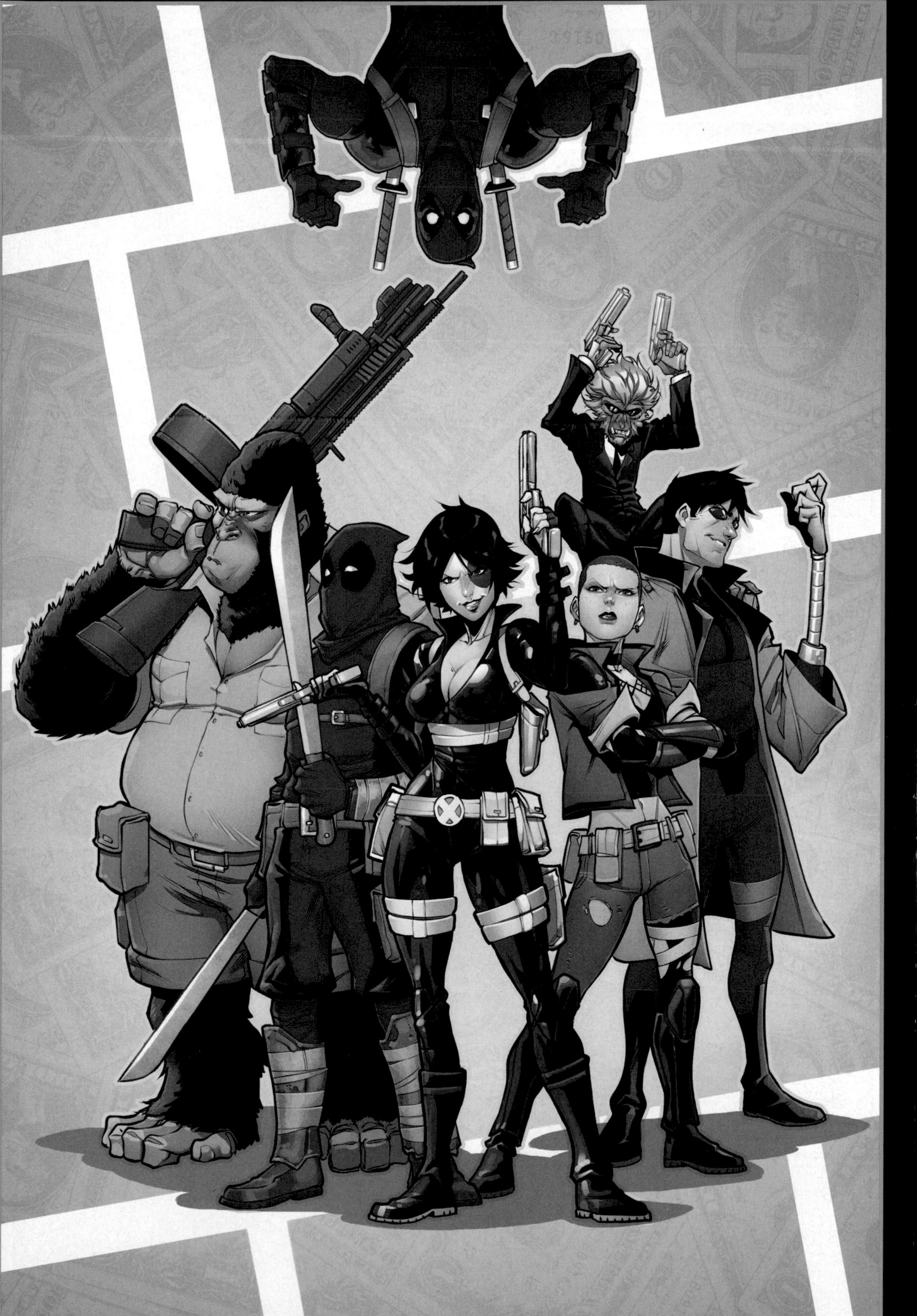

$ 4 $

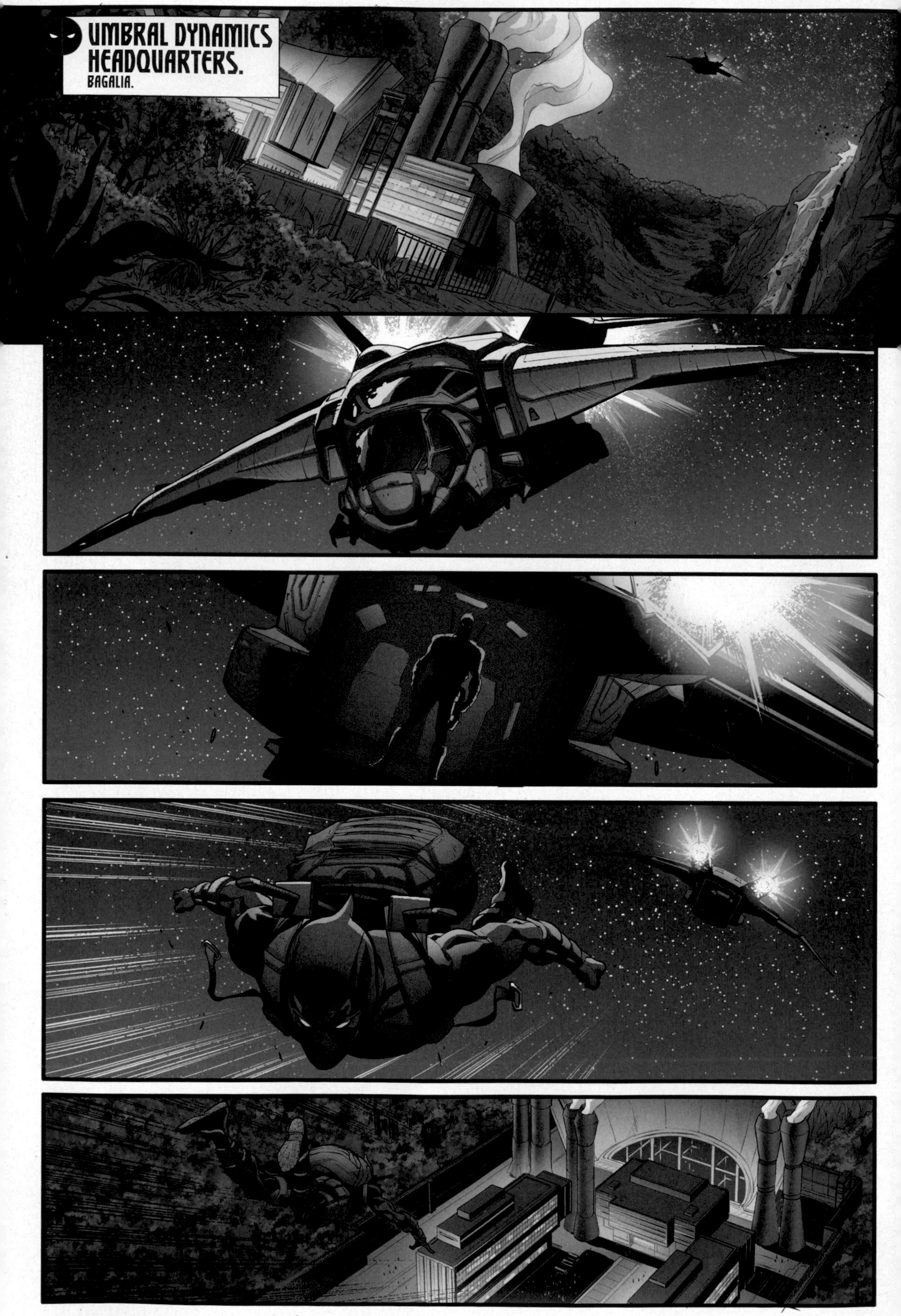
UMBRAL DYNAMICS HEADQUARTERS.
BAGALIA.

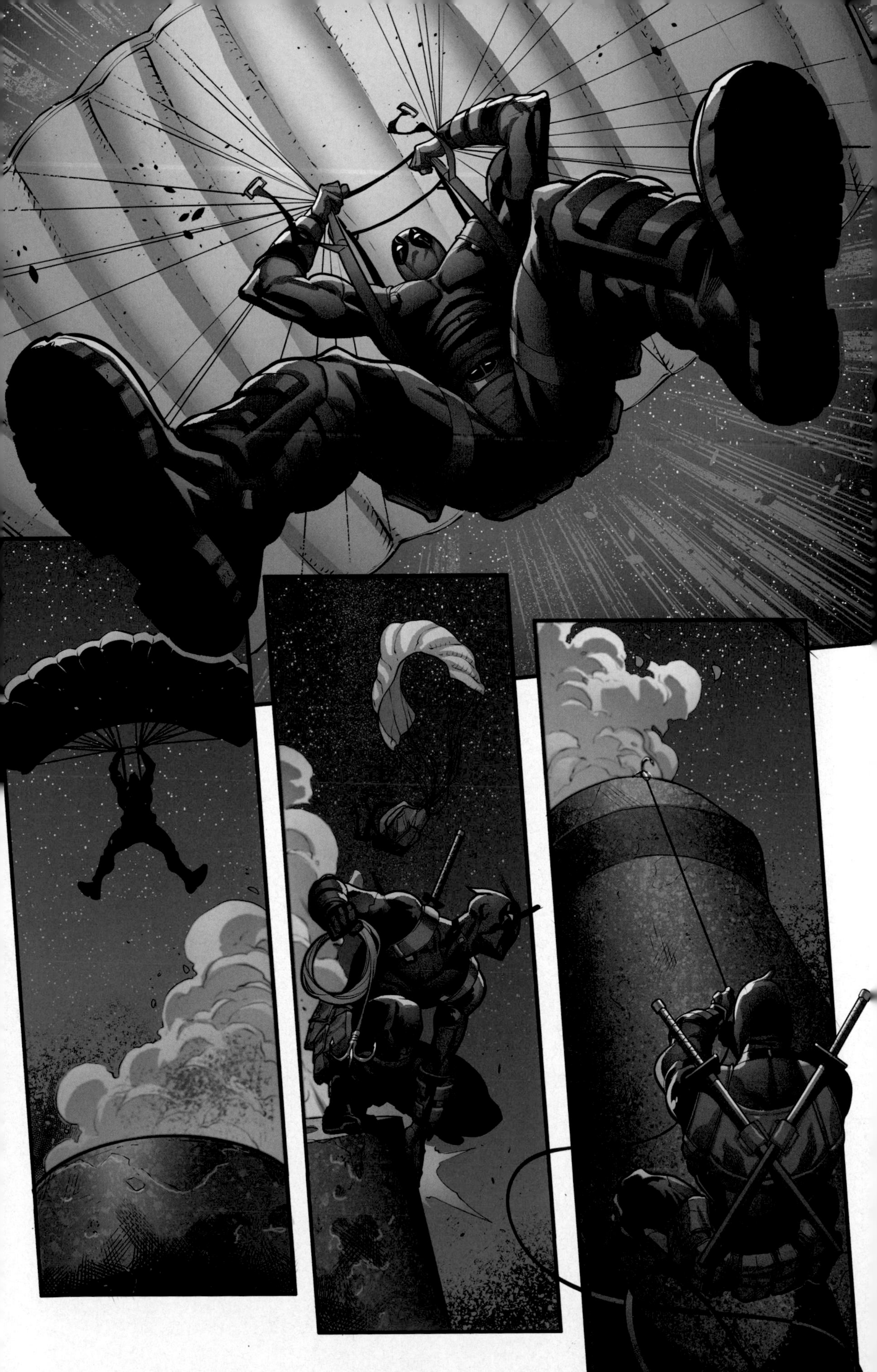

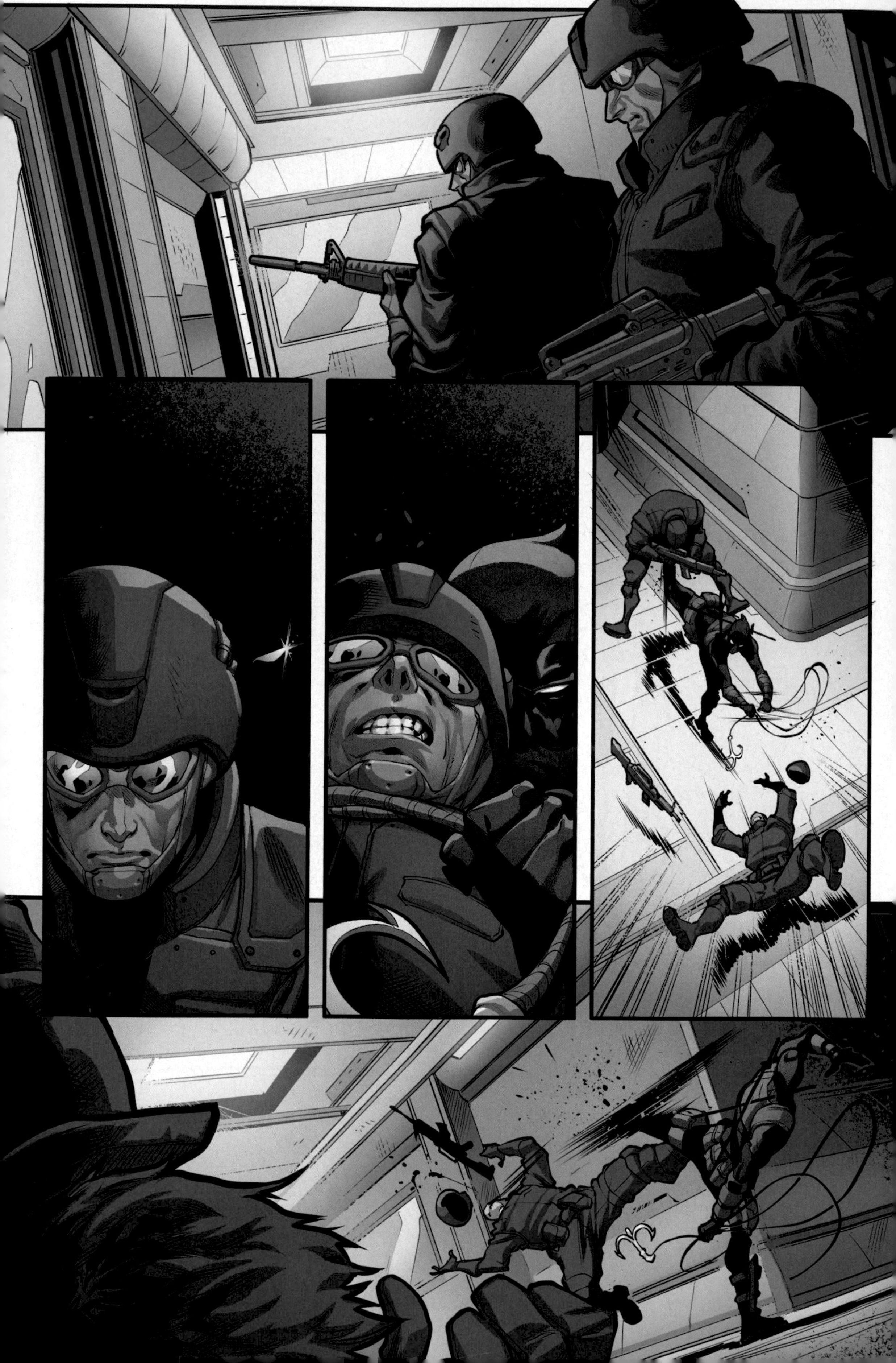

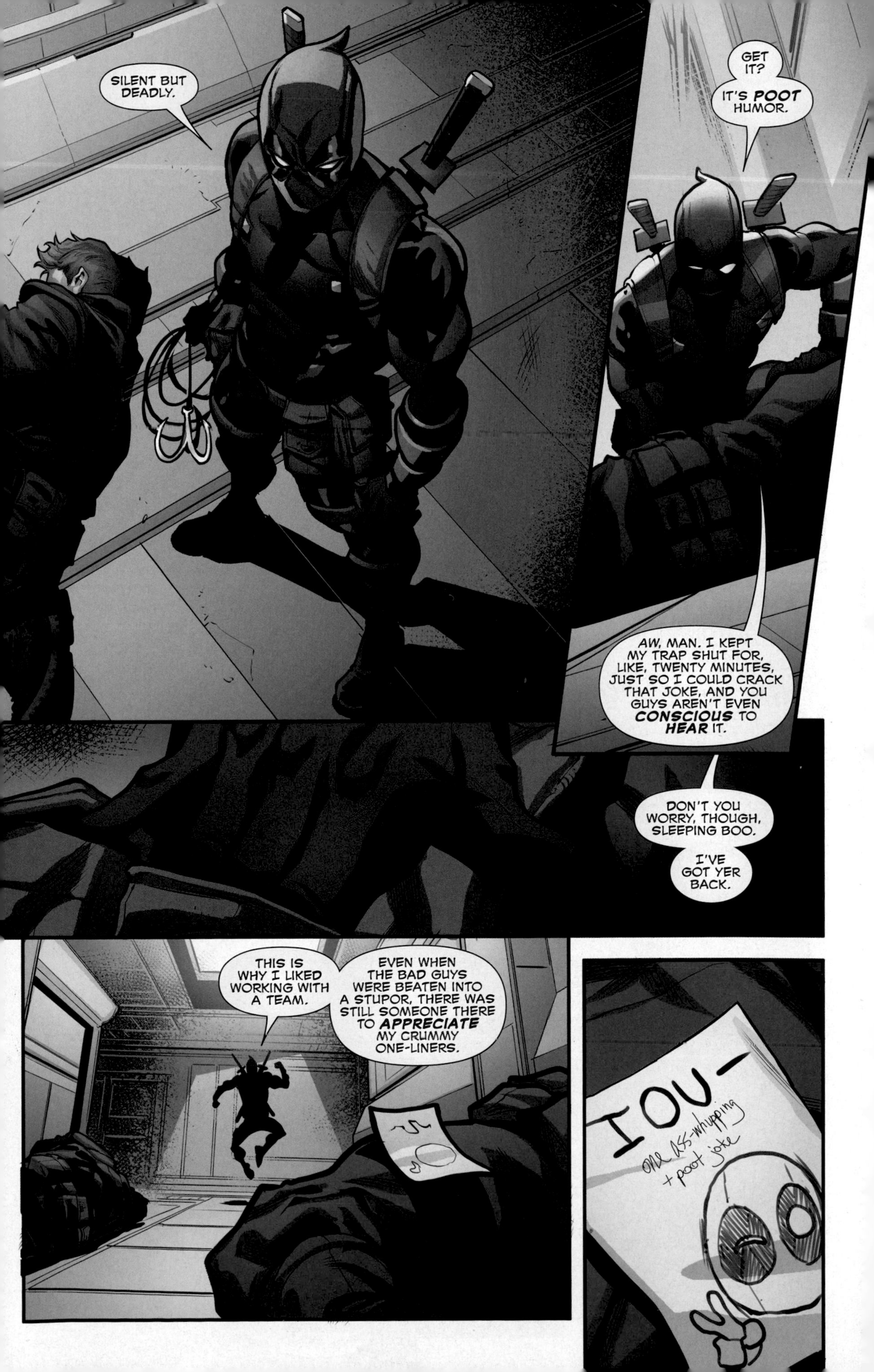
SILENT BUT DEADLY.
GET IT?
IT'S POOT HUMOR.
AW, MAN. I KEPT MY TRAP SHUT FOR, LIKE, TWENTY MINUTES, JUST SO I COULD CRACK THAT JOKE, AND YOU GUYS AREN'T EVEN CONSCIOUS TO HEAR IT.
DON'T YOU WORRY, THOUGH, SLEEPING BOO.
I'VE GOT YER BACK.
THIS IS WHY I LIKED WORKING WITH A TEAM.
EVEN WHEN THE BAD GUYS WERE BEATEN INTO A STUPOR, THERE WAS STILL SOMEONE THERE TO APPRECIATE MY CRUMMY ONE-LINERS.
IOU-
one ass-whipping
+ poot joke

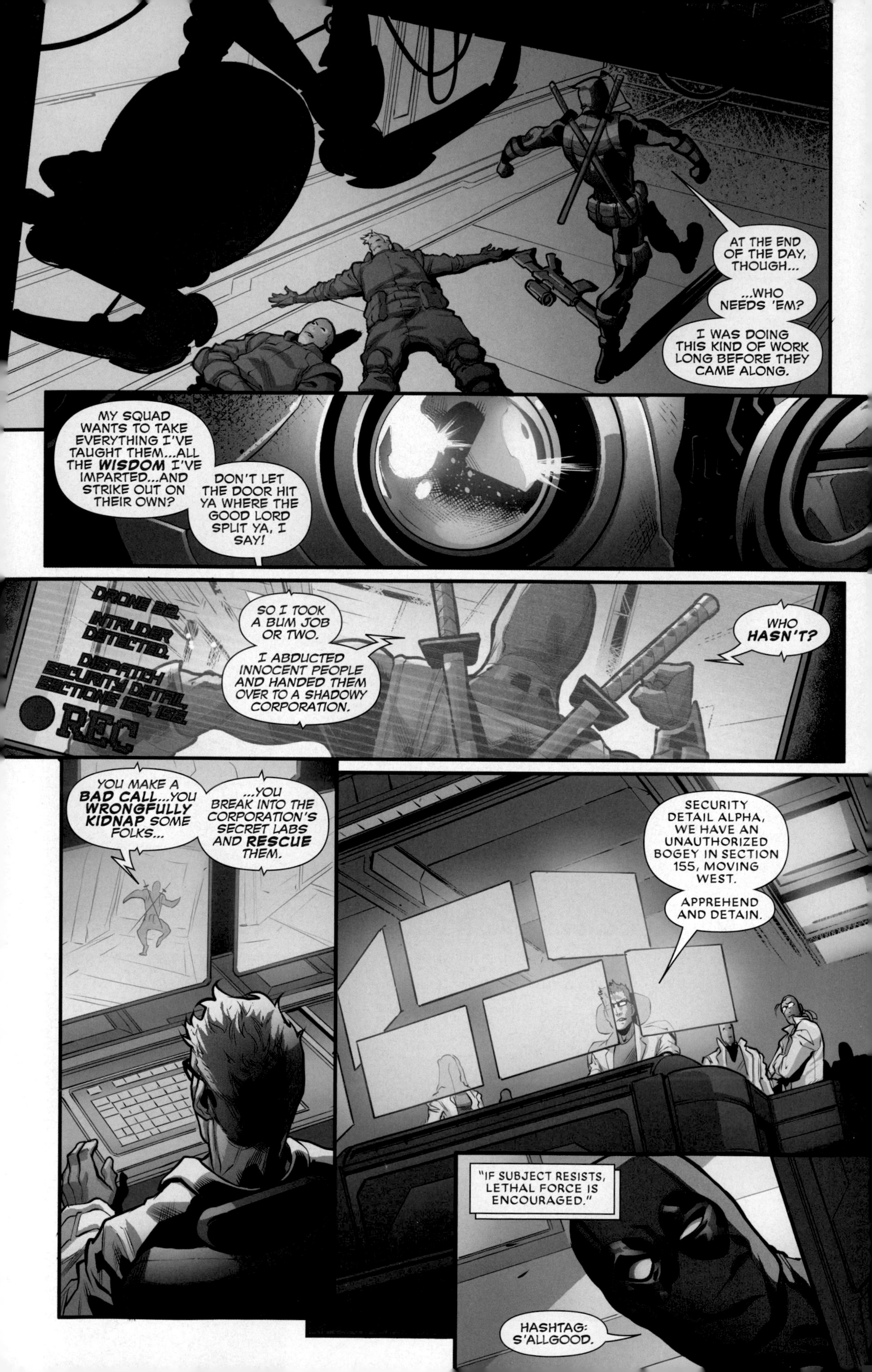
AT THE END OF THE DAY, THOUGH...
...WHO NEEDS 'EM?
I WAS DOING THIS KIND OF WORK LONG BEFORE THEY CAME ALONG.
MY SQUAD WANTS TO TAKE EVERYTHING I'VE TAUGHT THEM...ALL THE WISDOM I'VE IMPARTED...AND STRIKE OUT ON THEIR OWN?
DON'T LET THE DOOR HIT YA WHERE THE GOOD LORD SPLIT YA, I SAY!
DRONE 212. INTRUDER DETECTED. DISPATCH SECURITY DETAIL SECTIONS 155, 182.
REC
SO I TOOK A BUM JOB OR TWO.
I ABDUCTED INNOCENT PEOPLE AND HANDED THEM OVER TO A SHADOWY CORPORATION.
WHO HASN'T?
YOU MAKE A BAD CALL...YOU WRONGFULLY KIDNAP SOME FOLKS...
...YOU BREAK INTO THE CORPORATION'S SECRET LABS AND RESCUE THEM.
SECURITY DETAIL ALPHA, WE HAVE AN UNAUTHORIZED BOGEY IN SECTION 155, MOVING WEST.
APPREHEND AND DETAIN.
"IF SUBJECT RESISTS, LETHAL FORCE IS ENCOURAGED."
HASHTAG: S'ALLGOOD.

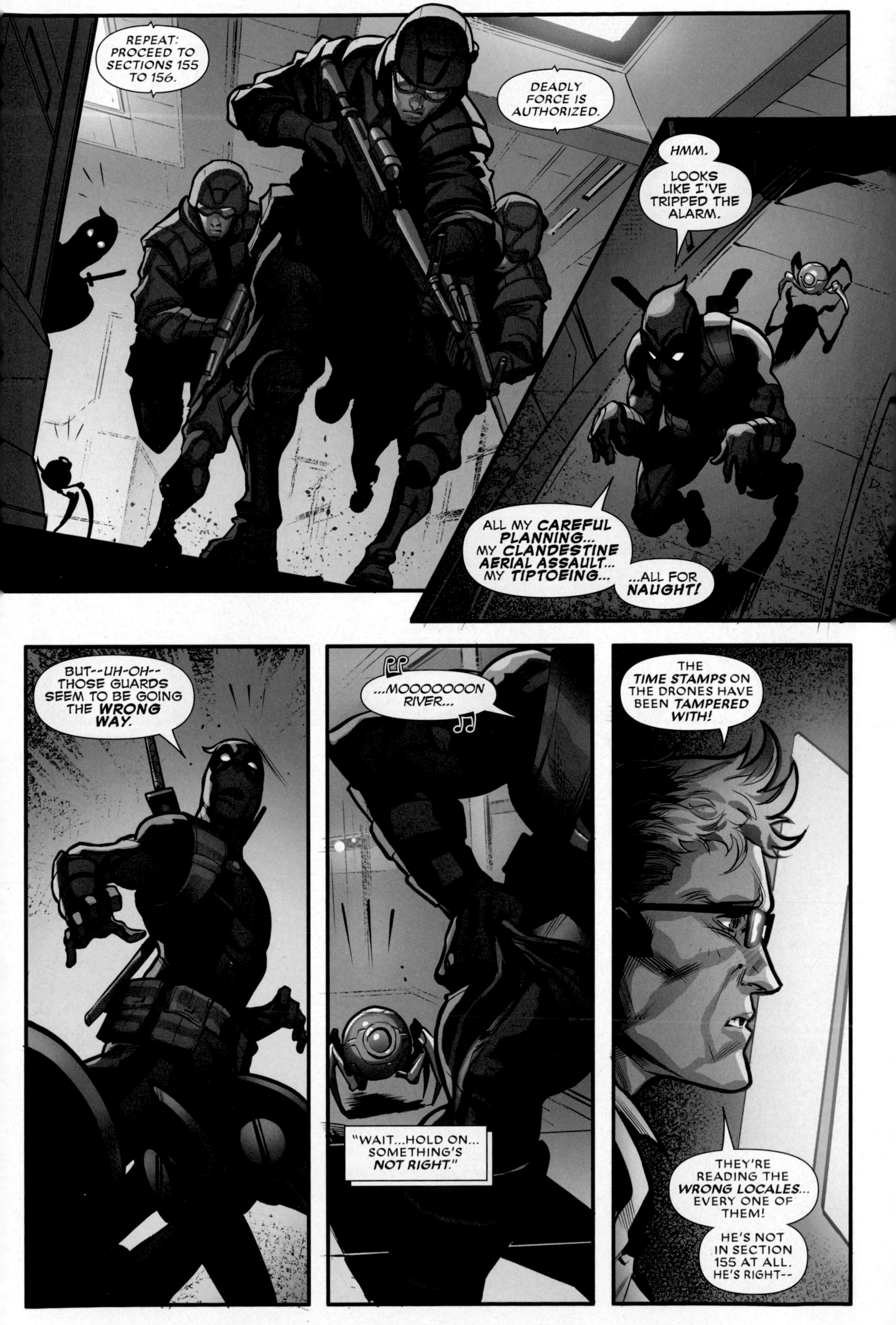
REPEAT: PROCEED TO SECTIONS 155 TO 156.
DEADLY FORCE IS AUTHORIZED.
HMM.
LOOKS LIKE I'VE TRIPPED THE ALARM.
ALL MY CAREFUL PLANNING... MY CLANDESTINE AERIAL ASSAULT... MY TIPTOEING...
...ALL FOR NAUGHT!
BUT--UH-OH--THOSE GUARDS SEEM TO BE GOING THE WRONG WAY.
...MOOOOOOON RIVER...
"WAIT...HOLD ON... SOMETHING'S NOT RIGHT."
THE TIME STAMPS ON THE DRONES HAVE BEEN TAMPERED WITH!
THEY'RE READING THE WRONG LOCALES... EVERY ONE OF THEM!
HE'S NOT IN SECTION 155 AT ALL. HE'S RIGHT--

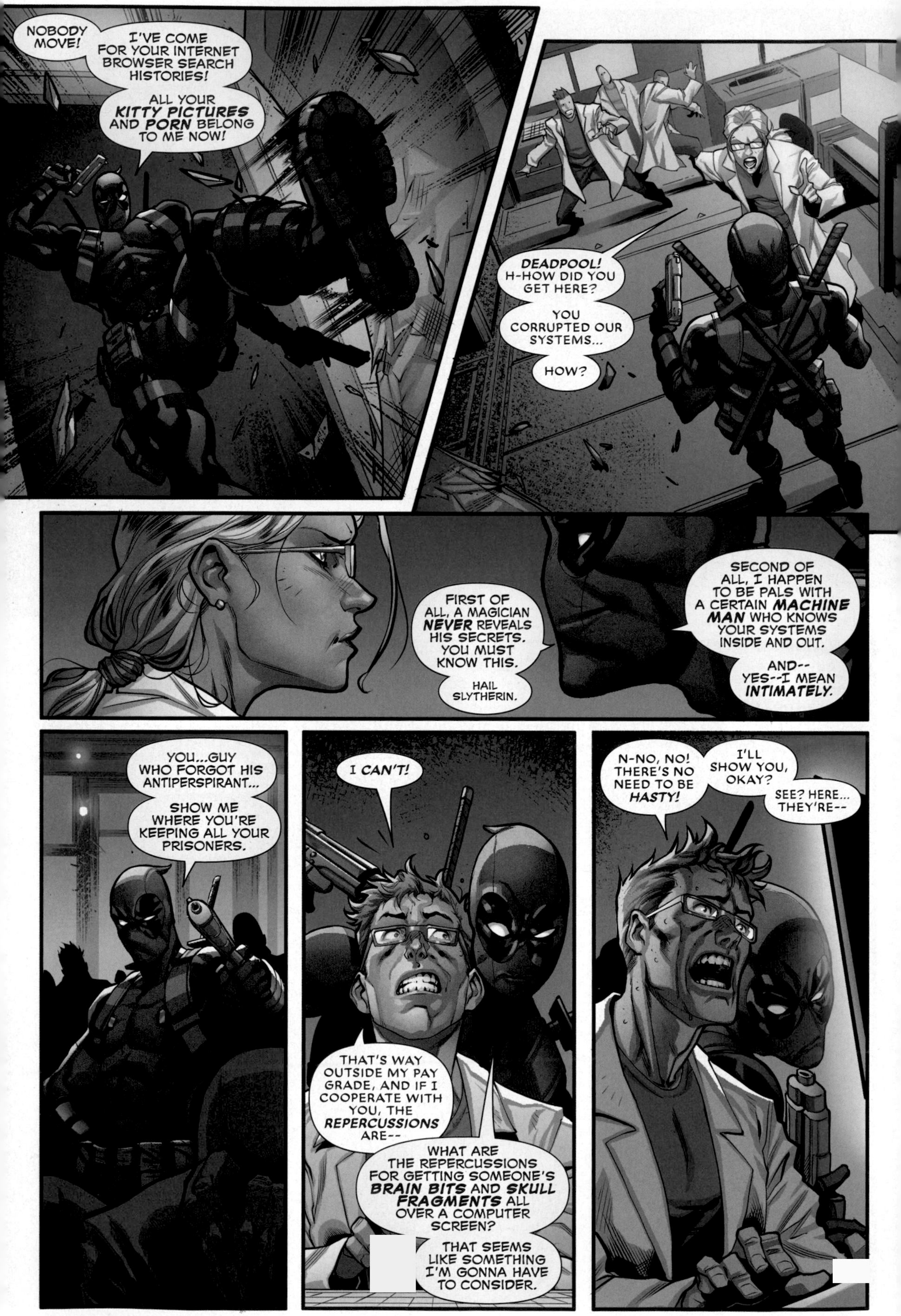
NOBODY MOVE!
I'VE COME FOR YOUR INTERNET BROWSER SEARCH HISTORIES!
ALL YOUR KITTY PICTURES AND PORN BELONG TO ME NOW!
DEADPOOL! H-HOW DID YOU GET HERE?
YOU CORRUPTED OUR SYSTEMS...
HOW?
FIRST OF ALL, A MAGICIAN NEVER REVEALS HIS SECRETS. YOU MUST KNOW THIS.
HAIL SLYTHERIN.
SECOND OF ALL, I HAPPEN TO BE PALS WITH A CERTAIN MACHINE MAN WHO KNOWS YOUR SYSTEMS INSIDE AND OUT.
AND-- YES--I MEAN INTIMATELY.
YOU...GUY WHO FORGOT HIS ANTIPERSPIRANT...
SHOW ME WHERE YOU'RE KEEPING ALL YOUR PRISONERS.
I CAN'T!
THAT'S WAY OUTSIDE MY PAY GRADE, AND IF I COOPERATE WITH YOU, THE REPERCUSSIONS ARE--
WHAT ARE THE REPERCUSSIONS FOR GETTING SOMEONE'S BRAIN BITS AND SKULL FRAGMENTS ALL OVER A COMPUTER SCREEN?
THAT SEEMS LIKE SOMETHING I'M GONNA HAVE TO CONSIDER.
N-NO, NO! THERE'S NO NEED TO BE HASTY!
I'LL SHOW YOU, OKAY?
SEE? HERE... THEY'RE--

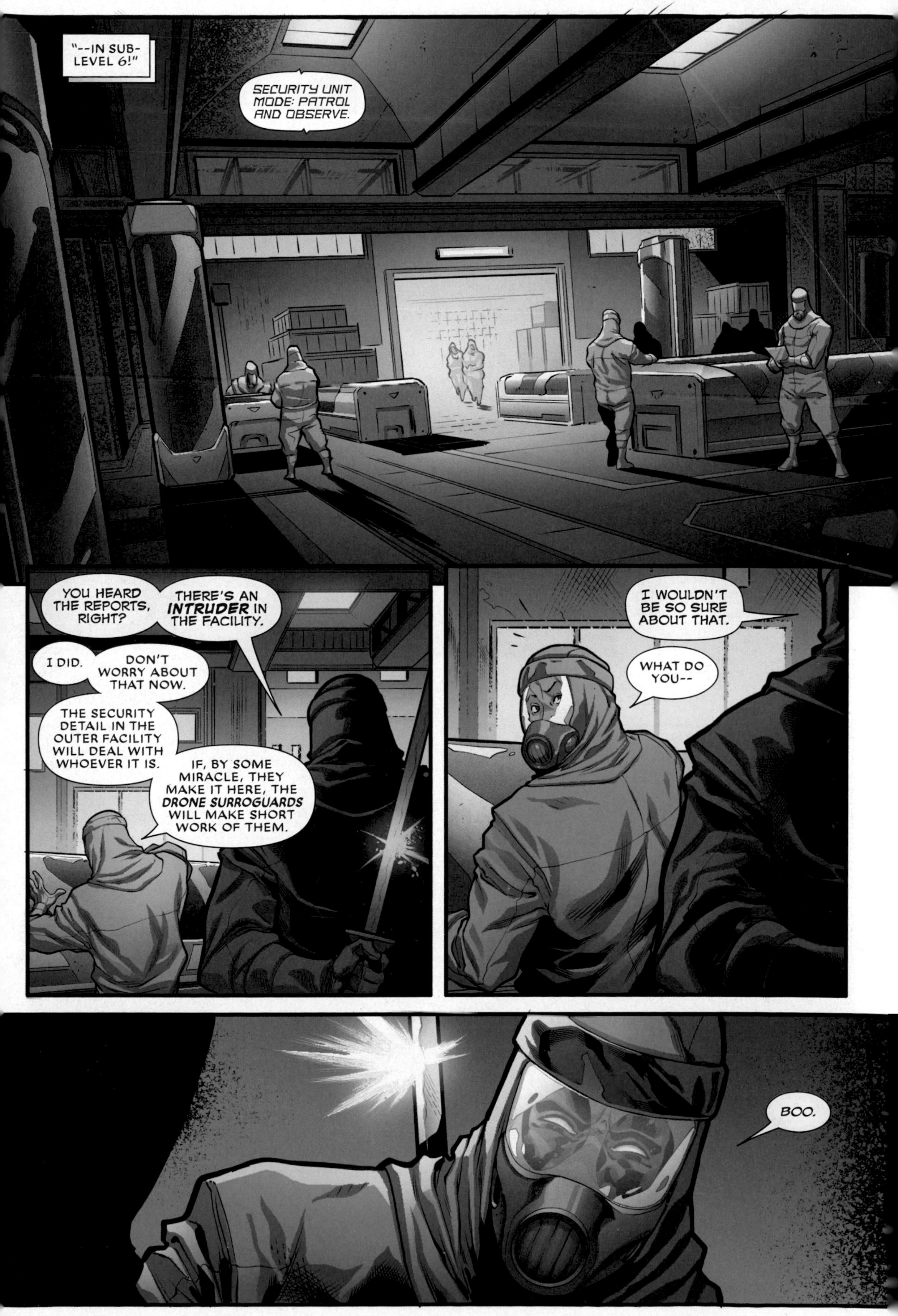
"--IN SUB-LEVEL 6!"
SECURITY UNIT MODE: PATROL AND OBSERVE.
YOU HEARD THE REPORTS, RIGHT?
THERE'S AN INTRUDER IN THE FACILITY.
I DID.
DON'T WORRY ABOUT THAT NOW.
THE SECURITY DETAIL IN THE OUTER FACILITY WILL DEAL WITH WHOEVER IT IS.
IF, BY SOME MIRACLE, THEY MAKE IT HERE, THE DRONE SURROGUARDS WILL MAKE SHORT WORK OF THEM.
I WOULDN'T BE SO SURE ABOUT THAT.
WHAT DO YOU--
BOO.

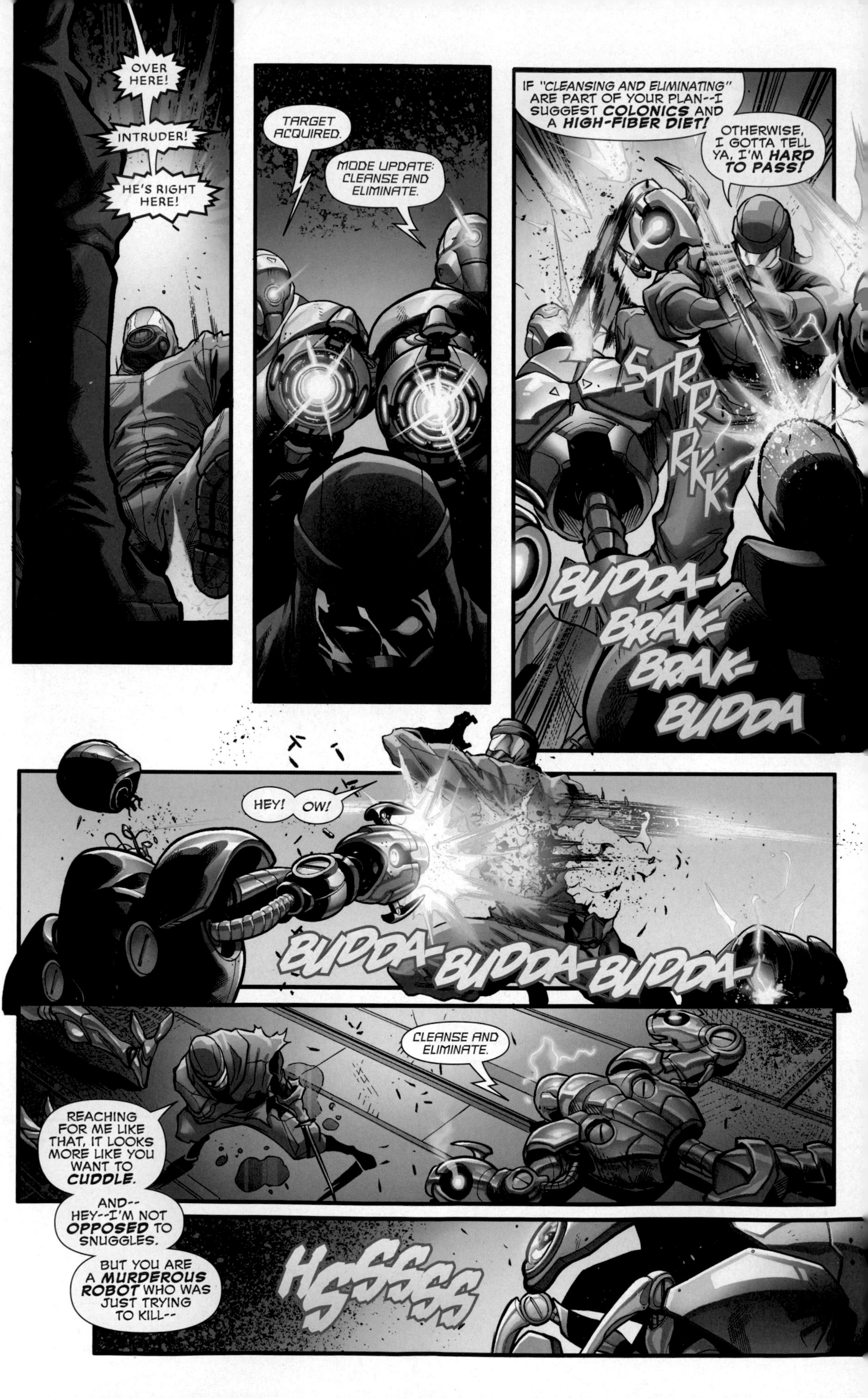
OVER HERE!
INTRUDER!
HE'S RIGHT HERE!
TARGET ACQUIRED.
MODE UPDATE: CLEANSE AND ELIMINATE.
IF "CLEANSING AND ELIMINATING" ARE PART OF YOUR PLAN--I SUGGEST COLONICS AND A HIGH-FIBER DIET!
OTHERWISE, I GOTTA TELL YA, I'M HARD TO PASS!
STRRRKK
BUDDA-BRAK-BRAK-BUDDA
HEY! OW!
BUDDA-BUDDA-BUDDA-
CLEANSE AND ELIMINATE.
REACHING FOR ME LIKE THAT, IT LOOKS MORE LIKE YOU WANT TO CUDDLE.
AND--HEY--I'M NOT OPPOSED TO SNUGGLES.
BUT YOU ARE A MURDEROUS ROBOT WHO WAS JUST TRYING TO KILL--
HSSSS

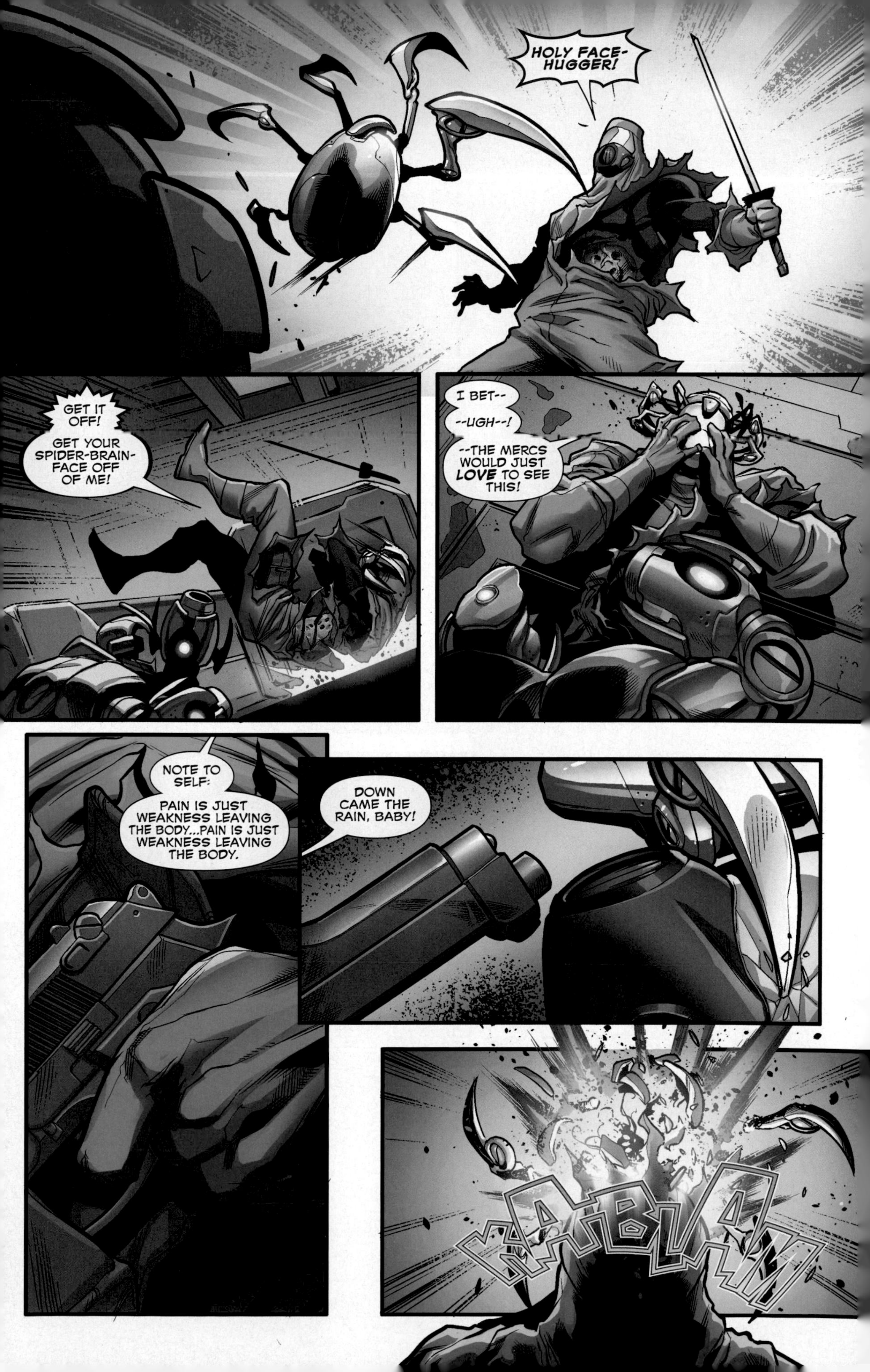
HOLY FACE-HUGGER!
GET IT OFF!
GET YOUR SPIDER-BRAIN-FACE OFF OF ME!
I BET--
--UGH--!
--THE MERCS WOULD JUST LOVE TO SEE THIS!
NOTE TO SELF:
PAIN IS JUST WEAKNESS LEAVING THE BODY...PAIN IS JUST WEAKNESS LEAVING THE BODY.
DOWN CAME THE RAIN, BABY!
KABLAM

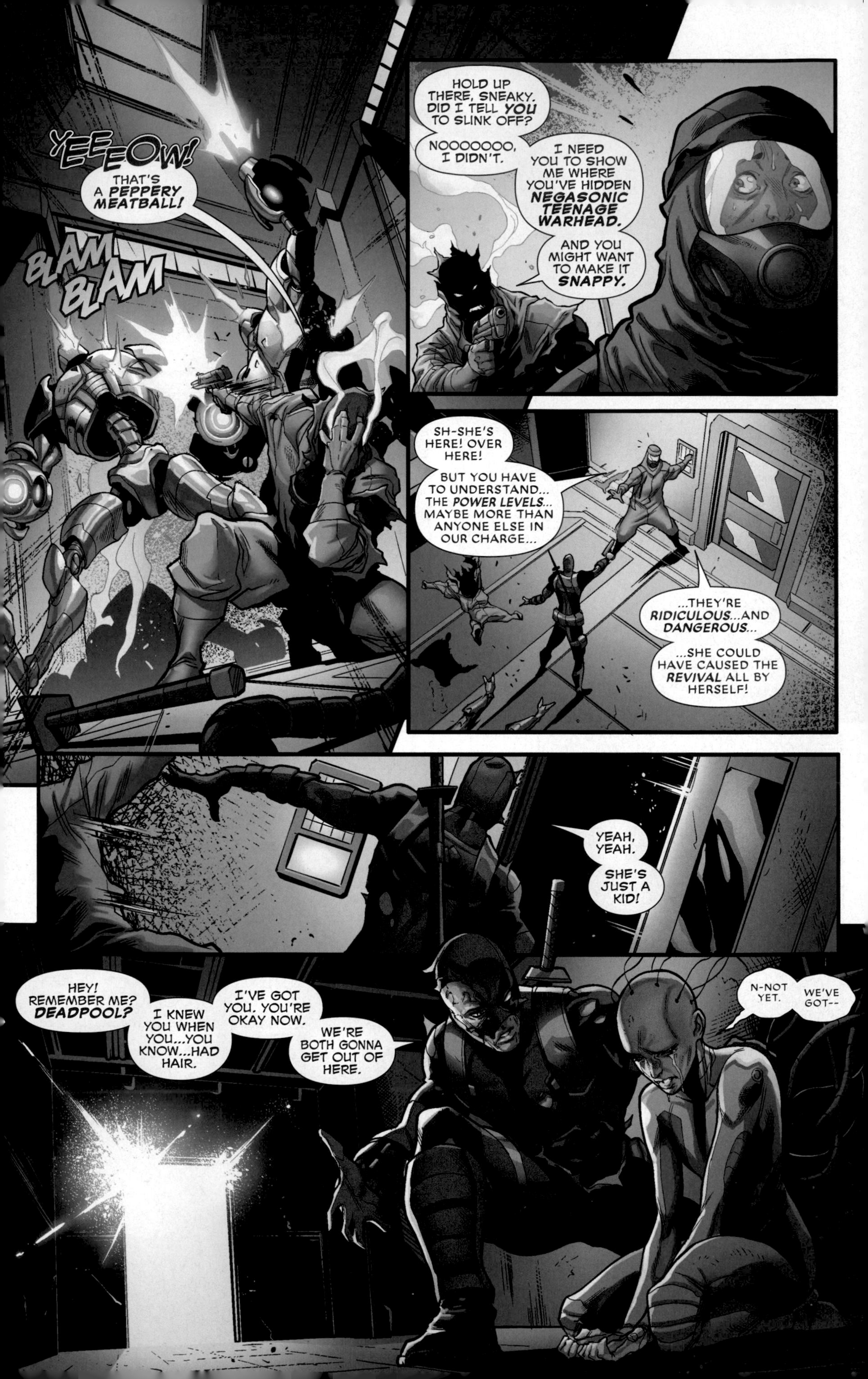
YEEEOW!
THAT'S A PEPPERY MEATBALL!
BLAM BLAM
HOLD UP THERE, SNEAKY. DID I TELL YOU TO SLINK OFF?
NOOOOOOO, I DIDN'T.
I NEED YOU TO SHOW ME WHERE YOU'VE HIDDEN NEGASONIC TEENAGE WARHEAD.
AND YOU MIGHT WANT TO MAKE IT SNAPPY.
SH-SHE'S HERE! OVER HERE!
BUT YOU HAVE TO UNDERSTAND... THE POWER LEVELS... MAYBE MORE THAN ANYONE ELSE IN OUR CHARGE...
...THEY'RE RIDICULOUS...AND DANGEROUS...
...SHE COULD HAVE CAUSED THE REVIVAL ALL BY HERSELF!
YEAH, YEAH.
SHE'S JUST A KID!
HEY! REMEMBER ME? DEADPOOL?
I KNEW YOU WHEN YOU...YOU KNOW...HAD HAIR.
I'VE GOT YOU. YOU'RE OKAY NOW.
WE'RE BOTH GONNA GET OUT OF HERE.
N-NOT YET.
WE'VE GOT--

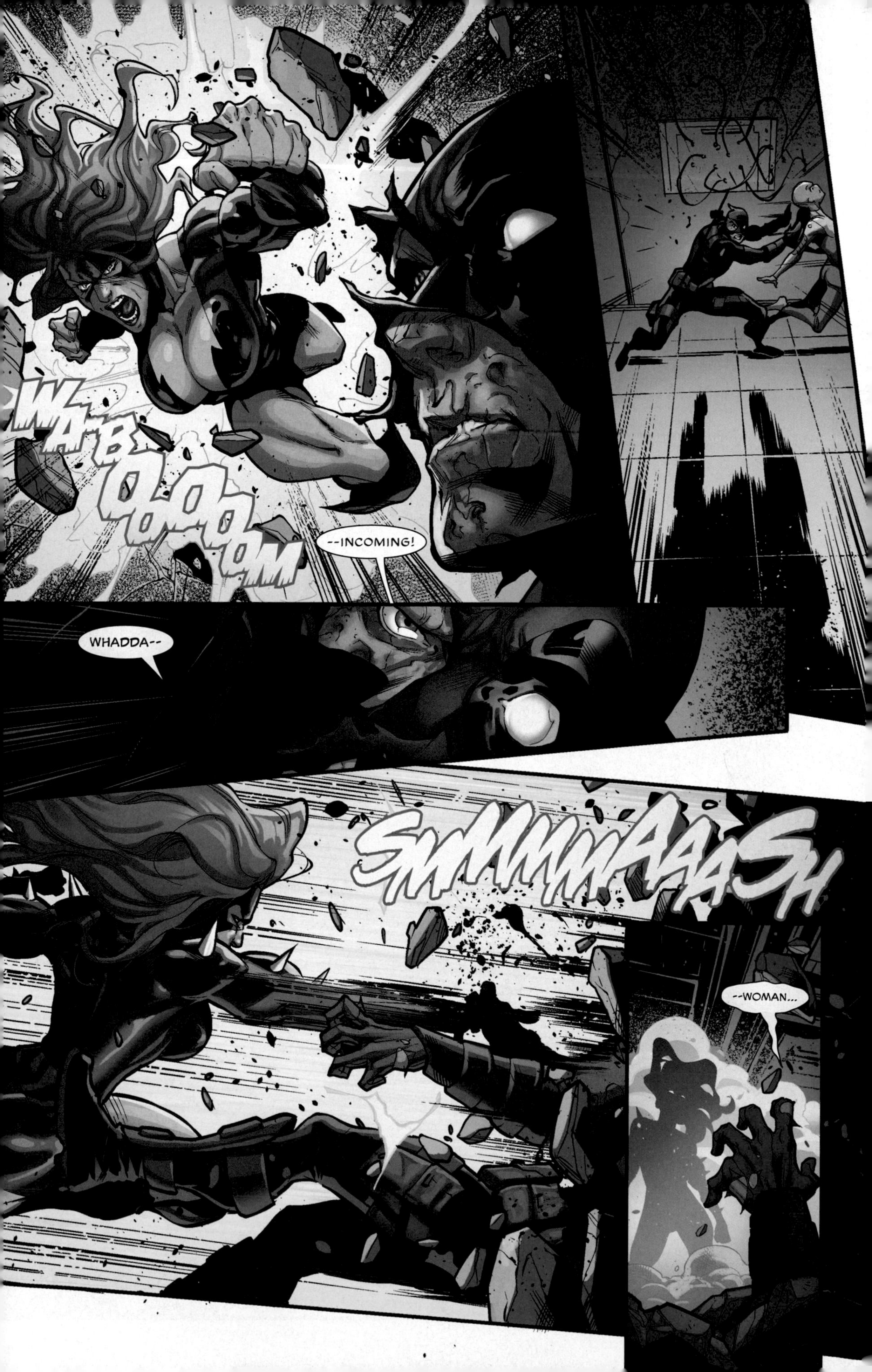
WABOOOOM
--INCOMING!
WHADDA--
SMMMMAAASH
--WOMAN...

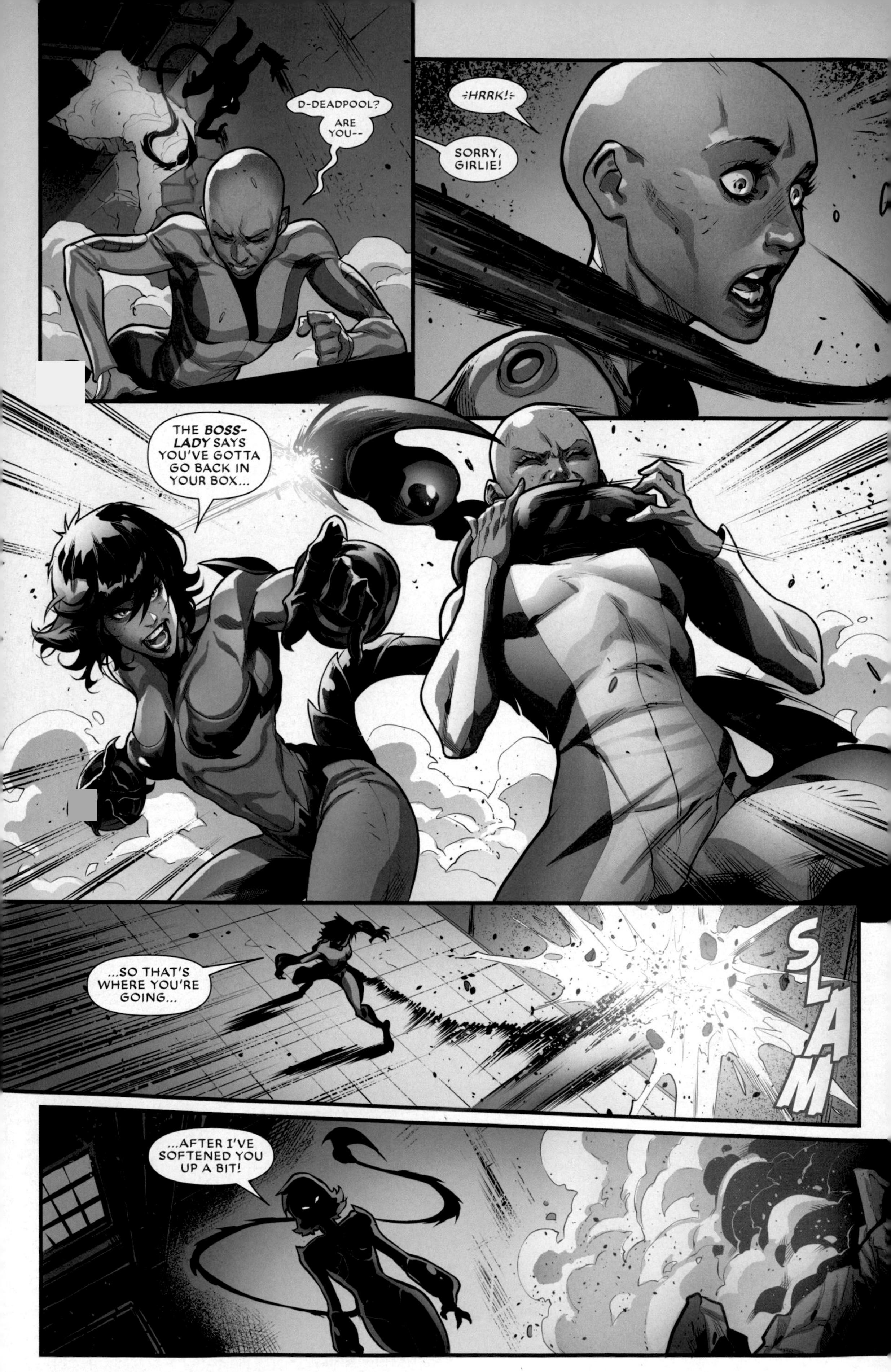
D-DEADPOOL? ARE YOU--
HRRK!
SORRY, GIRLIE!
THE BOSS-LADY SAYS YOU'VE GOTTA GO BACK IN YOUR BOX...
...SO THAT'S WHERE YOU'RE GOING...
SLAM
...AFTER I'VE SOFTENED YOU UP A BIT!

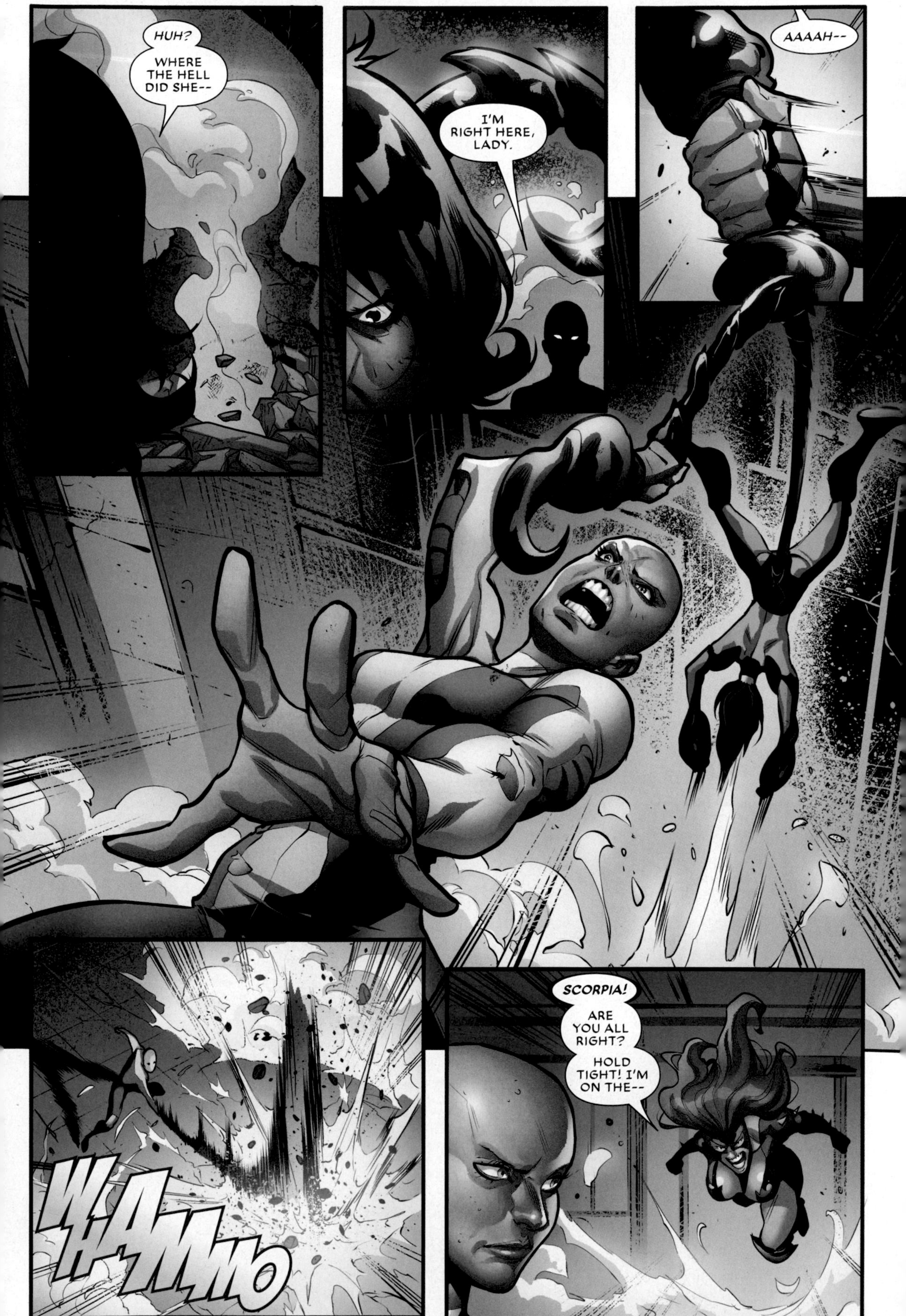
HUH?
WHERE THE HELL DID SHE--
I'M RIGHT HERE, LADY.
AAAAH--
WHAMMO
SCORPIA!
ARE YOU ALL RIGHT?
HOLD TIGHT! I'M ON THE--

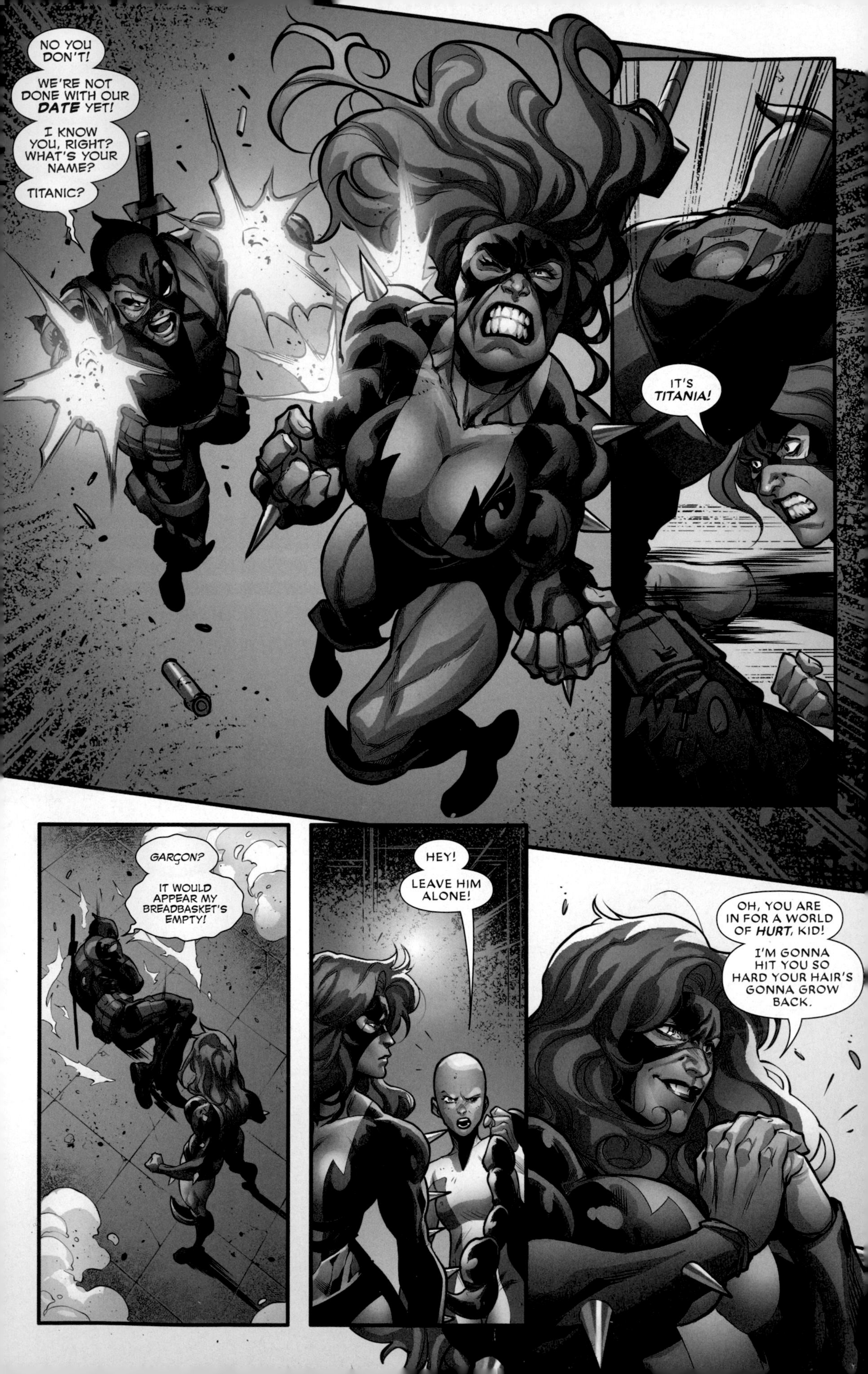
NO YOU DON'T!
WE'RE NOT DONE WITH OUR DATE YET!
I KNOW YOU, RIGHT? WHAT'S YOUR NAME?
TITANIC?
IT'S TITANIA!
GARÇON?
IT WOULD APPEAR MY BREADBASKET'S EMPTY!
HEY!
LEAVE HIM ALONE!
OH, YOU ARE IN FOR A WORLD OF HURT, KID!
I'M GONNA HIT YOU SO HARD YOUR HAIR'S GONNA GROW BACK.

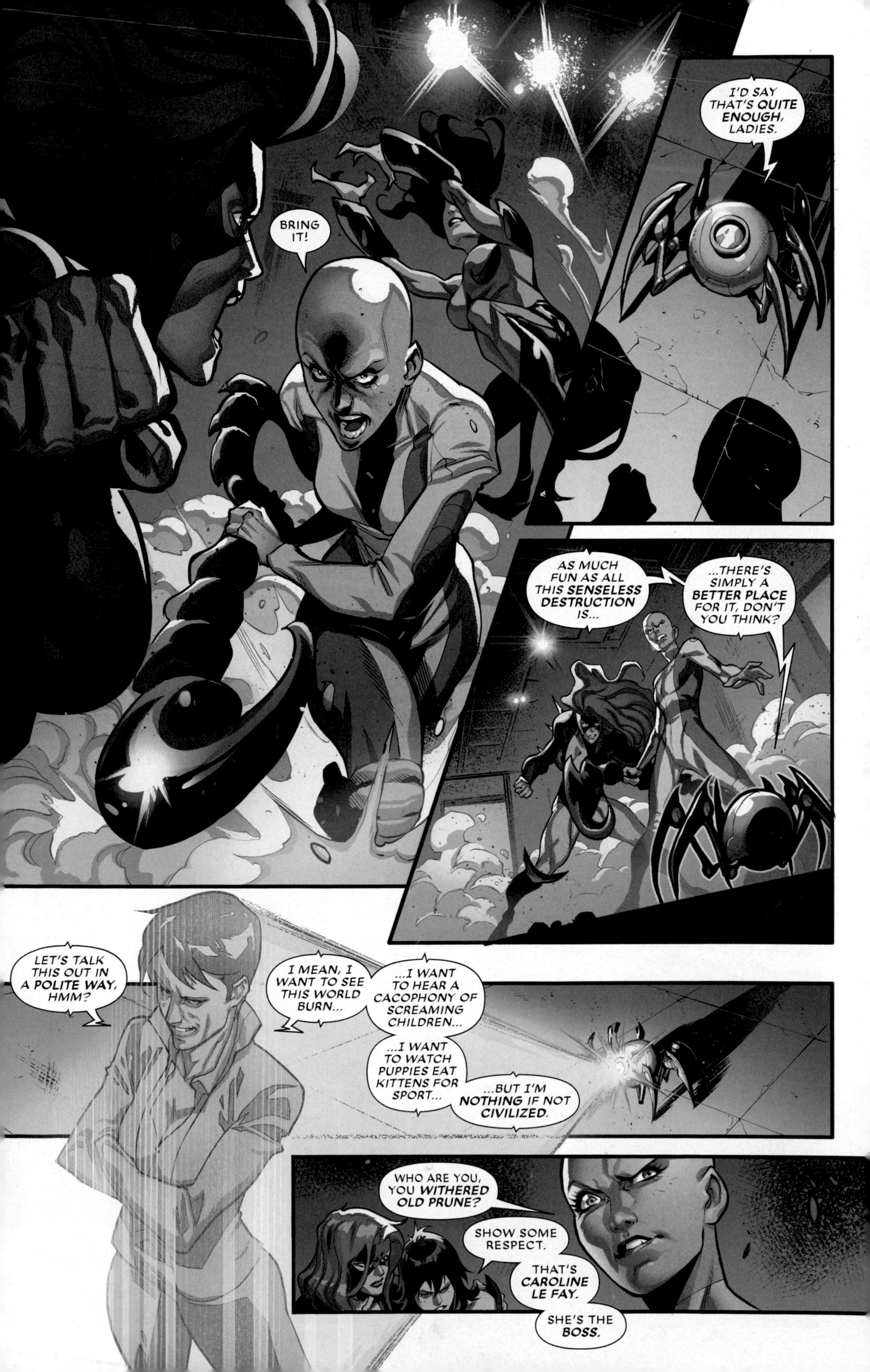

BRING IT!
I'D SAY THAT'S QUITE ENOUGH, LADIES.
AS MUCH FUN AS ALL THIS SENSELESS DESTRUCTION IS...
...THERE'S SIMPLY A BETTER PLACE FOR IT, DON'T YOU THINK?
LET'S TALK THIS OUT IN A POLITE WAY, HMM?
I MEAN, I WANT TO SEE THIS WORLD BURN...
...I WANT TO HEAR A CACOPHONY OF SCREAMING CHILDREN...
...I WANT TO WATCH PUPPIES EAT KITTENS FOR SPORT...
...BUT I'M NOTHING IF NOT CIVILIZED.
WHO ARE YOU, YOU WITHERED OLD PRUNE?
SHOW SOME RESPECT.
THAT'S CAROLINE LE FAY.
SHE'S THE BOSS.

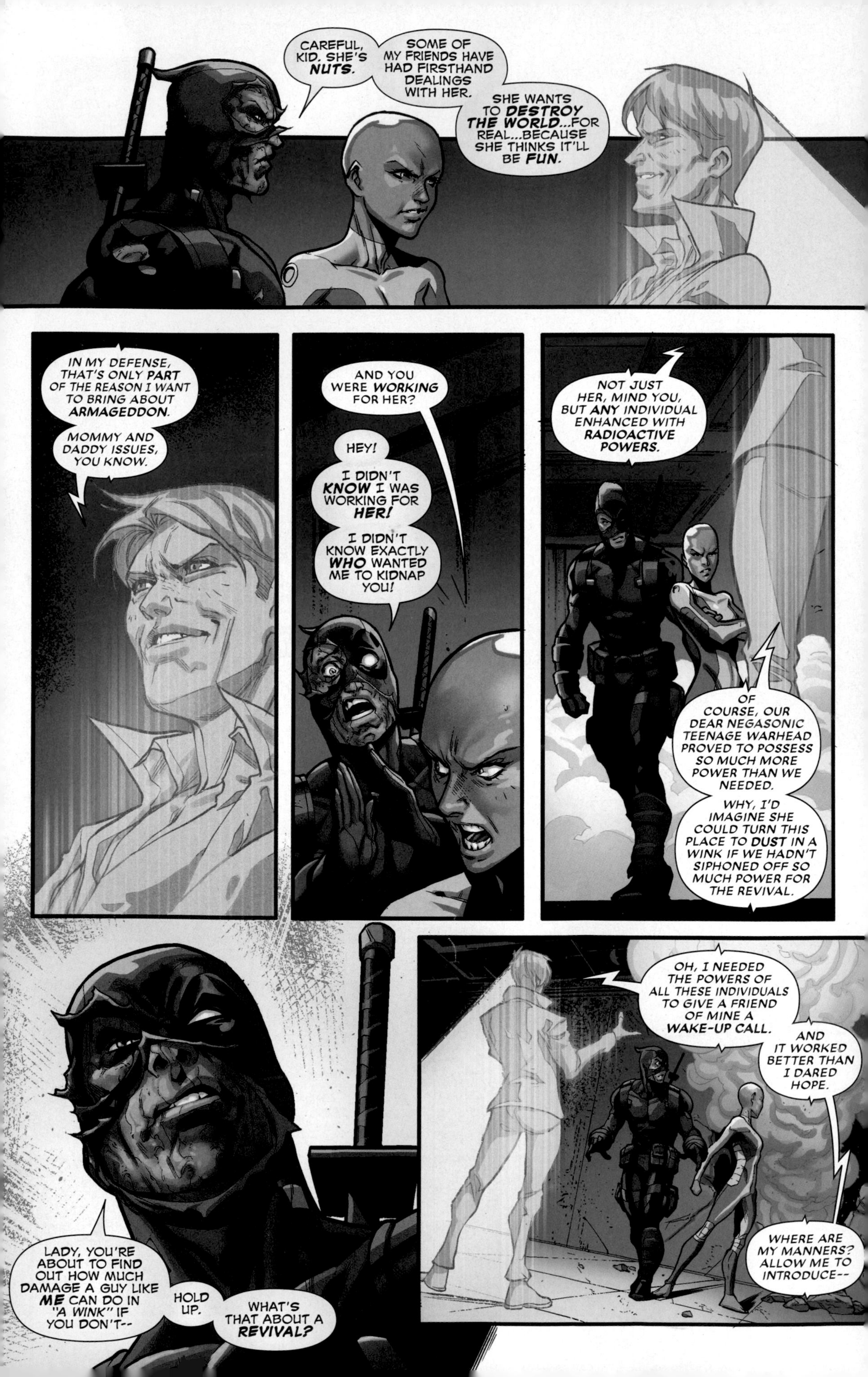

CAREFUL, KID. SHE'S NUTS.
SOME OF MY FRIENDS HAVE HAD FIRSTHAND DEALINGS WITH HER.
SHE WANTS TO DESTROY THE WORLD...FOR REAL...BECAUSE SHE THINKS IT'LL BE FUN.
IN MY DEFENSE, THAT'S ONLY PART OF THE REASON I WANT TO BRING ABOUT ARMAGEDDON.
MOMMY AND DADDY ISSUES, YOU KNOW.
AND YOU WERE WORKING FOR HER?
HEY!
I DIDN'T KNOW I WAS WORKING FOR HER!
I DIDN'T KNOW EXACTLY WHO WANTED ME TO KIDNAP YOU!
NOT JUST HER, MIND YOU, BUT ANY INDIVIDUAL ENHANCED WITH RADIOACTIVE POWERS.
OF COURSE, OUR DEAR NEGASONIC TEENAGE WARHEAD PROVED TO POSSESS SO MUCH MORE POWER THAN WE NEEDED.
WHY, I'D IMAGINE SHE COULD TURN THIS PLACE TO DUST IN A WINK IF WE HADN'T SIPHONED OFF SO MUCH POWER FOR THE REVIVAL.
LADY, YOU'RE ABOUT TO FIND OUT HOW MUCH DAMAGE A GUY LIKE ME CAN DO IN "A WINK" IF YOU DON'T--
HOLD UP.
WHAT'S THAT ABOUT A REVIVAL?
OH, I NEEDED THE POWERS OF ALL THESE INDIVIDUALS TO GIVE A FRIEND OF MINE A WAKE-UP CALL.
AND IT WORKED BETTER THAN I DARED HOPE.
WHERE ARE MY MANNERS? ALLOW ME TO INTRODUCE--

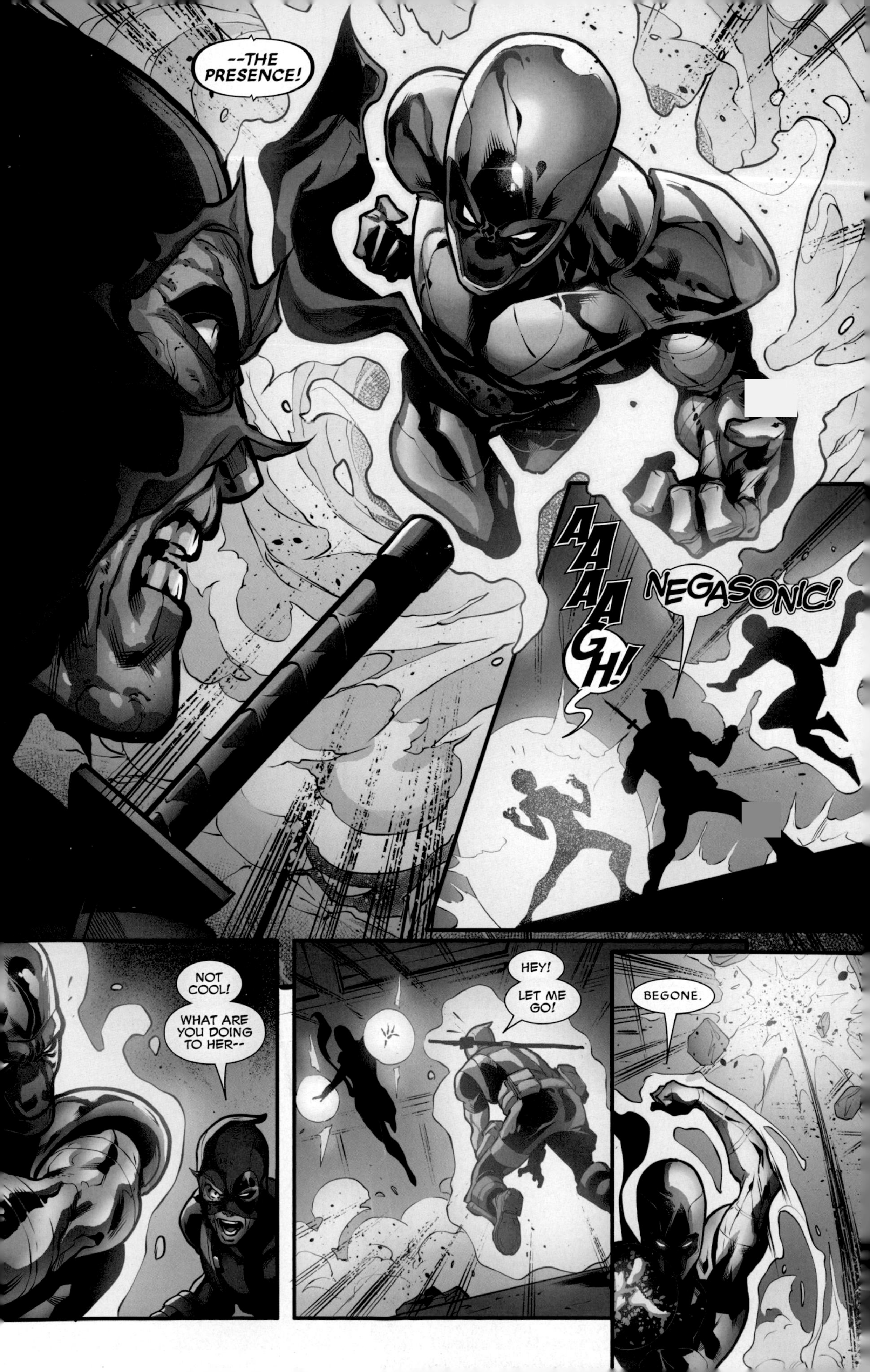
--THE PRESENCE!
AAAAAGH!
NEGASONIC!
NOT COOL!
WHAT ARE YOU DOING TO HER--
HEY!
LET ME GO!
BEGONE.

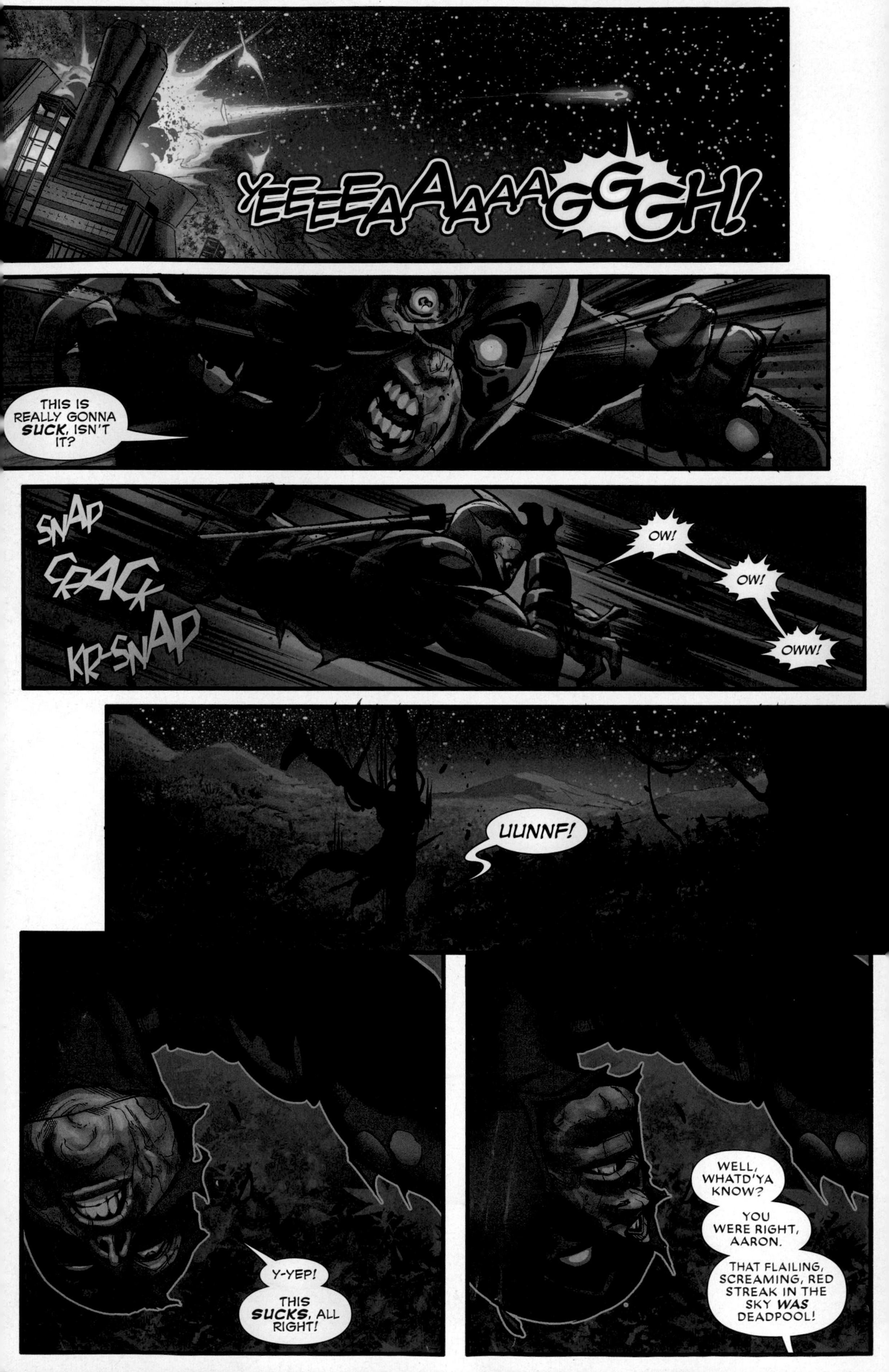
YEEEEAAAAAGGGGH!
THIS IS REALLY GONNA SUCK, ISN'T IT?
SNAP
CRACK
KR-SNAP
OW!
OW!
OWW!
UUNNF!
Y-YEP!
THIS SUCKS, ALL RIGHT!
WELL, WHATD'YA KNOW?
YOU WERE RIGHT, AARON.
THAT FLAILING, SCREAMING, RED STREAK IN THE SKY WAS DEADPOOL!

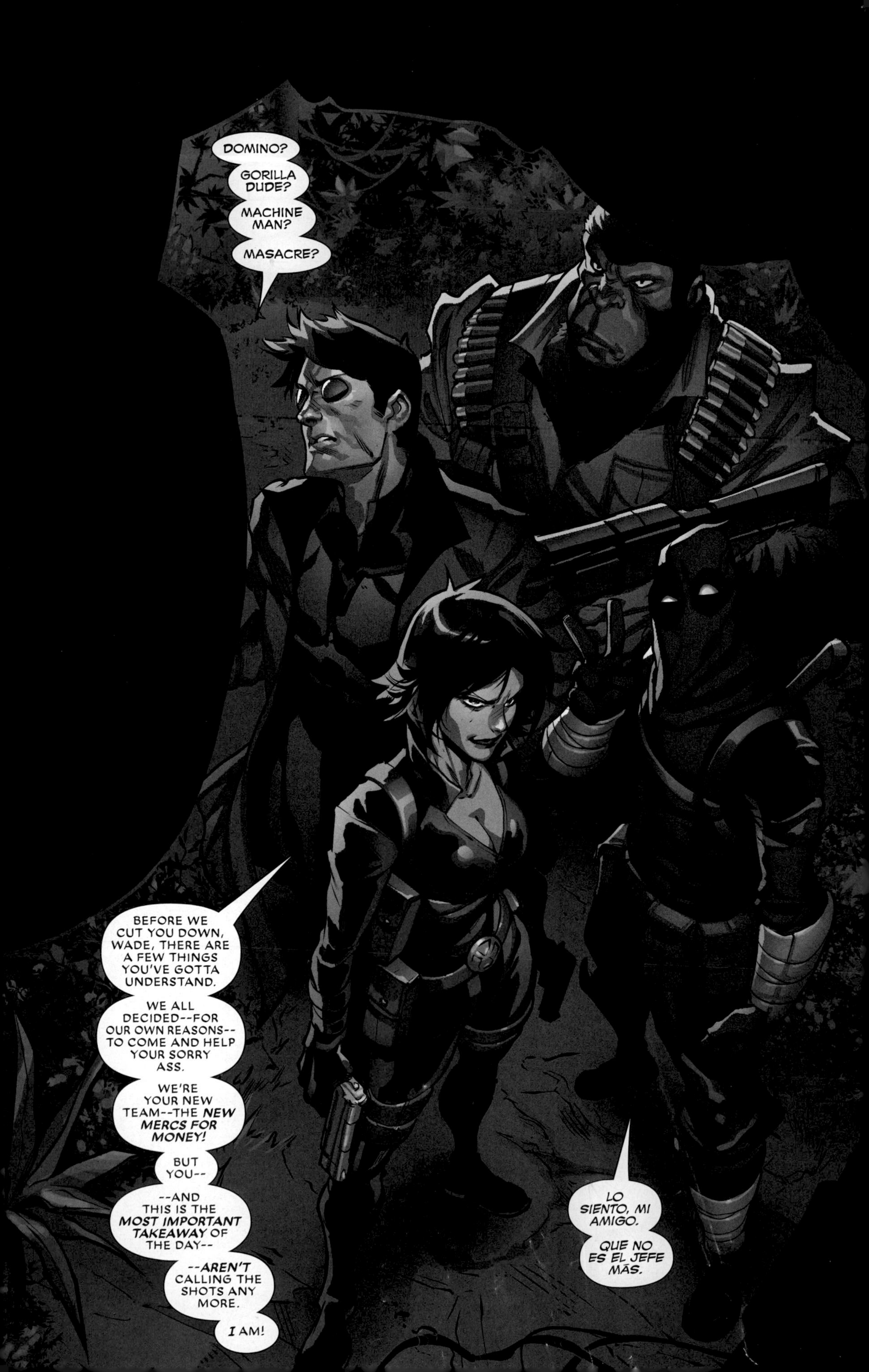
DOMINO?
GORILLA DUDE?
MACHINE MAN?
MASACRE?
BEFORE WE CUT YOU DOWN, WADE, THERE ARE A FEW THINGS YOU'VE GOTTA UNDERSTAND.
WE ALL DECIDED--FOR OUR OWN REASONS--TO COME AND HELP YOUR SORRY ASS.
WE'RE YOUR NEW TEAM--THE NEW MERCS FOR MONEY!
BUT YOU--
--AND THIS IS THE MOST IMPORTANT TAKEAWAY OF THE DAY--
--AREN'T CALLING THE SHOTS ANY MORE.
I AM!
LO SIENTO, MI AMIGO.
QUE NO ES EL JEFE MÁS.

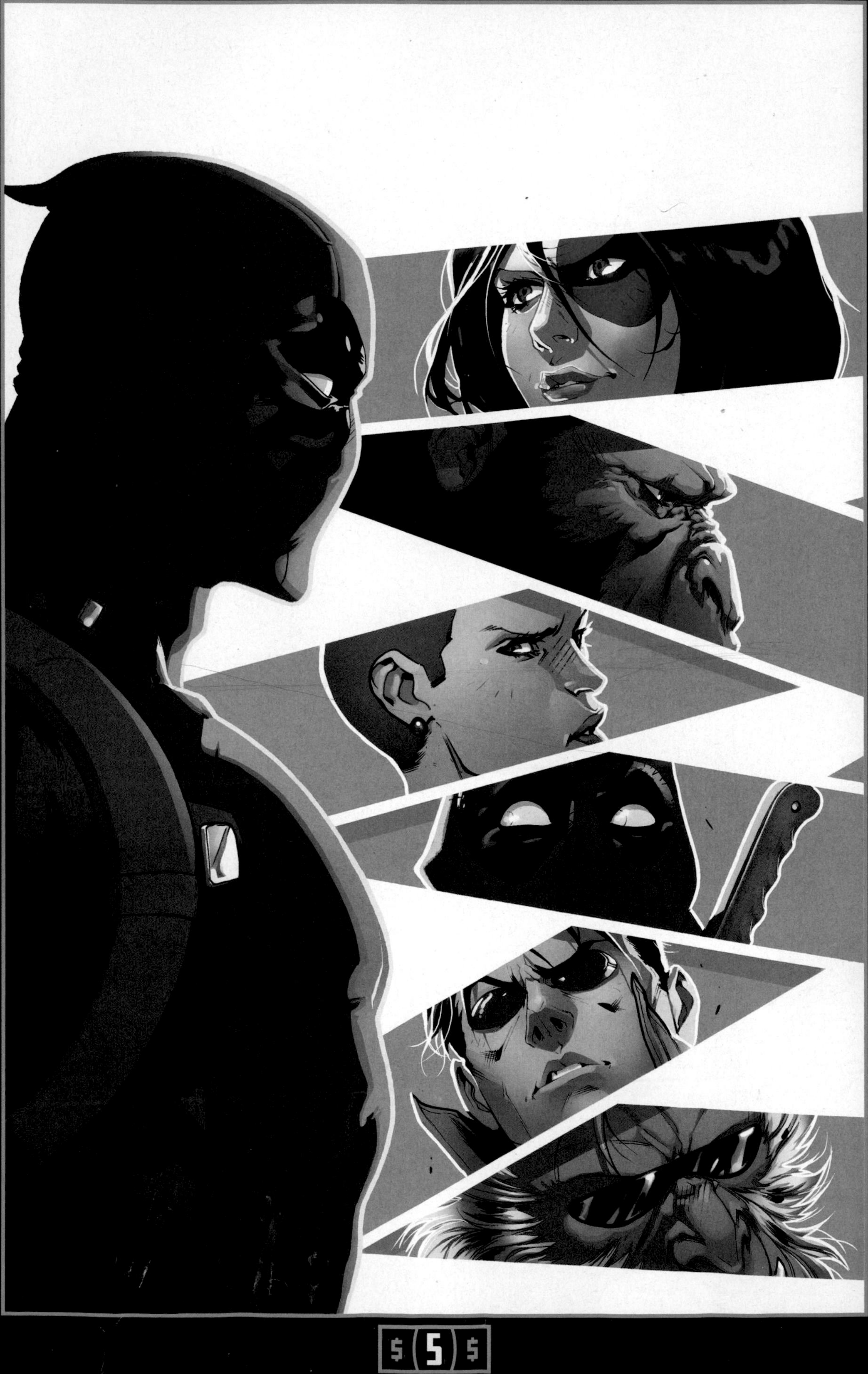
$ 5 $

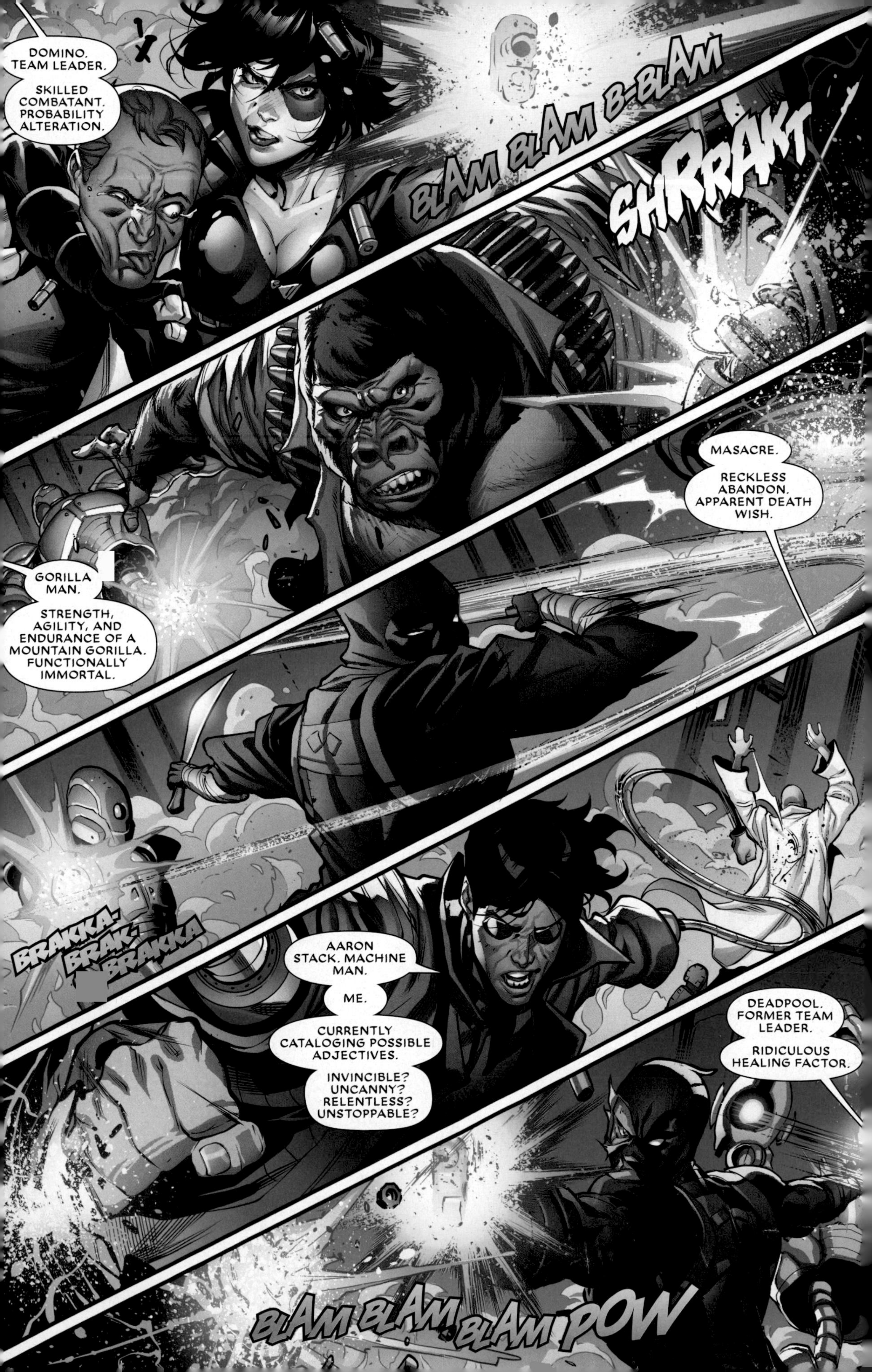
DOMINO. TEAM LEADER.
SKILLED COMBATANT. PROBABILITY ALTERATION.
BLAM BLAM B-BLAM
SHRRAKT
GORILLA MAN.
STRENGTH, AGILITY, AND ENDURANCE OF A MOUNTAIN GORILLA. FUNCTIONALLY IMMORTAL.
MASACRE.
RECKLESS ABANDON. APPARENT DEATH WISH.
BRAKKA-BRAK-BRAKKA
AARON STACK. MACHINE MAN.
ME.
CURRENTLY CATALOGING POSSIBLE ADJECTIVES.
INVINCIBLE? UNCANNY? RELENTLESS? UNSTOPPABLE?
DEADPOOL. FORMER TEAM LEADER.
RIDICULOUS HEALING FACTOR.
BLAM BLAM BLAM POW

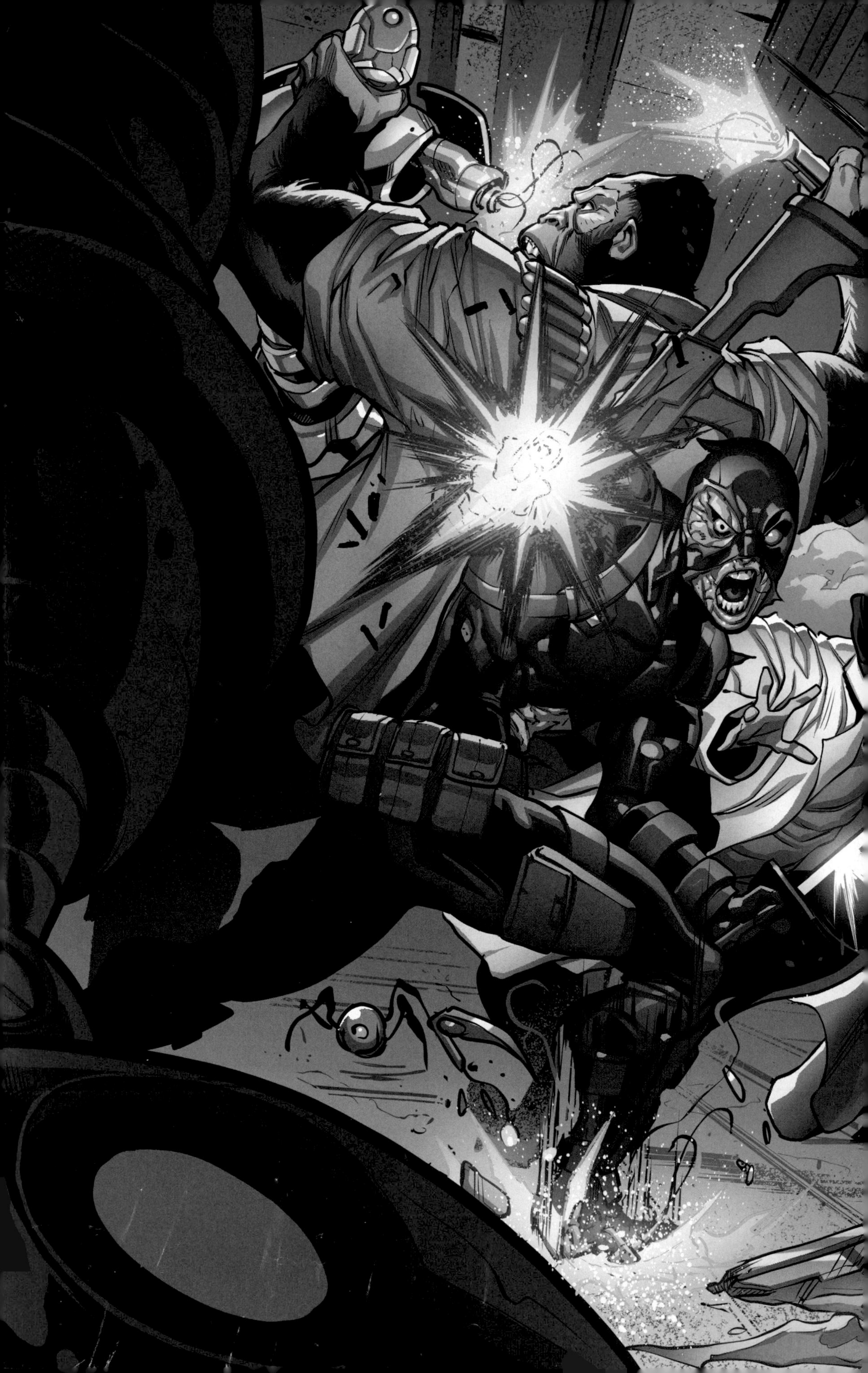

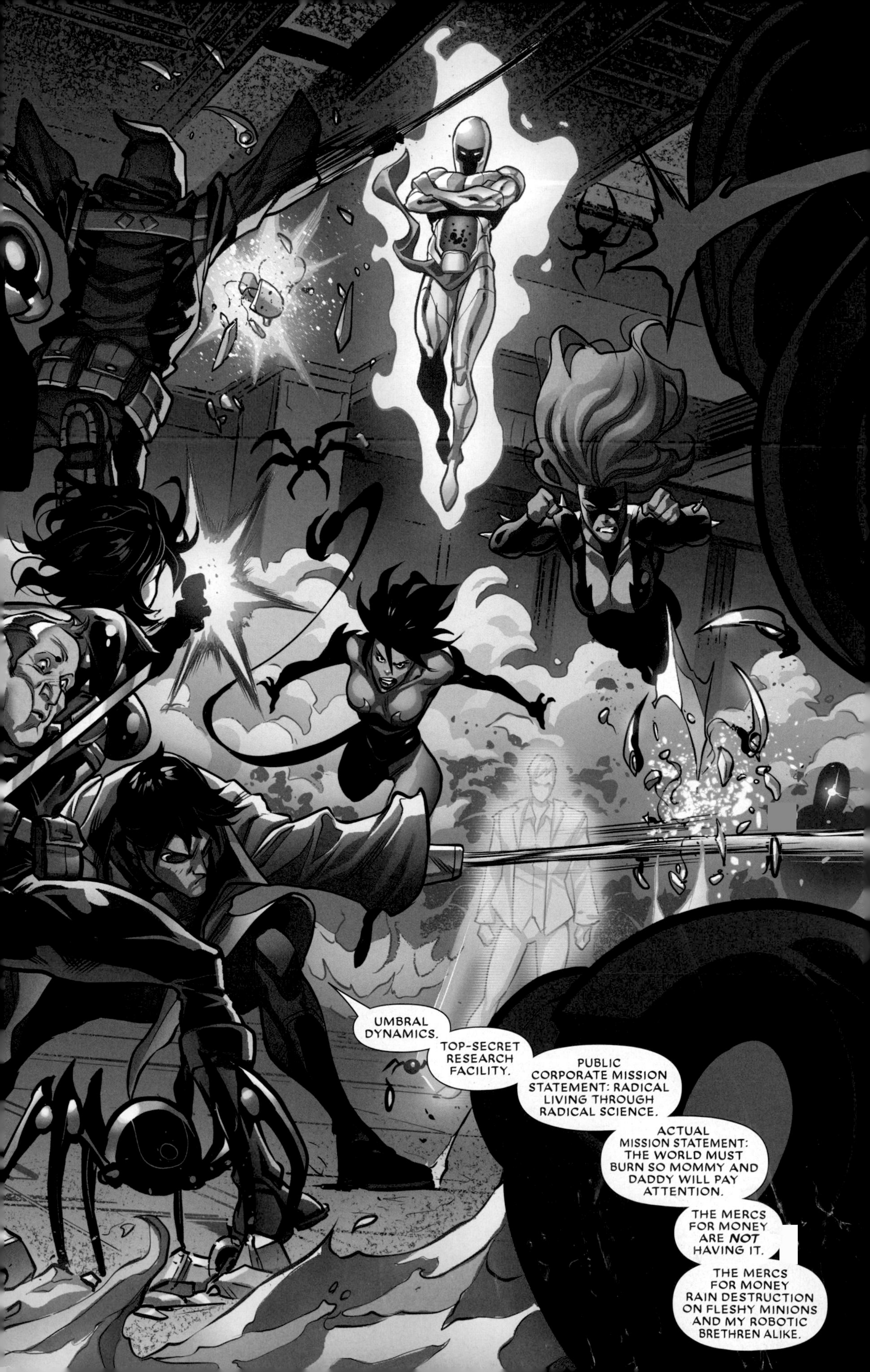
UMBRAL DYNAMICS.
TOP-SECRET RESEARCH FACILITY.
PUBLIC CORPORATE MISSION STATEMENT: RADICAL LIVING THROUGH RADICAL SCIENCE.
ACTUAL MISSION STATEMENT: THE WORLD MUST BURN SO MOMMY AND DADDY WILL PAY ATTENTION.
THE MERCS FOR MONEY ARE NOT HAVING IT.
THE MERCS FOR MONEY RAIN DESTRUCTION ON FLESHY MINIONS AND MY ROBOTIC BRETHREN ALIKE.

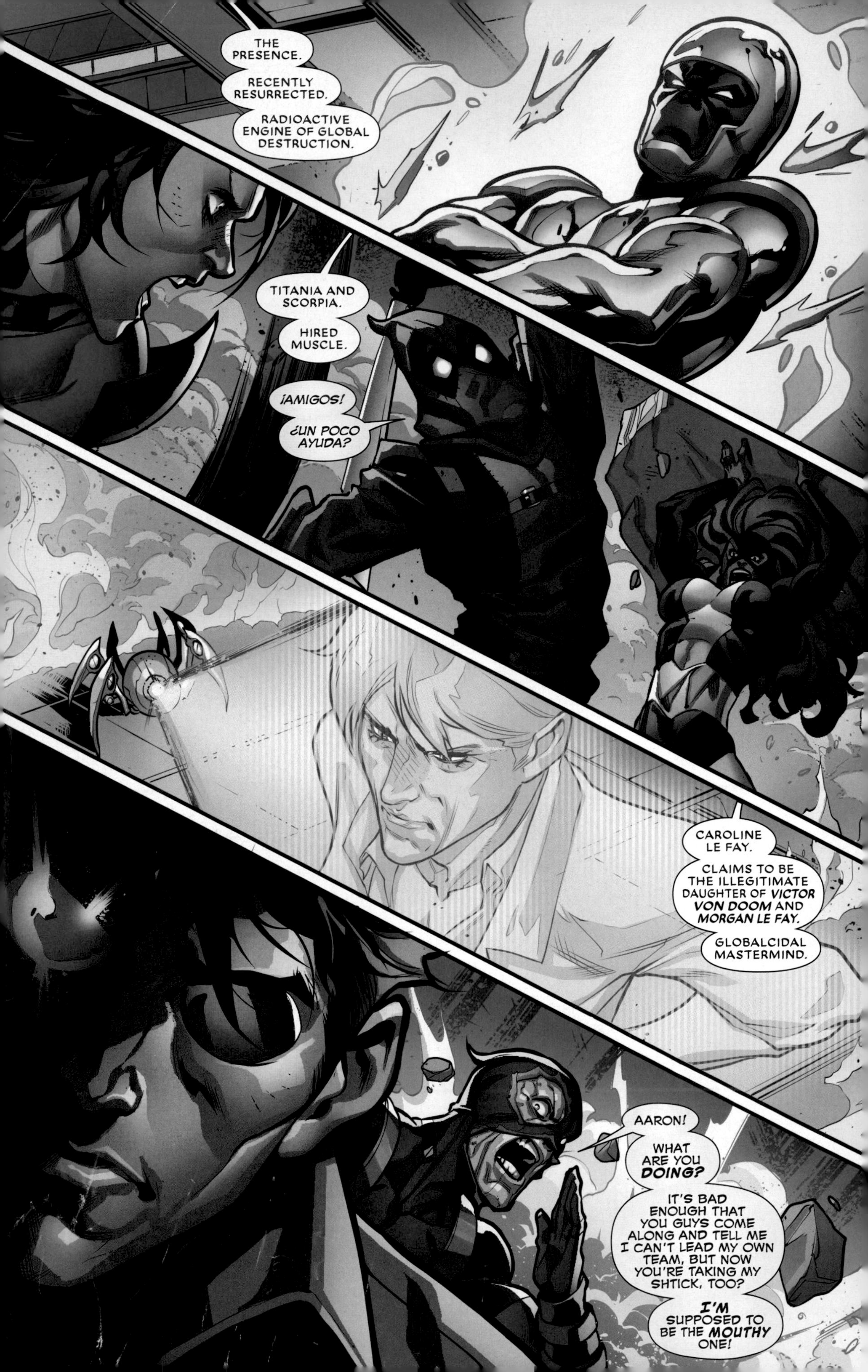
THE PRESENCE.
RECENTLY RESURRECTED.
RADIOACTIVE ENGINE OF GLOBAL DESTRUCTION.
TITANIA AND SCORPIA.
HIRED MUSCLE.
¡AMIGOS!
¿UN POCO AYUDA?
CAROLINE LE FAY.
CLAIMS TO BE THE ILLEGITIMATE DAUGHTER OF VICTOR VON DOOM AND MORGAN LE FAY.
GLOBALCIDAL MASTERMIND.
AARON!
WHAT ARE YOU DOING?
IT'S BAD ENOUGH THAT YOU GUYS COME ALONG AND TELL ME I CAN'T LEAD MY OWN TEAM, BUT NOW YOU'RE TAKING MY SHTICK, TOO?
I'M SUPPOSED TO BE THE MOUTHY ONE!

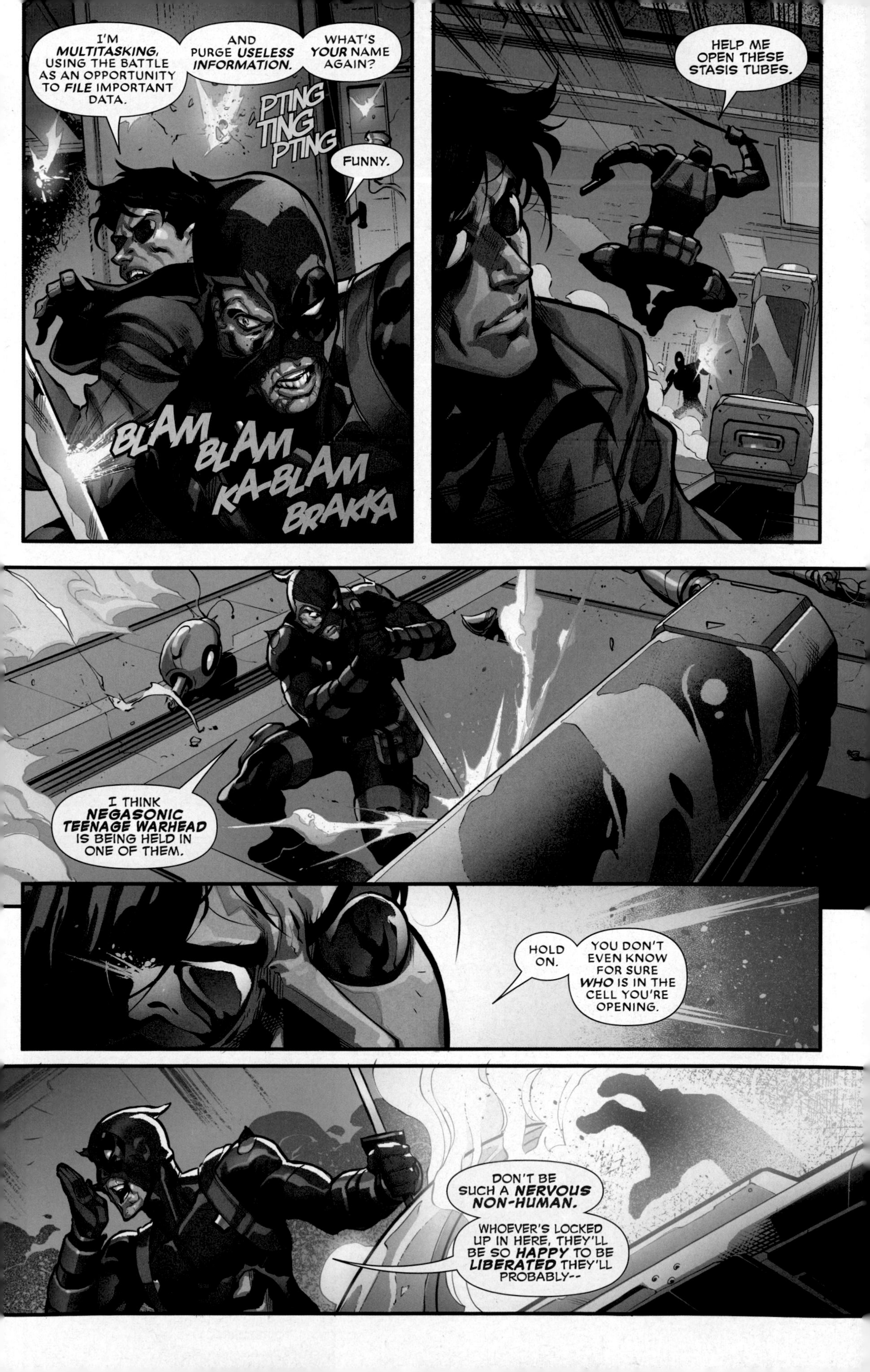
I'M MULTITASKING, USING THE BATTLE AS AN OPPORTUNITY TO FILE IMPORTANT DATA.
AND PURGE USELESS INFORMATION.
WHAT'S YOUR NAME AGAIN?
PTING TING PTING
FUNNY.
BLAM BLAM KA-BLAM BRAKKA
HELP ME OPEN THESE STASIS TUBES.
I THINK NEGASONIC TEENAGE WARHEAD IS BEING HELD IN ONE OF THEM.
HOLD ON.
YOU DON'T EVEN KNOW FOR SURE WHO IS IN THE CELL YOU'RE OPENING.
DON'T BE SUCH A NERVOUS NON-HUMAN.
WHOEVER'S LOCKED UP IN HERE, THEY'LL BE SO HAPPY TO BE LIBERATED THEY'LL PROBABLY--

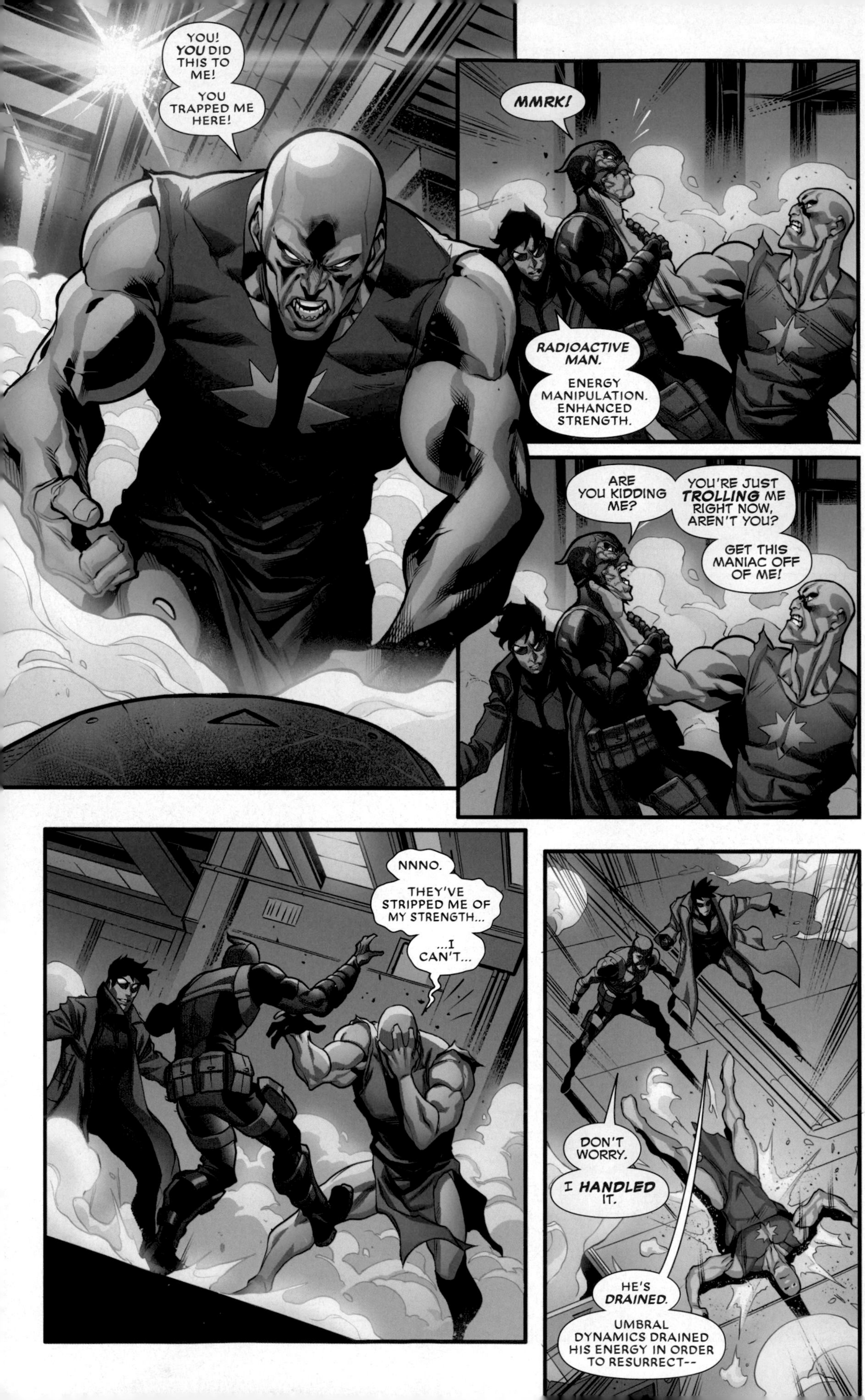
YOU! *YOU* DID THIS TO ME!
YOU TRAPPED ME HERE!
MMRK!
RADIOACTIVE MAN.
ENERGY MANIPULATION. ENHANCED STRENGTH.
ARE YOU KIDDING ME?
YOU'RE JUST *TROLLING* ME RIGHT NOW, AREN'T YOU?
GET THIS MANIAC OFF OF ME!
NNNO.
THEY'VE STRIPPED ME OF MY STRENGTH...
...I CAN'T...
DON'T WORRY.
I *HANDLED* IT.
HE'S *DRAINED.*
UMBRAL DYNAMICS DRAINED HIS ENERGY IN ORDER TO RESURRECT--

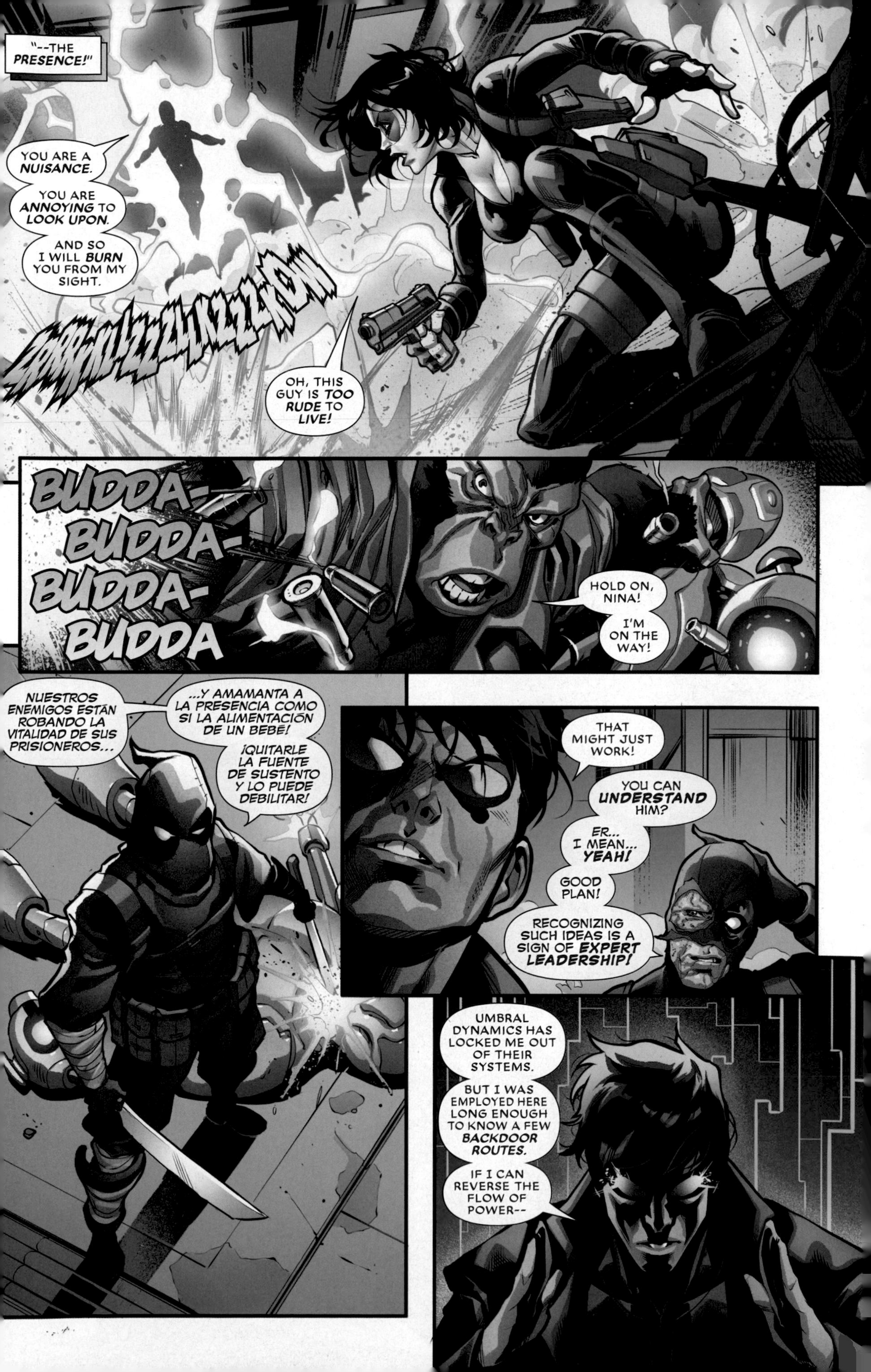
"--THE PRESENCE!"
YOU ARE A NUISANCE.
YOU ARE ANNOYING TO LOOK UPON.
AND SO I WILL BURN YOU FROM MY SIGHT.
OH, THIS GUY IS TOO RUDE TO LIVE!
BUDDA-BUDDA-BUDDA-BUDDA
HOLD ON, NINA!
I'M ON THE WAY!
NUESTROS ENEMIGOS ESTÁN ROBANDO LA VITALIDAD DE SUS PRISIONEROS...
...Y AMAMANTA A LA PRESENCIA COMO SI LA ALIMENTACIÓN DE UN BEBÉ!
¡QUITARLE LA FUENTE DE SUSTENTO Y LO PUEDE DEBILITAR!
THAT MIGHT JUST WORK!
YOU CAN UNDERSTAND HIM?
ER... I MEAN... YEAH!
GOOD PLAN!
RECOGNIZING SUCH IDEAS IS A SIGN OF EXPERT LEADERSHIP!
UMBRAL DYNAMICS HAS LOCKED ME OUT OF THEIR SYSTEMS.
BUT I WAS EMPLOYED HERE LONG ENOUGH TO KNOW A FEW BACKDOOR ROUTES.
IF I CAN REVERSE THE FLOW OF POWER--

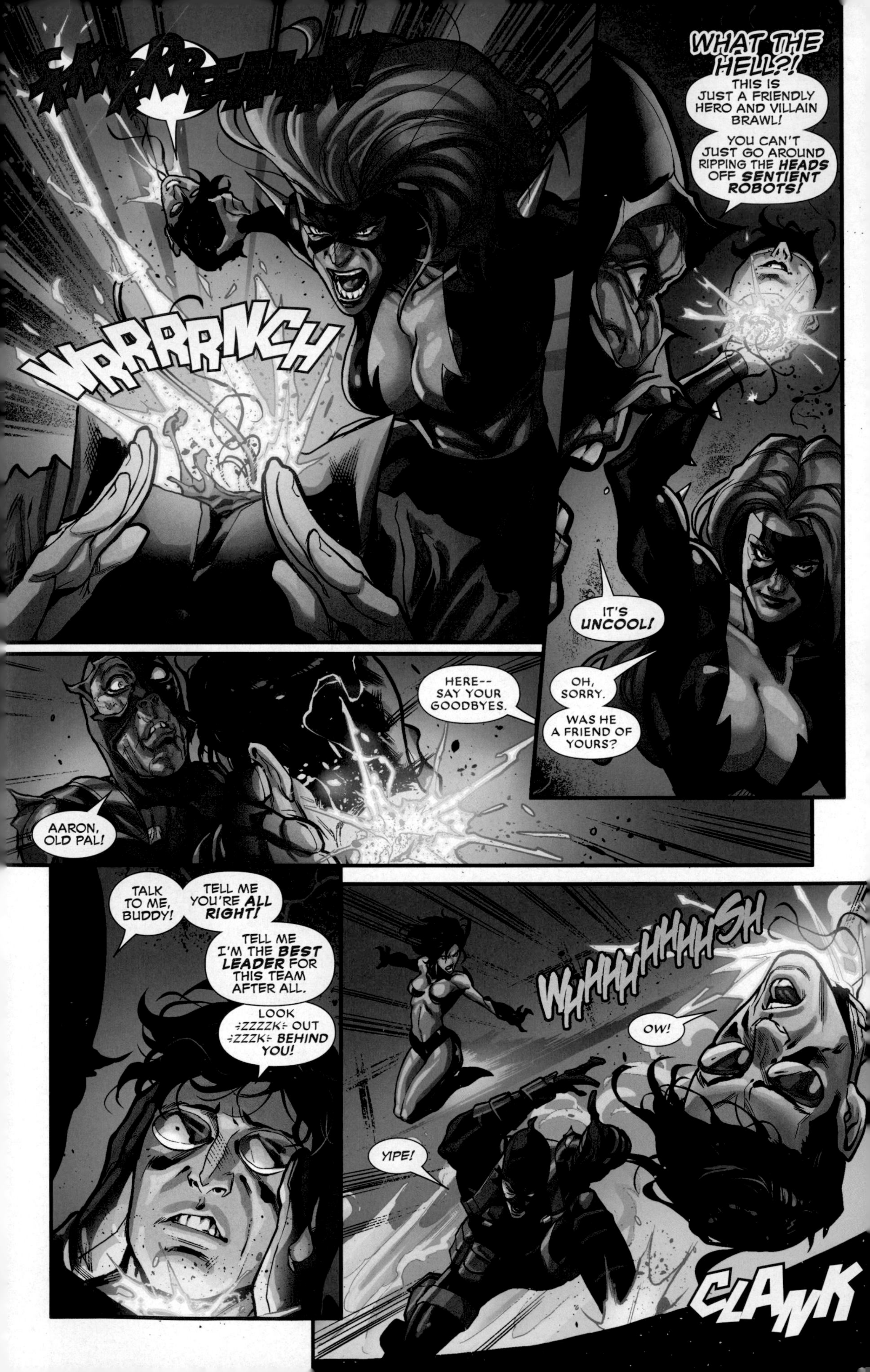
WRRRRNCH
WHAT THE HELL?! THIS IS JUST A FRIENDLY HERO AND VILLAIN BRAWL!
YOU CAN'T JUST GO AROUND RIPPING THE HEADS OFF SENTIENT ROBOTS!
IT'S UNCOOL!
OH, SORRY.
WAS HE A FRIEND OF YOURS?
HERE-- SAY YOUR GOODBYES.
AARON, OLD PAL!
TALK TO ME, BUDDY!
TELL ME YOU'RE ALL RIGHT!
TELL ME I'M THE BEST LEADER FOR THIS TEAM AFTER ALL.
LOOK ÷ZZZZK÷ OUT ÷ZZZK÷ BEHIND YOU!
WHHHHHHHHSH
OW!
YIPE!
CLANK

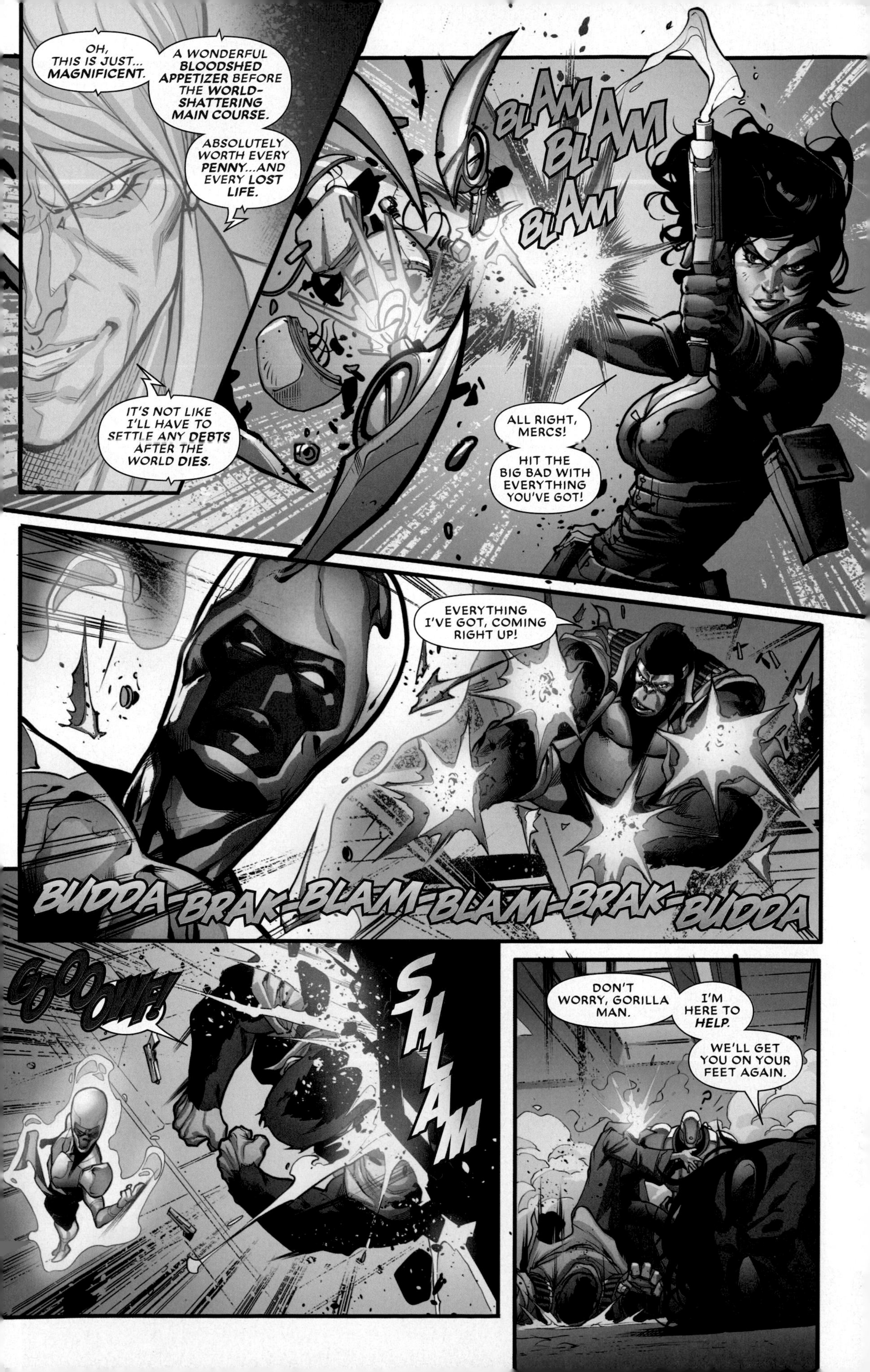
OH, THIS IS JUST... MAGNIFICENT.
A WONDERFUL BLOODSHED APPETIZER BEFORE THE WORLD-SHATTERING MAIN COURSE.
ABSOLUTELY WORTH EVERY PENNY...AND EVERY LOST LIFE.
IT'S NOT LIKE I'LL HAVE TO SETTLE ANY DEBTS AFTER THE WORLD DIES.
BLAM BLAM BLAM
ALL RIGHT, MERCS!
HIT THE BIG BAD WITH EVERYTHING YOU'VE GOT!
EVERYTHING I'VE GOT, COMING RIGHT UP!
BUDDA-BRAK-BLAM-BLAM-BRAK-BUDDA
GOOOOWF!
SHLAM
DON'T WORRY, GORILLA MAN.
I'M HERE TO HELP.
WE'LL GET YOU ON YOUR FEET AGAIN.
?

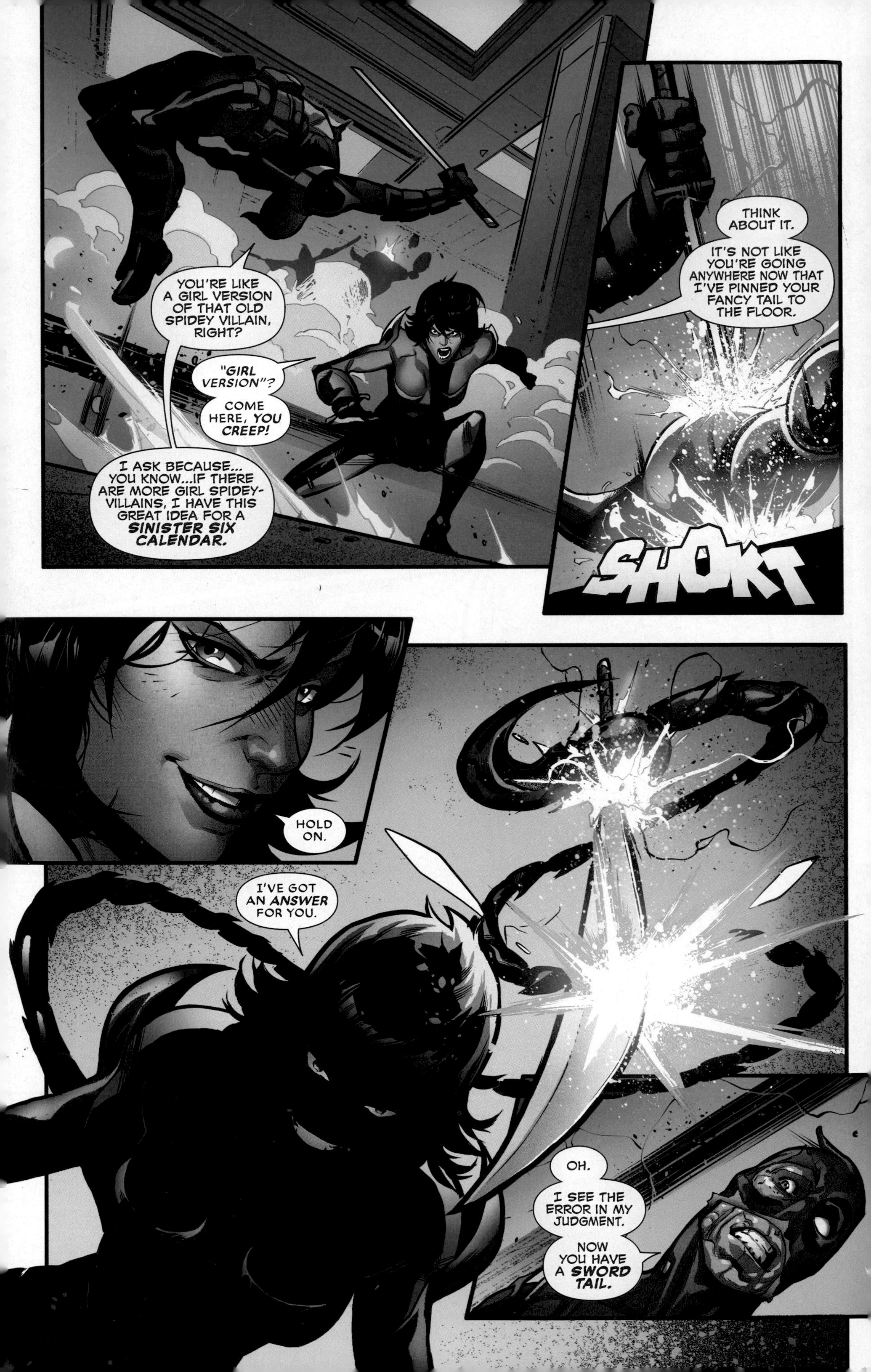

YOU'RE LIKE A GIRL VERSION OF THAT OLD SPIDEY VILLAIN, RIGHT?
"GIRL VERSION"?
COME HERE, YOU CREEP!
I ASK BECAUSE... YOU KNOW...IF THERE ARE MORE GIRL SPIDEY-VILLAINS, I HAVE THIS GREAT IDEA FOR A SINISTER SIX CALENDAR.
THINK ABOUT IT.
IT'S NOT LIKE YOU'RE GOING ANYWHERE NOW THAT I'VE PINNED YOUR FANCY TAIL TO THE FLOOR.
SHOKT
HOLD ON.
I'VE GOT AN ANSWER FOR YOU.
OH.
I SEE THE ERROR IN MY JUDGMENT.
NOW YOU HAVE A SWORD TAIL.

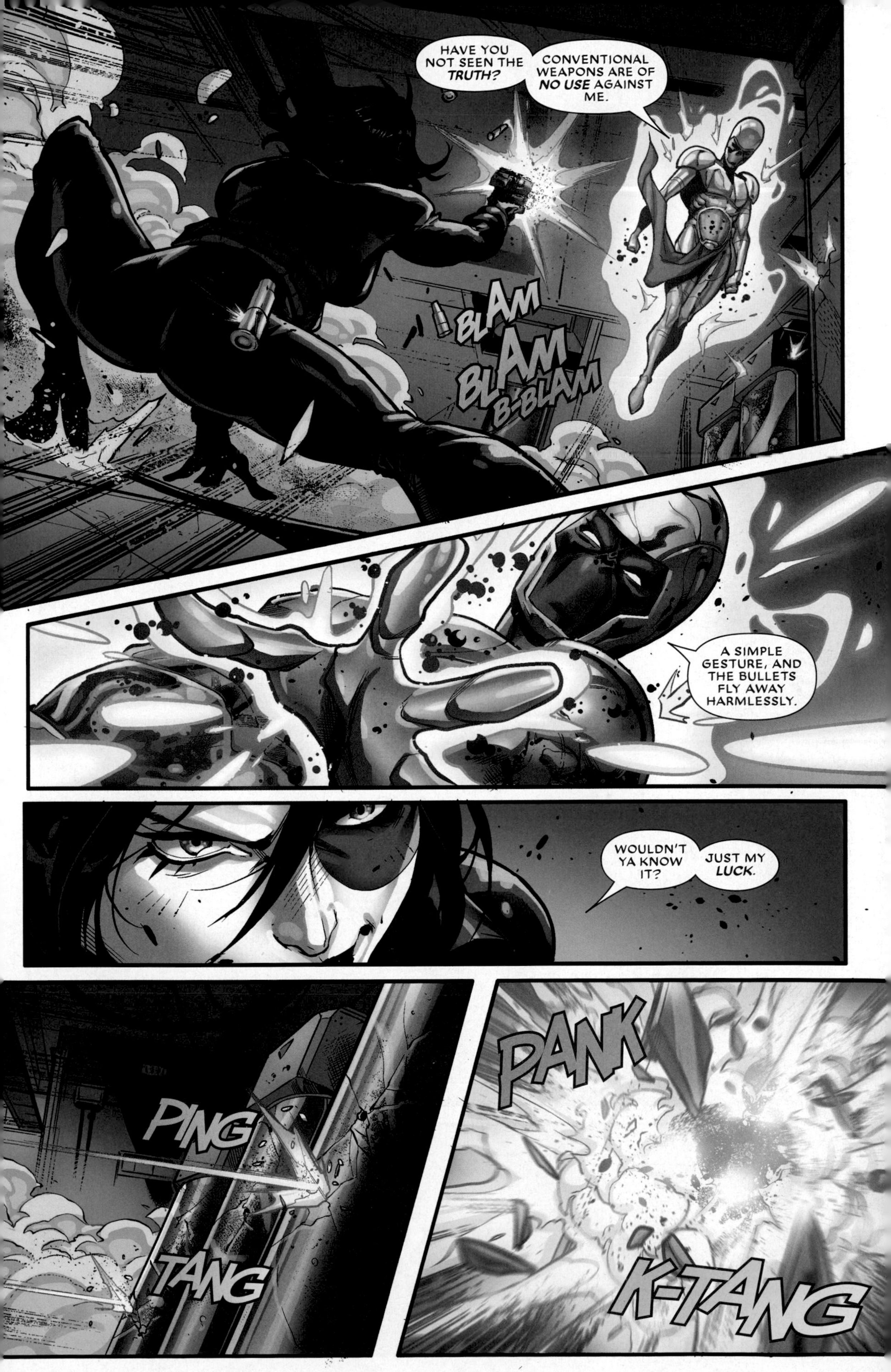

HAVE YOU NOT SEEN THE TRUTH?
CONVENTIONAL WEAPONS ARE OF NO USE AGAINST ME.
BLAM
BLAM
BLAM
B-BLAM
A SIMPLE GESTURE, AND THE BULLETS FLY AWAY HARMLESSLY.
WOULDN'T YA KNOW IT?
JUST MY LUCK.
PING
TANG
PANK
K-TANG

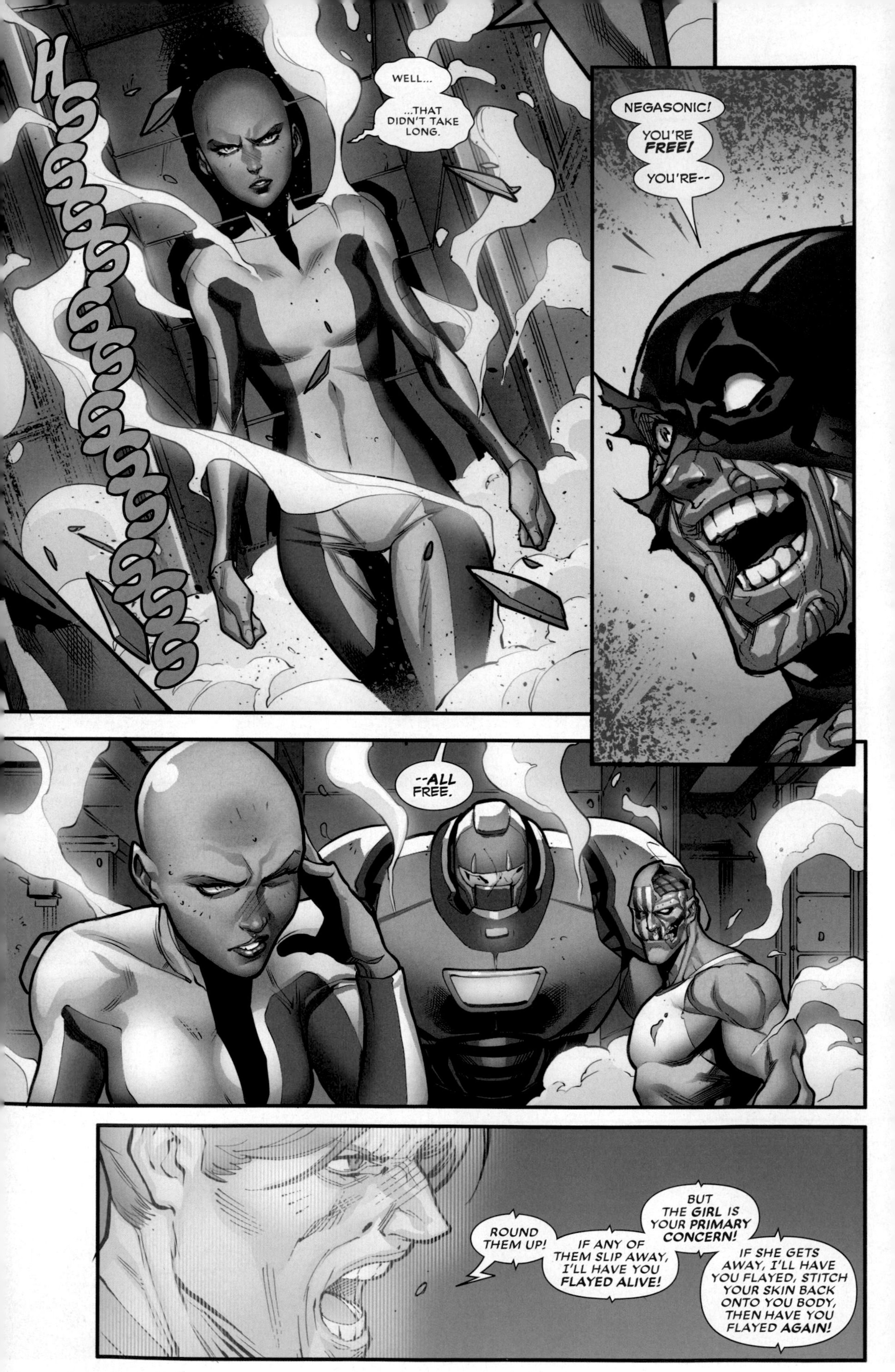
HSSSSSSSSSSSSSSS
WELL...
...THAT DIDN'T TAKE LONG.
NEGASONIC!
YOU'RE **FREE!**
YOU'RE--
--**ALL** FREE.
ROUND THEM UP!
IF ANY OF THEM SLIP AWAY, I'LL HAVE YOU **FLAYED ALIVE!**
BUT THE **GIRL** IS YOUR **PRIMARY CONCERN!**
IF SHE GETS AWAY, I'LL HAVE YOU FLAYED, STITCH YOUR SKIN BACK ONTO YOU BODY, THEN HAVE YOU FLAYED **AGAIN!**

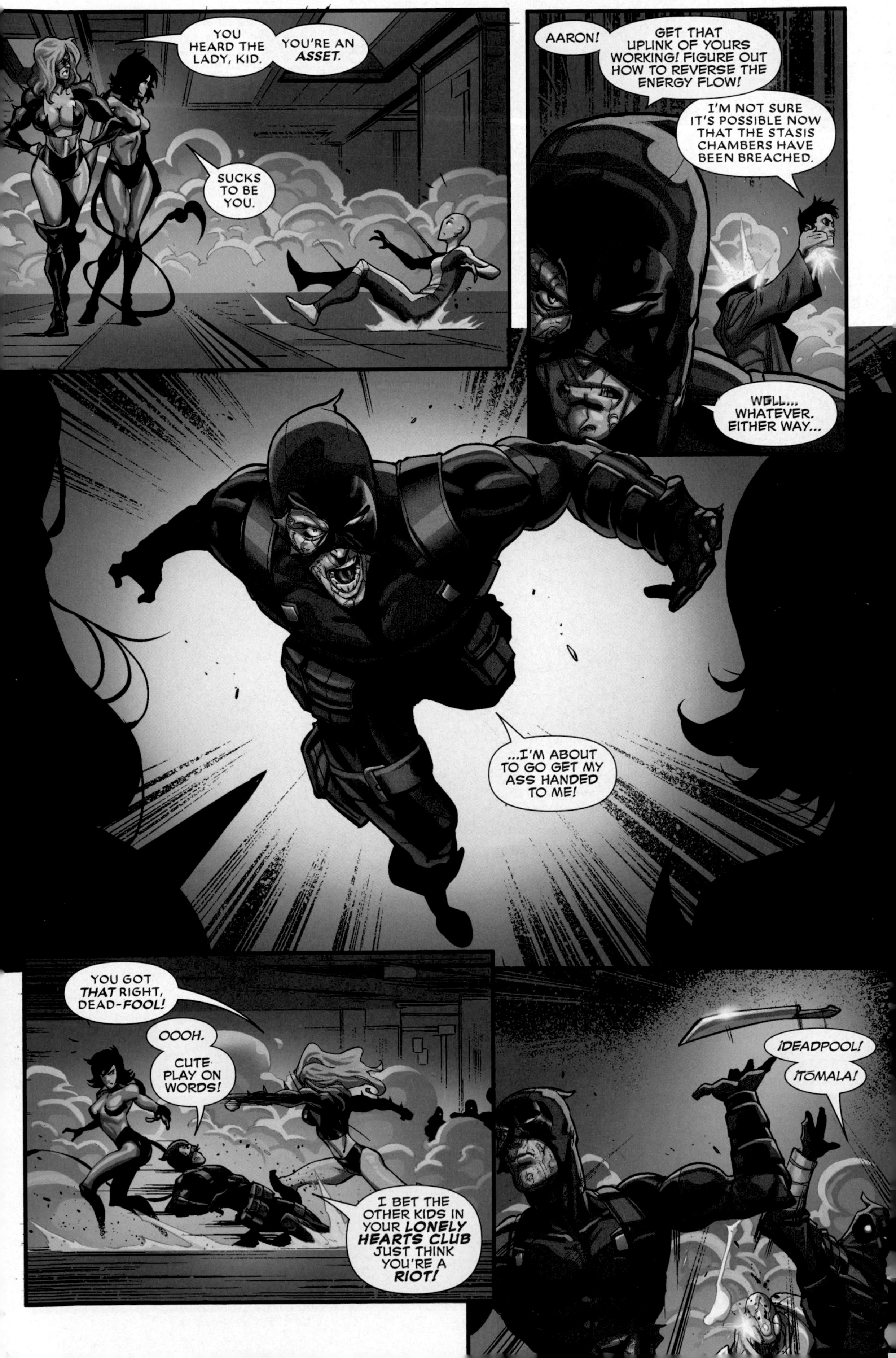
YOU HEARD THE LADY, KID.
YOU'RE AN *ASSET*.
SUCKS TO BE YOU.
AARON!
GET THAT UPLINK OF YOURS WORKING! FIGURE OUT HOW TO REVERSE THE ENERGY FLOW!
I'M NOT SURE IT'S POSSIBLE NOW THAT THE STASIS CHAMBERS HAVE BEEN BREACHED.
WELL... WHATEVER. EITHER WAY...
...I'M ABOUT TO GO GET MY ASS HANDED TO ME!
YOU GOT *THAT* RIGHT, DEAD-*FOOL*!
OOOH.
CUTE PLAY ON WORDS!
I BET THE OTHER KIDS IN YOUR *LONELY HEARTS CLUB* JUST THINK YOU'RE A *RIOT!*
¡DEADPOOL!
¡TÓMALA!

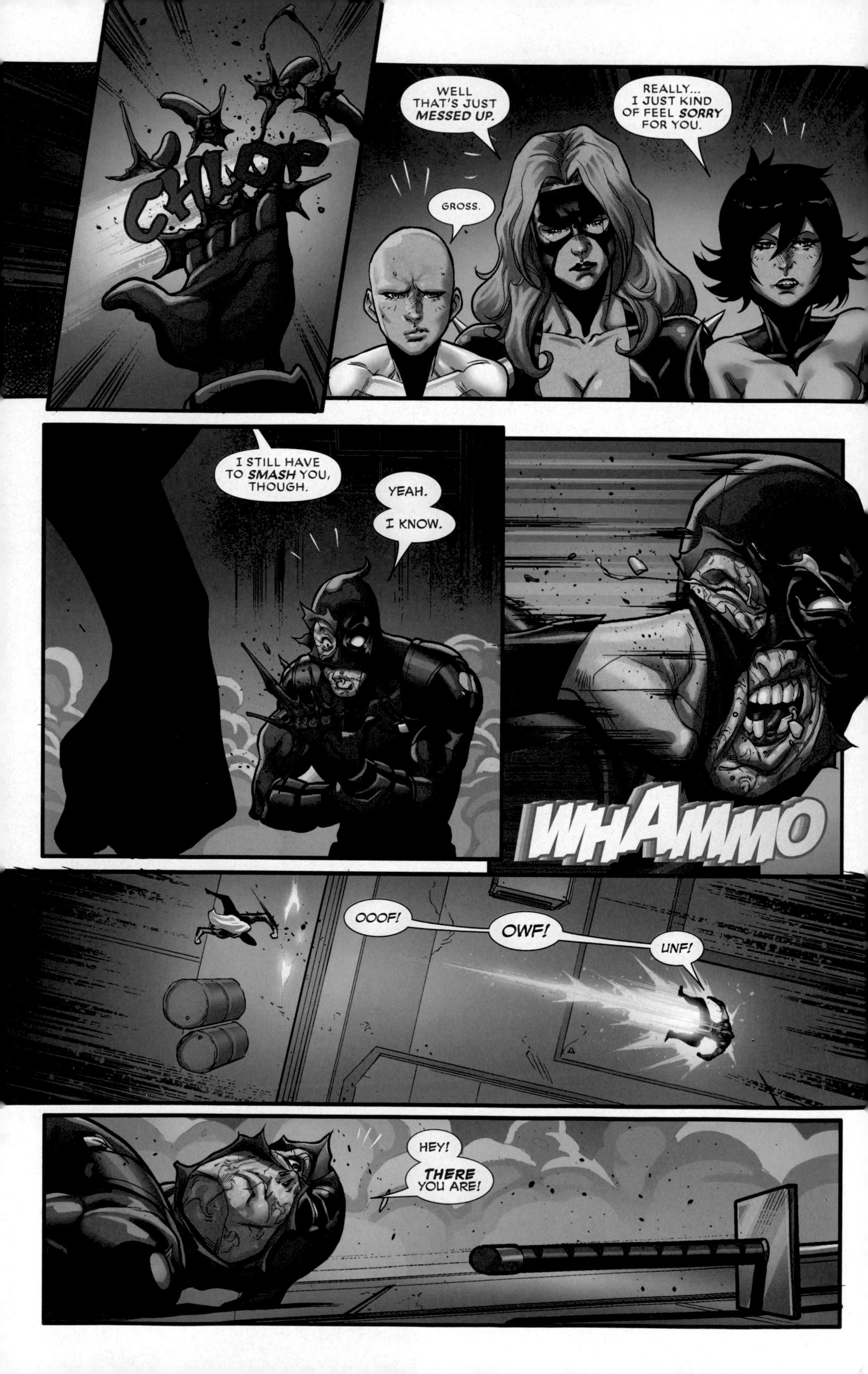
CHLOP
WELL THAT'S JUST MESSED UP.
GROSS.
REALLY... I JUST KIND OF FEEL SORRY FOR YOU.
I STILL HAVE TO SMASH YOU, THOUGH.
YEAH.
I KNOW.
WHAMMO
OOOF!
OWF!
UNF!
HEY!
THERE YOU ARE!

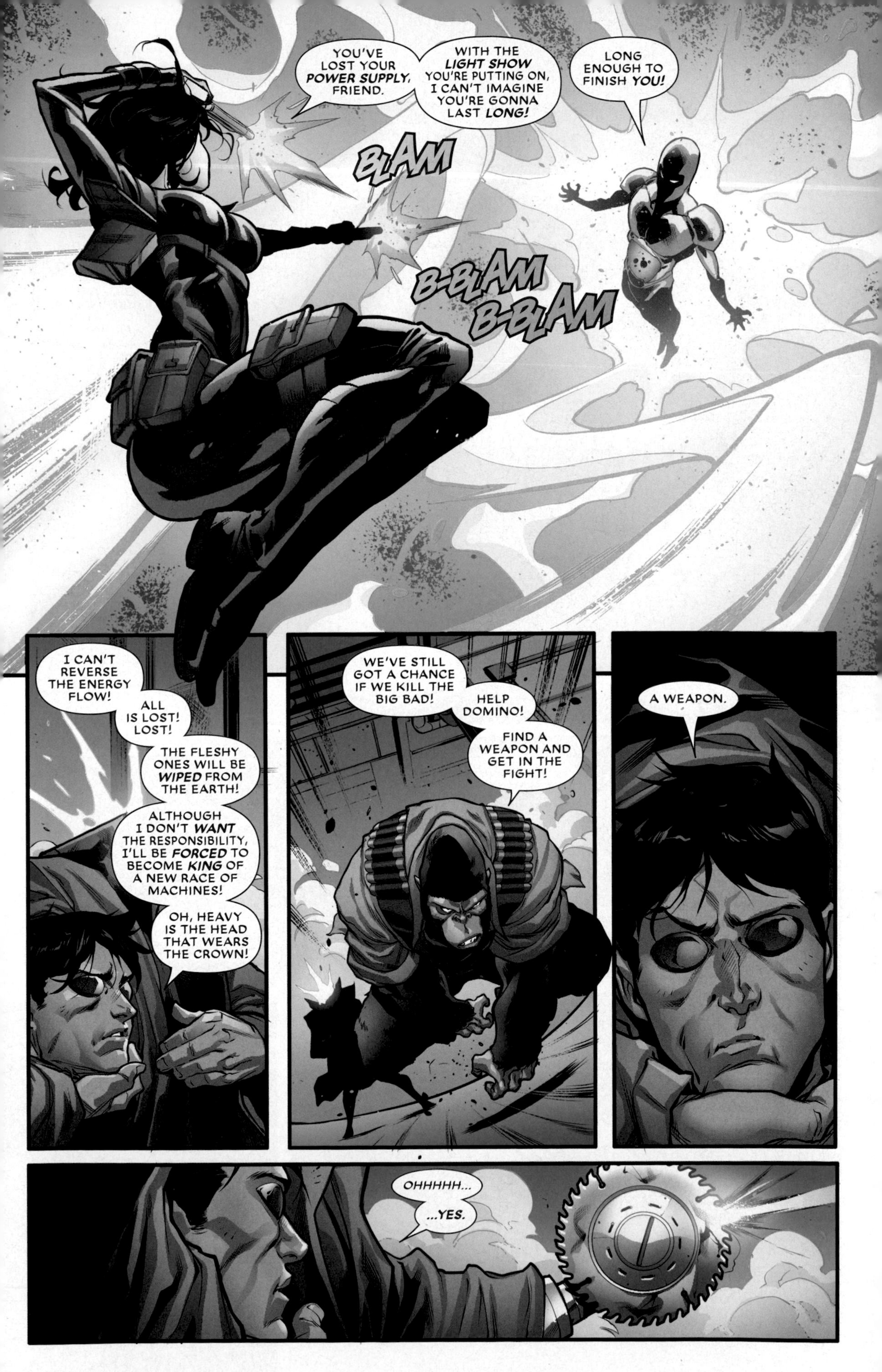
YOU'VE LOST YOUR POWER SUPPLY, FRIEND.
WITH THE LIGHT SHOW YOU'RE PUTTING ON, I CAN'T IMAGINE YOU'RE GONNA LAST LONG!
LONG ENOUGH TO FINISH YOU!
BLAM
B-BLAM
B-BLAM
I CAN'T REVERSE THE ENERGY FLOW!
ALL IS LOST! LOST!
THE FLESHY ONES WILL BE WIPED FROM THE EARTH!
ALTHOUGH I DON'T WANT THE RESPONSIBILITY, I'LL BE FORCED TO BECOME KING OF A NEW RACE OF MACHINES!
OH, HEAVY IS THE HEAD THAT WEARS THE CROWN!
WE'VE STILL GOT A CHANCE IF WE KILL THE BIG BAD!
HELP DOMINO!
FIND A WEAPON AND GET IN THE FIGHT!
A WEAPON.
OHHHHH...
...YES.

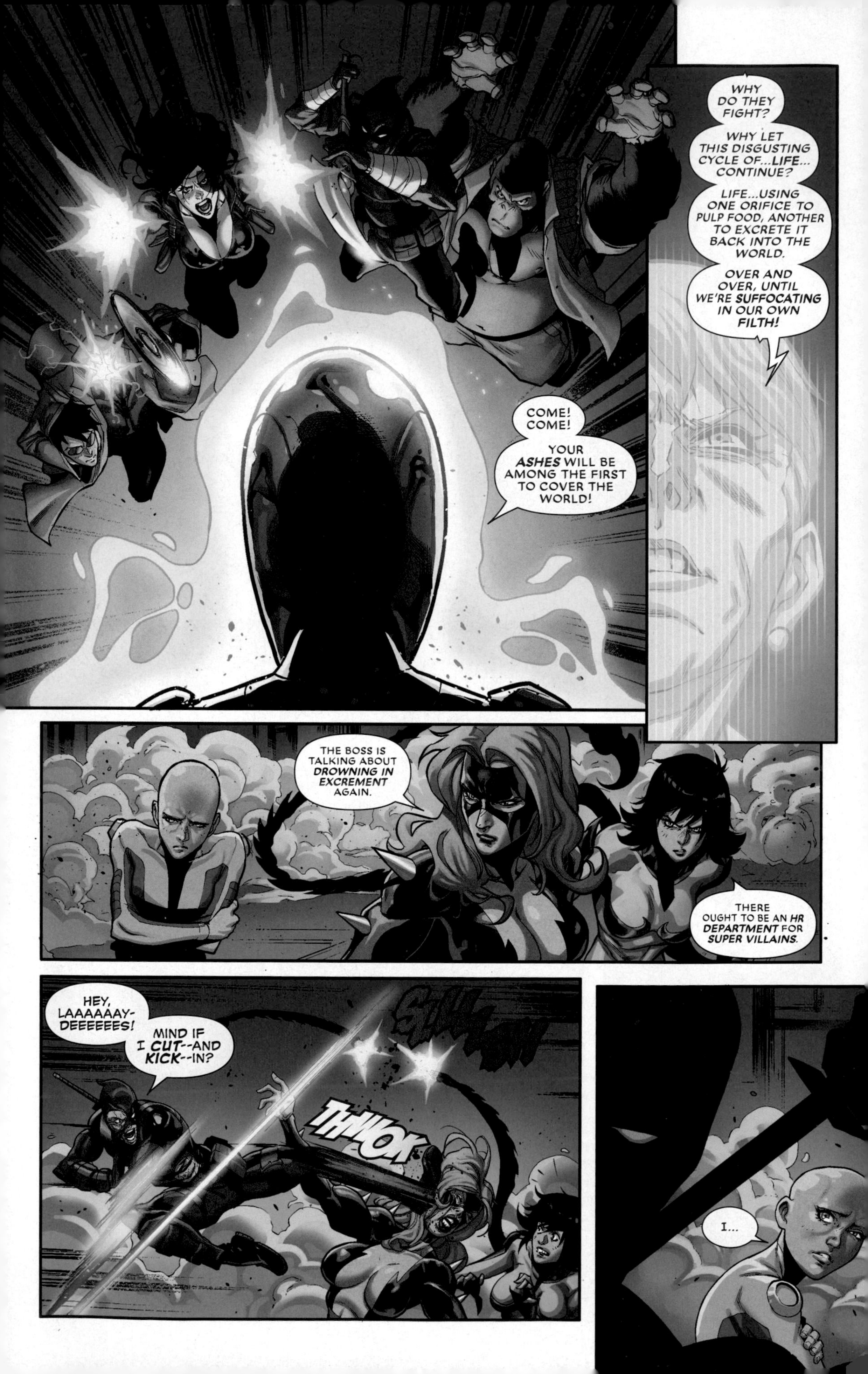
WHY DO THEY FIGHT?
WHY LET THIS DISGUSTING CYCLE OF...LIFE... CONTINUE?
LIFE...USING ONE ORIFICE TO PULP FOOD, ANOTHER TO EXCRETE IT BACK INTO THE WORLD.
OVER AND OVER, UNTIL WE'RE SUFFOCATING IN OUR OWN FILTH!
COME! COME!
YOUR ASHES WILL BE AMONG THE FIRST TO COVER THE WORLD!
THE BOSS IS TALKING ABOUT DROWNING IN EXCREMENT AGAIN.
THERE OUGHT TO BE AN HR DEPARTMENT FOR SUPER VILLAINS.
HEY, LAAAAAAY-DEEEEEES!
MIND IF I CUT--AND KICK--IN?
THWOK
I...

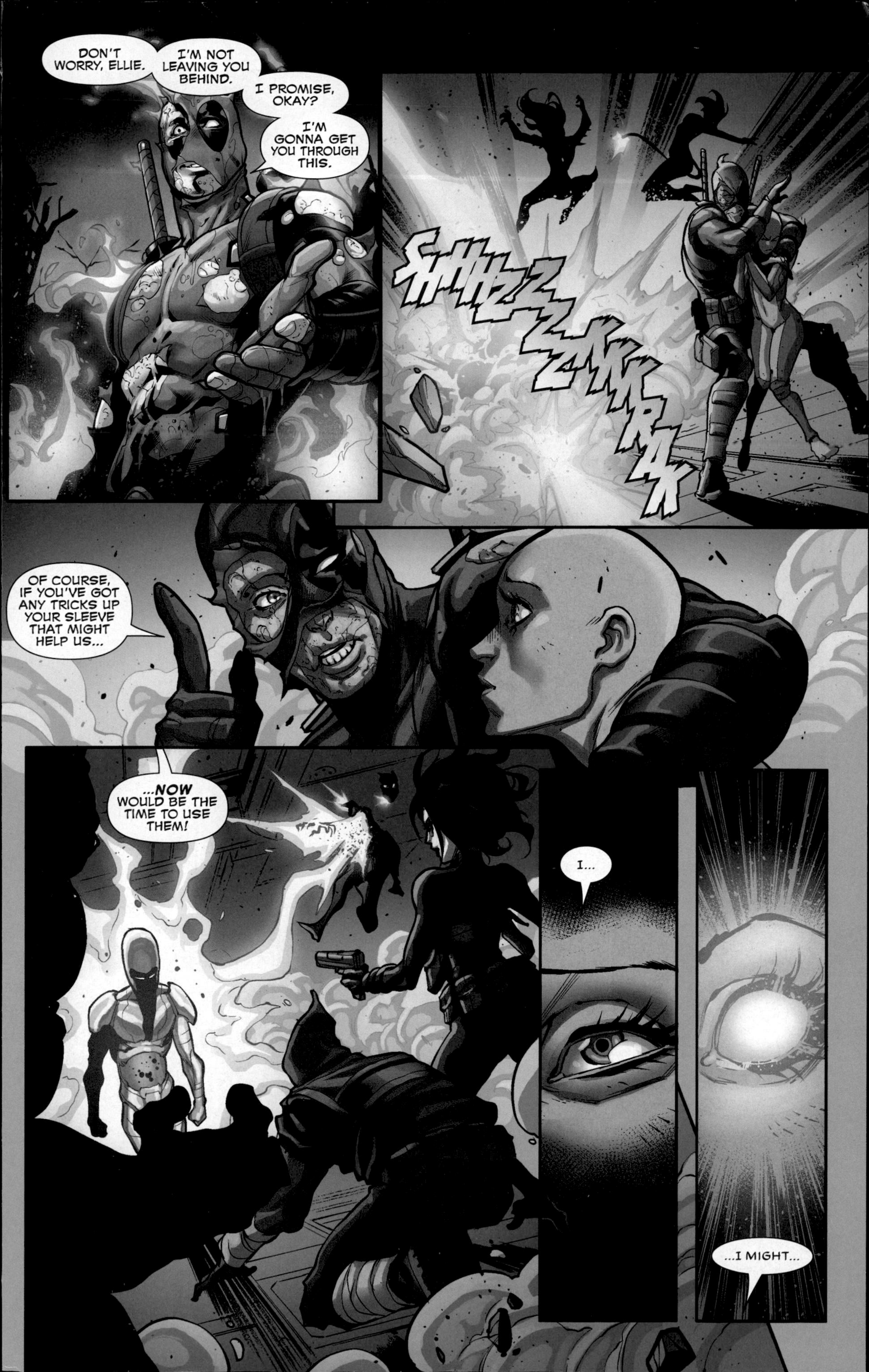
DON'T WORRY, ELLIE.
I'M NOT LEAVING YOU BEHIND.
I PROMISE, OKAY?
I'M GONNA GET YOU THROUGH THIS.
SHHHZZZZZAKKRAK
OF COURSE, IF YOU'VE GOT ANY TRICKS UP YOUR SLEEVE THAT MIGHT HELP US...
...NOW WOULD BE THE TIME TO USE THEM!
I...
...I MIGHT...

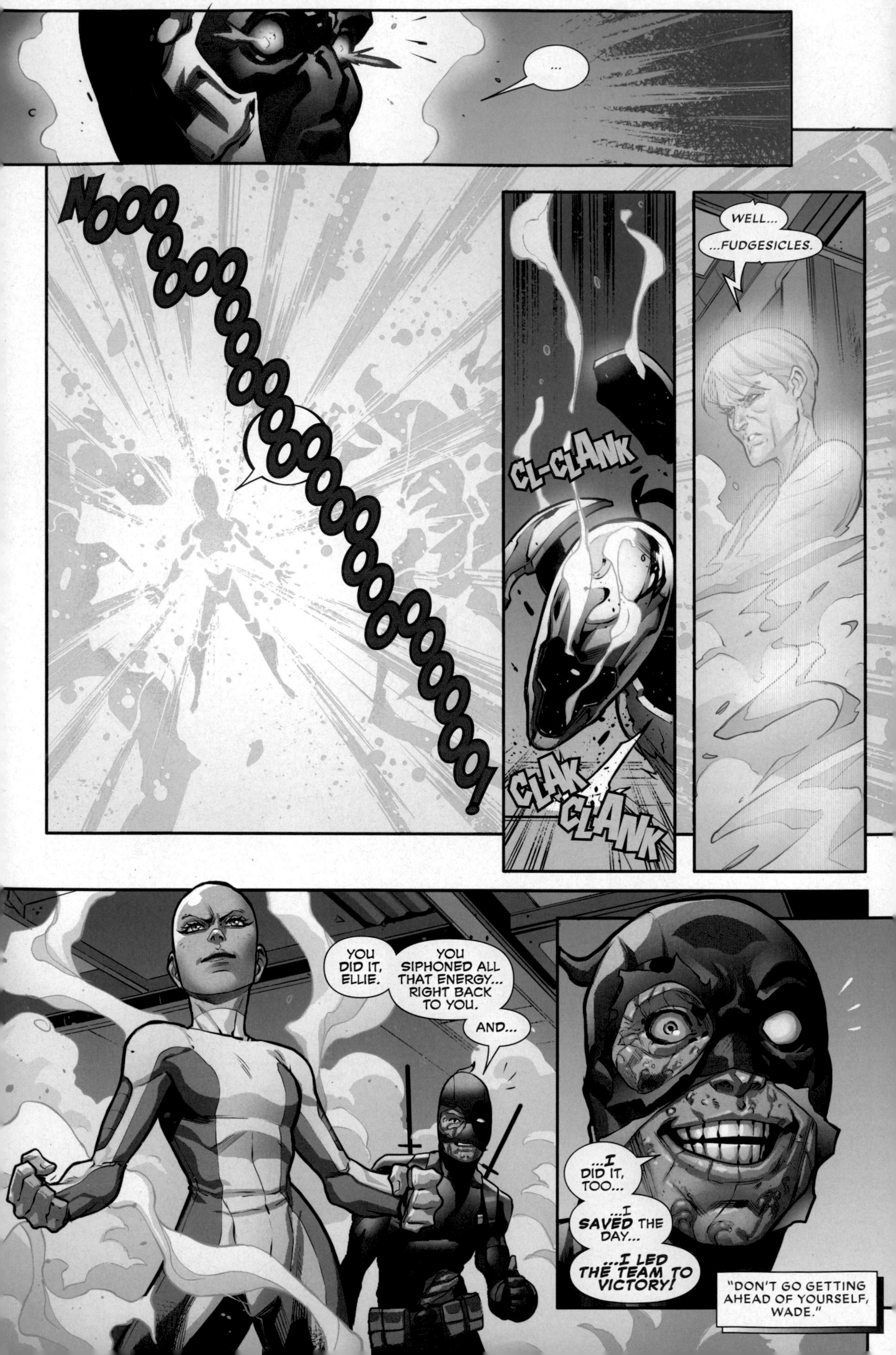
...
NOOOOOOOOOOOOOOOOOOOOOOOOOOOOOO!
CL-CLANK
CLAK
CLANK
WELL...
...FUDGESICLES.
YOU DID IT, ELLIE.
YOU SIPHONED ALL THAT ENERGY... RIGHT BACK TO YOU.
AND...
...I DID IT, TOO...
...I SAVED THE DAY...
...I LED THE TEAM TO VICTORY!
"DON'T GO GETTING AHEAD OF YOURSELF, WADE."

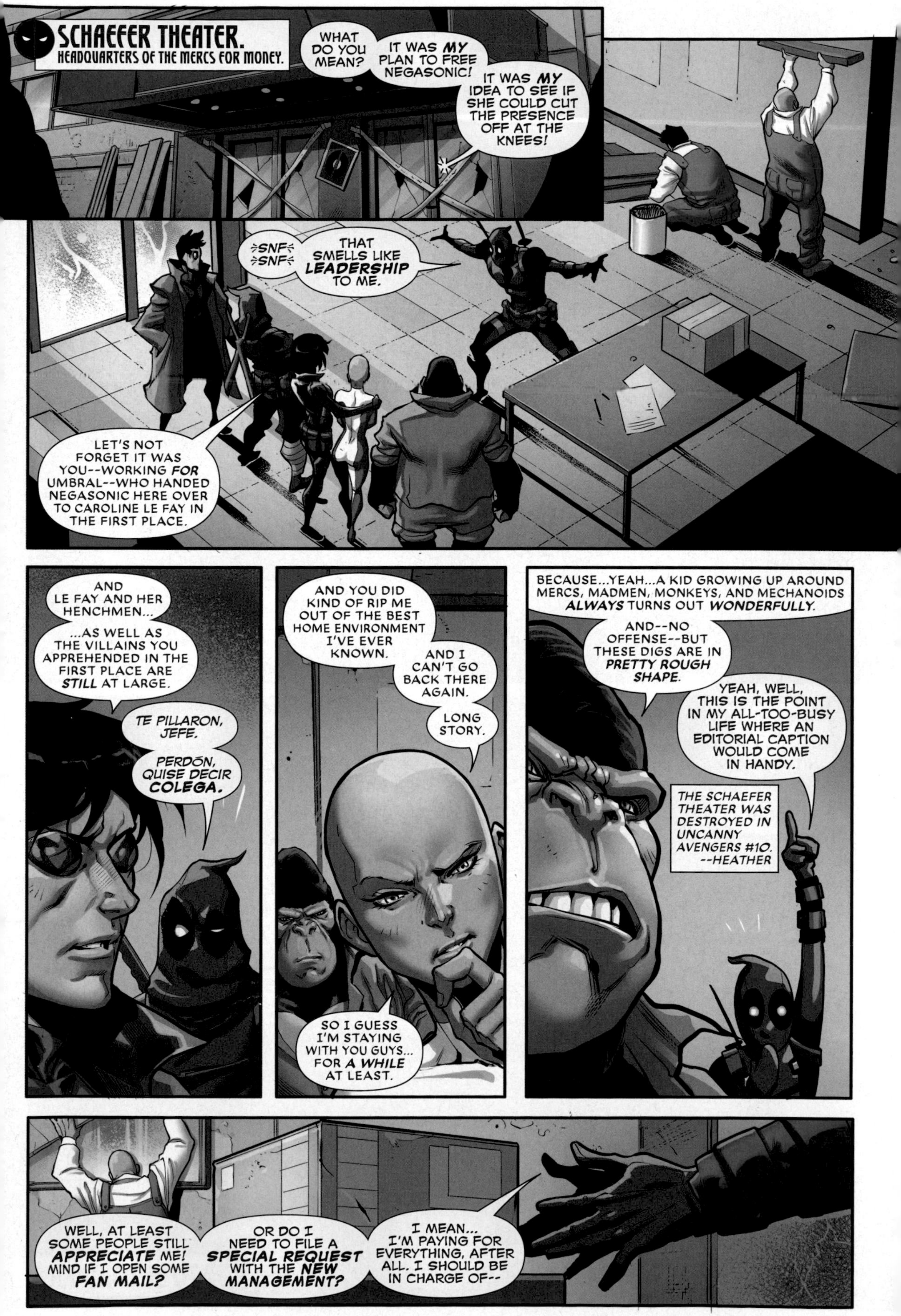
SCHAEFER THEATER.
HEADQUARTERS OF THE MERCS FOR MONEY.
WHAT DO YOU MEAN?
IT WAS MY PLAN TO FREE NEGASONIC!
IT WAS MY IDEA TO SEE IF SHE COULD CUT THE PRESENCE OFF AT THE KNEES!
SNF SNF
THAT SMELLS LIKE LEADERSHIP TO ME.
LET'S NOT FORGET IT WAS YOU--WORKING FOR UMBRAL--WHO HANDED NEGASONIC HERE OVER TO CAROLINE LE FAY IN THE FIRST PLACE.
AND LE FAY AND HER HENCHMEN...
...AS WELL AS THE VILLAINS YOU APPREHENDED IN THE FIRST PLACE ARE STILL AT LARGE.
TE PILLARON, JEFE.
PERDÓN, QUISE DECIR COLEGA.
AND YOU DID KIND OF RIP ME OUT OF THE BEST HOME ENVIRONMENT I'VE EVER KNOWN.
AND I CAN'T GO BACK THERE AGAIN.
LONG STORY.
SO I GUESS I'M STAYING WITH YOU GUYS... FOR A WHILE AT LEAST.
BECAUSE...YEAH...A KID GROWING UP AROUND MERCS, MADMEN, MONKEYS, AND MECHANOIDS ALWAYS TURNS OUT WONDERFULLY.
AND--NO OFFENSE--BUT THESE DIGS ARE IN PRETTY ROUGH SHAPE.
YEAH, WELL, THIS IS THE POINT IN MY ALL-TOO-BUSY LIFE WHERE AN EDITORIAL CAPTION WOULD COME IN HANDY.
THE SCHAEFER THEATER WAS DESTROYED IN UNCANNY AVENGERS #10. --HEATHER
WELL, AT LEAST SOME PEOPLE STILL APPRECIATE ME! MIND IF I OPEN SOME FAN MAIL?
OR DO I NEED TO FILE A SPECIAL REQUEST WITH THE NEW MANAGEMENT?
I MEAN... I'M PAYING FOR EVERYTHING, AFTER ALL. I SHOULD BE IN CHARGE OF--

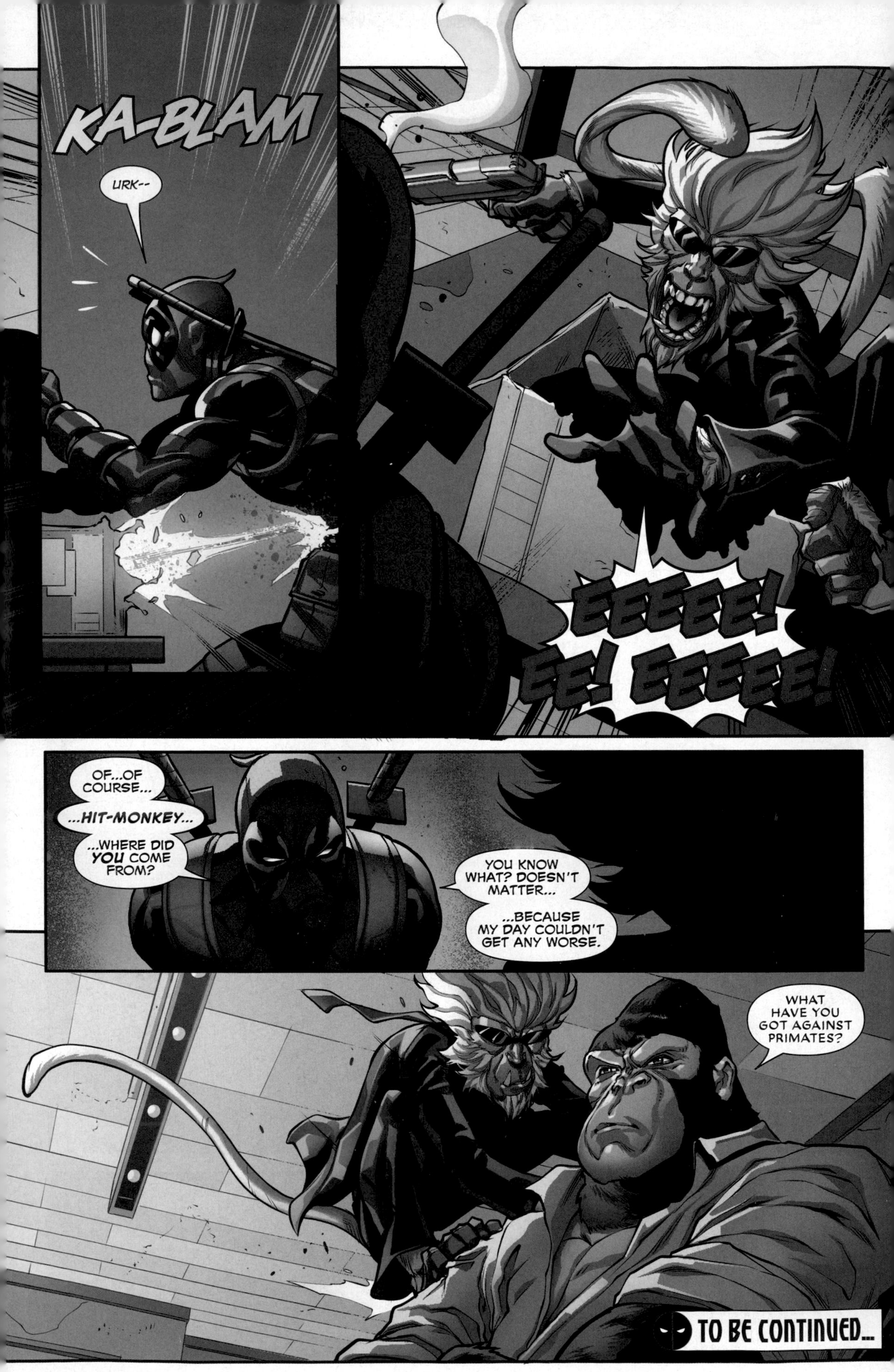
KA-BLAM
URK--
EEEEE! EE! EEEEE!
OF...OF COURSE...
...HIT-MONKEY...
...WHERE DID YOU COME FROM?
YOU KNOW WHAT? DOESN'T MATTER...
...BECAUSE MY DAY COULDN'T GET ANY WORSE.
WHAT HAVE YOU GOT AGAINST PRIMATES?
TO BE CONTINUED...

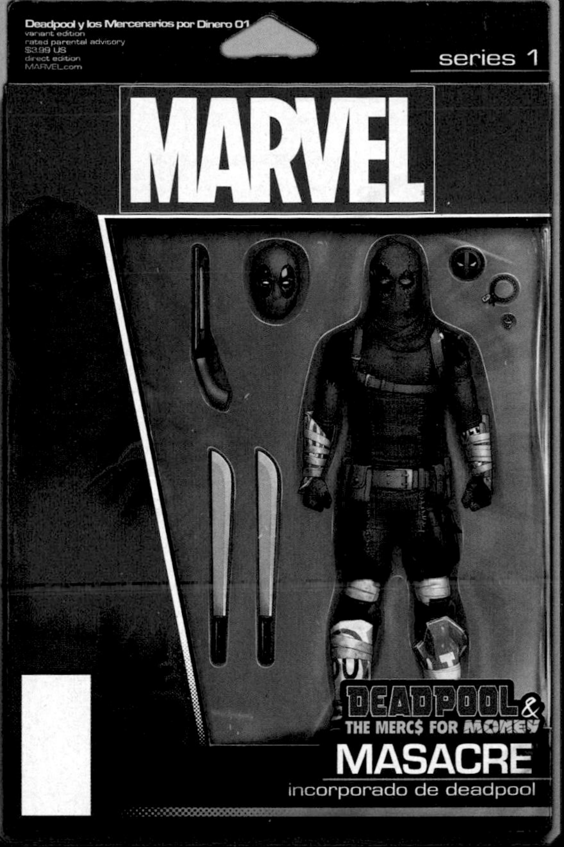

Deadpool y los Mercenarios por Dinero 01
variant edition
rated parental advisory
$3.99 US
direct edition
MARVEL.com
series 1
MARVEL
DEADPOOL & THE MERC$ FOR MONEY
MASACRE
incorporado de deadpool

JOHN TYLER CHRISTOPHER

#1 action figure variant

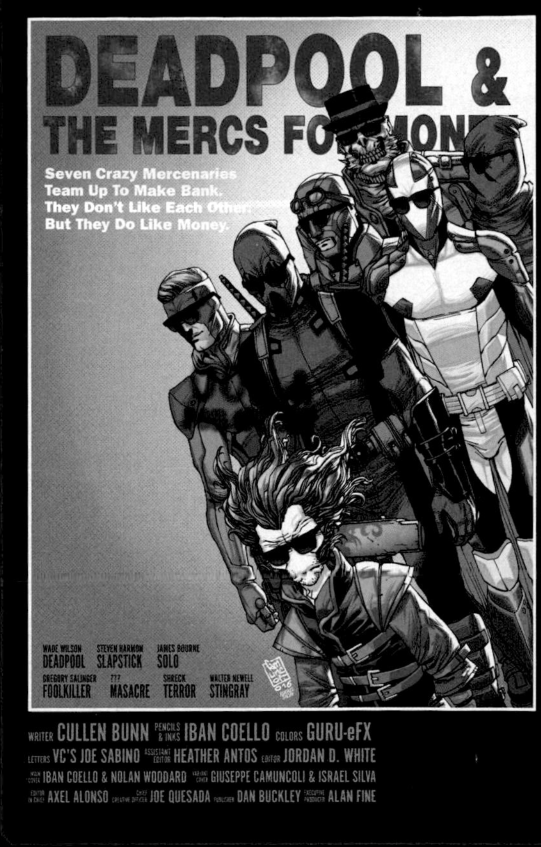

DEADPOOL & THE MERCS FOR MONEY
Seven Crazy Mercenaries
Team Up To Make Bank.
They Don't Like Each Other.
But They Do Like Money.
WADE WILSON DEADPOOL
STEVEN HARMON SLAPSTICK
JAMES BOURNE SOLO
GREGORY SALINGER FOOLKILLER
??? MASACRE
SHRECK TERROR
WALTER NEWELL STINGRAY
WRITER CULLEN BUNN PENCILS & INKS IBAN COELLO COLORS GURU-eFX
LETTERS VC'S JOE SABINO ASSISTANT EDITOR HEATHER ANTOS EDITOR JORDAN D. WHITE
MAIN COVER IBAN COELLO & NOLAN WOODARD VARIANT COVER GIUSEPPE CAMUNCOLI & ISRAEL SILVA
EDITOR IN CHIEF AXEL ALONSO CHIEF CREATIVE OFFICER JOE QUESADA PUBLISHER DAN BUCKLEY EXECUTIVE PRODUCER ALAN FINE

GIUSEPPE CAMUNCOLI & ISRAEL SILVA

#1 variant

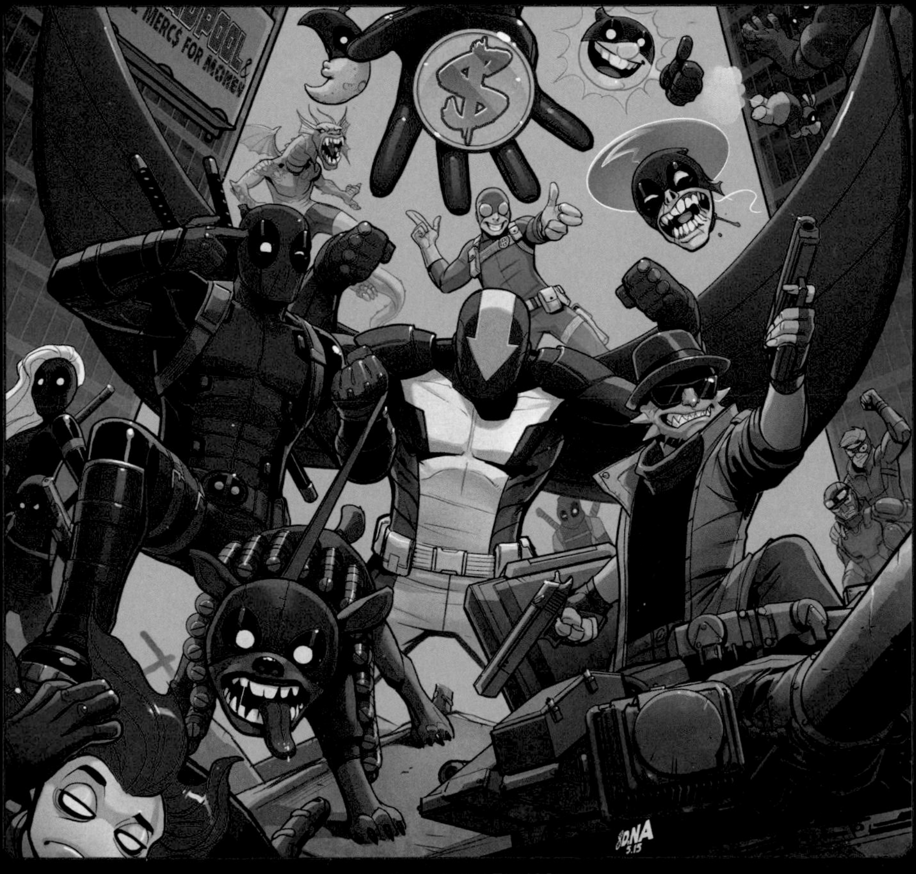

DEADPOOL & THE MERC$ FOR MONEY

DAVID NAKAYAMA

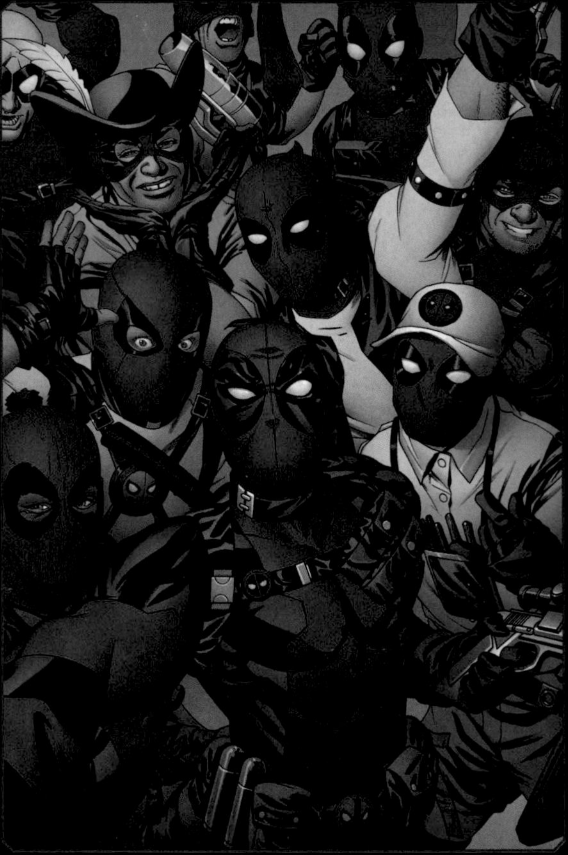

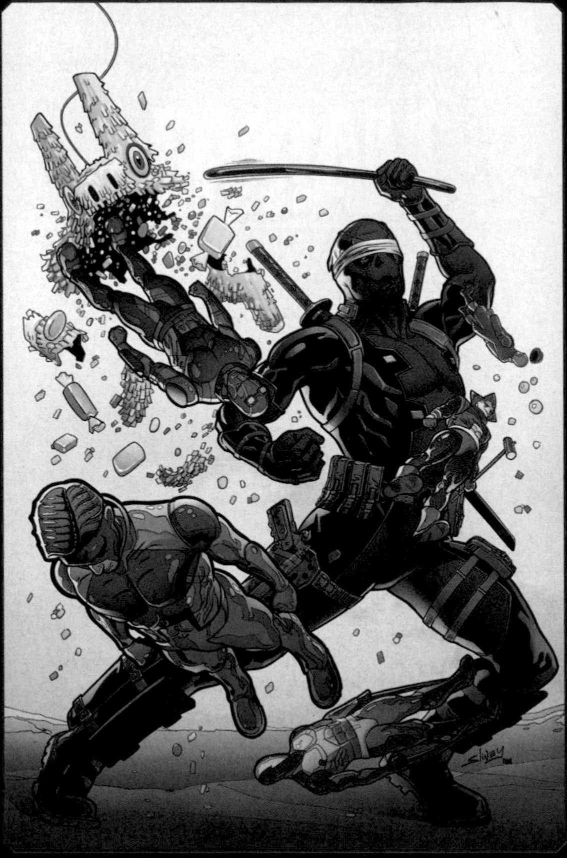

MIKE MCKONE & FRANK D'ARMATA
#1 variant

WILL SLINEY & FRANK D'ARMATA
#2 variant

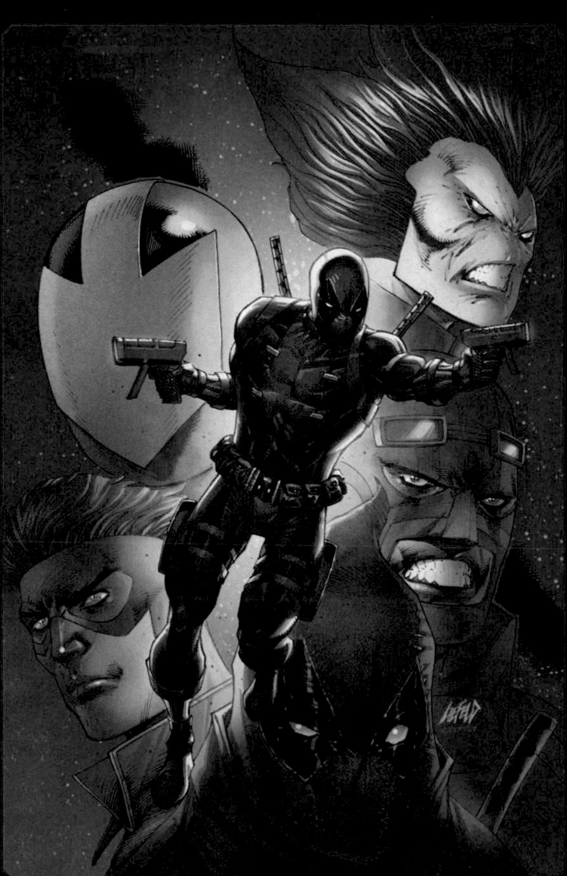

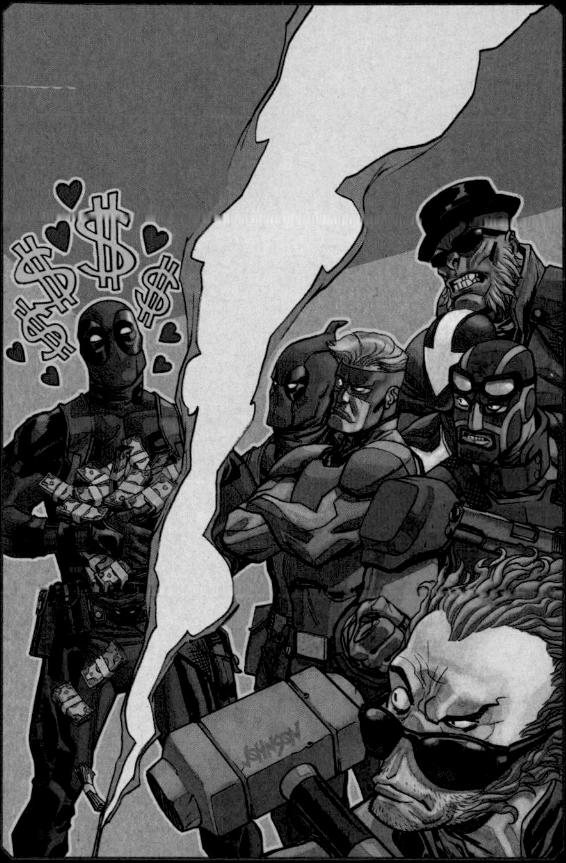
JOHNSON

DAVE JOHNSON
#4 story thus far variant

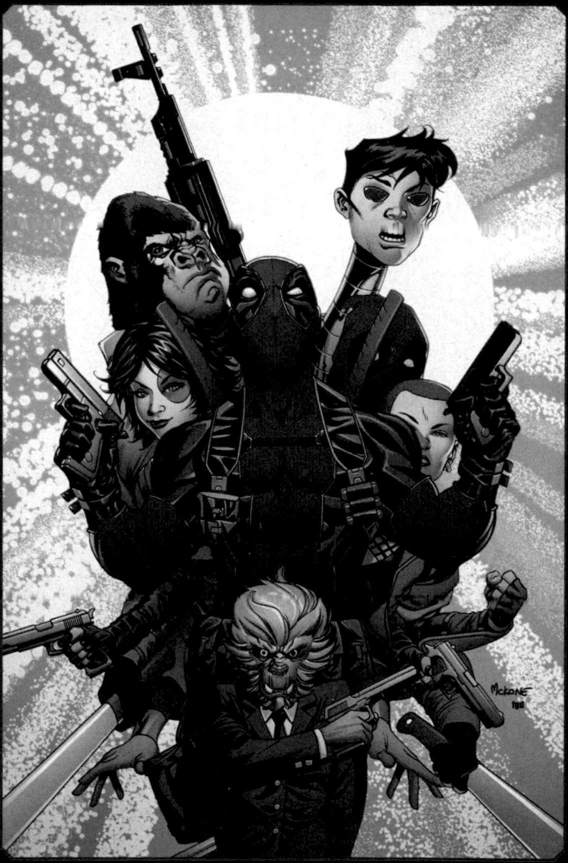
MCKONE

MIKE MCKONE & FRANK D'ARMATA
#4 variant

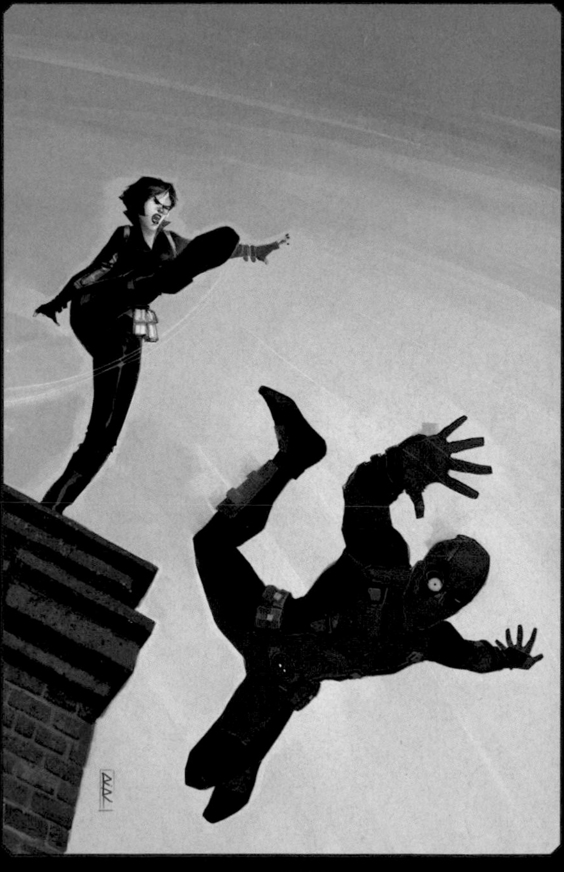

ROD REIS
#4 character variant

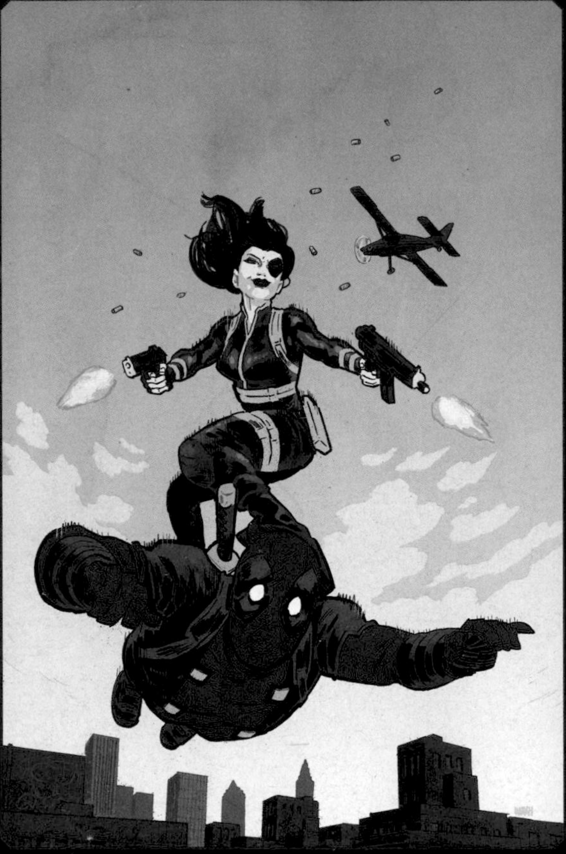

MICHAEL WALSH
#5 variant

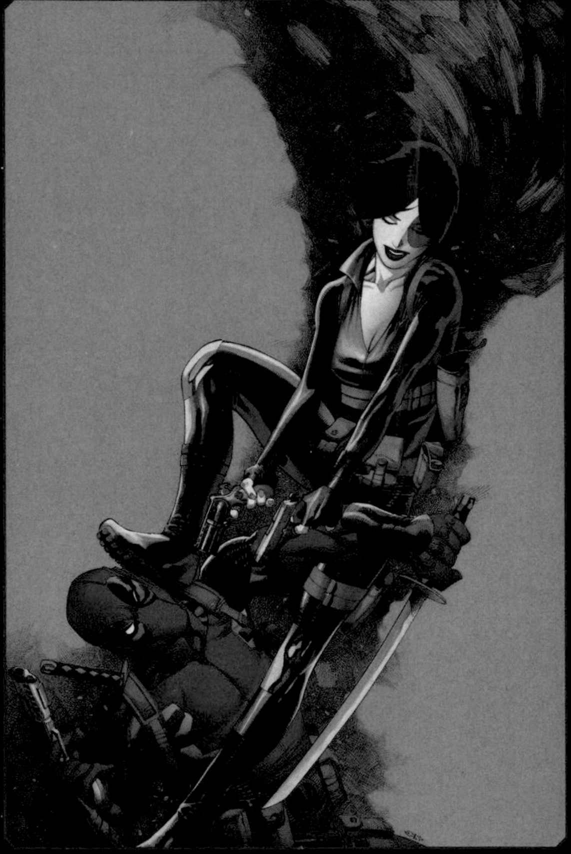

CHRISTOPHER STEVENS & FRANK MARTIN
#5 divided we stand variant

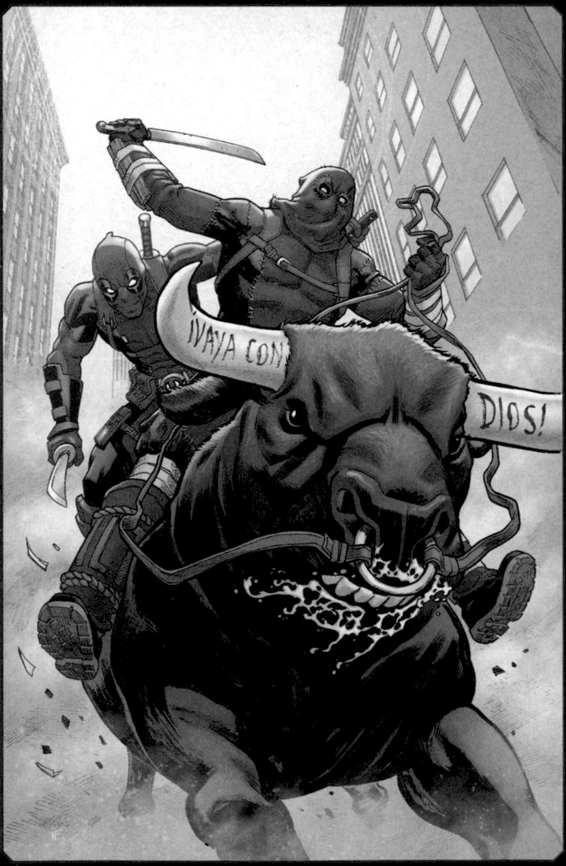
¡VAYA CON
DIOS!

MIKE HAWTHORNE & NATHAN FAIRBAIRN
#5 character variant